Helion & Company Limited
Unit 8 Amherst Business Centre
Budbrooke Road
Warwick
CV34 5WE
England
Tel. 01926 499 619
Email: info@helion.co.uk
Website: www.helion.co.uk
Twitter: @helionbooks
Visit our blog http://blog.helion.co.uk/

Designed and typeset by Farr out Publications, Wokingham, Berkshire
Cover design by Paul Hewitt, Battlefield Design (www.battlefield-design.co.uk)

ISBN 978-1-804510-21-6

British Library Cataloguing-in-Publication Data
A catalogue record for this book is available from the British Library

We always welcome receiving book proposals from prospective authors.

CONTENTS

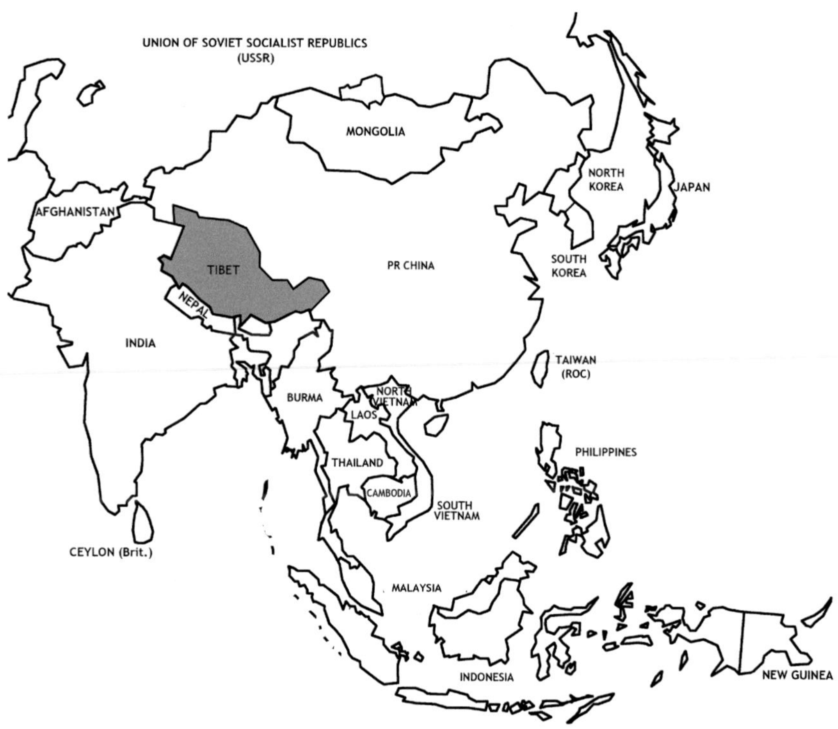

Note: In order to simplify the use of this book, all names, locations and geographic designations are as provided in *The Times World Atlas*, or other traditionally accepted major sources of reference, as of the time of described events.

ABBREVIATIONS

ARC	Aviation Research Centre
CAT	Civil Air Transport
CFA	Committee for a Free Asia
CIA	Central Intelligence Agency
ELINT	Electronic intelligence
NEFA	Northeast Frontier Agency
NSA	National Security Agency
NVDA	National Volunteer Defense Army
PLA	People's Liberation Army (China)
PRC	People's Republic of China
RAW	Research and Analysis Wing
ROC	Republic of China (Taiwan)
SAT	Southern Air Transport
SFF	Special Frontier Force
ST BARNUM	The codename for the aerial support for the CIA paramilitary effort in Tibet
ST CIRCUS	The codename of the overall CIA paramilitary effort in Tibet
STOL	Short take-off and landing
ST WHALE	Joint US-ROC covert paramilitary project in Tibet
USAF	US Air Force

1
FIRST CONTACT

Averaging almost five kilometres above sea level and covering an area the size of the American Southwest, Tibet is surrounded by some of the planet's highest mountain ranges: the Himalayas to the south, the Karakoram to the west, and the Kunlun to the north. Within these imposing natural borders, most of northern and western Tibet is a barren mountain desert of wind-blown dunes crusted with salt deposits. In the northeast — in a zone known among Tibetans as the province of Amdo — the terrain is akin to the Mongolian steppes, with its grassy veneer sustaining a sparse population of hardy alpine fauna. In the southeast quadrant known as Kham, Tibet drops slightly in altitude, and the topography devolves into the exaggerated slopes, impossibly narrow valleys, and gnarled conifers normally associated with Chinese watercolours.

It is the central plateau, however, that has become synonymous with the landscape of Tibet. Encompassing the provinces of U and Tsang, it is a harsh, rocky land of hypnotic beauty where, because of the altitude, light seems to intensify colour and detail.

The cultures of Tibet reflect these various ecosystems. In the northern and western deserts, the parched, frigid dunes have traditionally kept the region free of human habitation, save for transient trade caravans. To the northeast, the sparse population of Amdo finds little recourse on the steppes other than to eke out a living as semi-nomadic herdsmen — or marauding bandits that prey on the same. In the southeast, residents of Kham make the most of river valleys, using them for both pastureland and terraced agricultural plots. Tall for Asians and often lacking the Mongoloid eye fold (giving them a passing resemblance to American Indians), Khampas have earned a reputation for being clannish, courageous, and often socially unpolished.

Once again, it is in the central plateau where stereotypical Tibetan culture can be found. Clustered around arable meadows, inhabitants of this zone focus on animal husbandry and growing the most robust of crops, such as barley. Significantly, central Tibetans have maintained a lock on the country's political power. Dominating the thin upper strata of Tibet's religious bureaucracy and lay aristocracy, they often assume a pampered, elitist air toward the more rural Khampas and Amdowas.

Despite such diversity, all the peoples of Tibet share two basic historical truths. The first is the prominent role of religion — specifically, their unique brand of Buddhism — in daily life. The second historical truth is that geography has been Tibet's saviour. Occupying a strategic crossroads at the heart of the Eurasian landmass, Tibet has been coveted for centuries by surrounding empires. As a consequence, it has repeatedly suffered the humiliation of occupation by various neighbours.

Subjugation of the Tibetan population is a wholly different matter. Owing to its high altitude, invaders from the lowlands invariably weaken in Tibet's thin air. Aside from more lasting incursions onto the edge of the Amdo plains or across the river valley of Kham, foreign expeditions against the central plateau soon found the cost of sustaining a military presence prohibitive, affording the Tibetan heartland extended periods of de facto independence. Indeed, Tibet for generations fielded its own government and army.

By the start of the twentieth century, however, these historical truths were under pressure. In 1928, Chiang Kai-shek's Kuomintang party took the reins of power within China's republican government. Stoking Han nationalist sentiment, the Kuomintang emphasised the goal of a unified China that included Tibet. To realise this goal in part, that same year they announced plans to formally absorb Amdo and Kham as the new Chinese provinces of Tsing-hai and Sikang, respectively.

While the Koumintang began to gain momentum, Tibet won a reprieve when the Second World War overtook Asia. Shrewdly walking a neutralist tightrope, Tibet emerged from the war with its traditional way of life intact. However, all this changed in 1949, when the Chinese Civil War came to a head and the Koumintang fled offshore to the island sanctuary of Taiwan. On 1 October, a victorious Communist Party under Chairman Mao Zedong formally inaugurated the People's Republic of China (PRC) from a new capital in Beijing. Its grip, however, was far from consolidated. Besides facing republican strongholds on Taiwan and on the tropical island of Hainan to the south, the PRC saw itself as heir to the Kuomintang claim over Tibet. Making no secret of its intentions, on 1 January 1950 communist state radio declared that the liberation of

The Dalai Lama and his entourage fleeing to India in 1959. (Photo courtesy The Tibet Museum)

all three — Taiwan, Hainan, and Tibet — was the goal of the People's Liberation Army (PLA) for the upcoming calendar year.

Of these three, Tibet posed a unique set of difficulties. Like the Mongols, Manchus, and Koumintang before them, the PLA had to confront both distance and altitude to reach the central Tibetan plateau. With no drivable roads or airfields, trucks and transport aircraft were of little help.

Still, there were compelling reasons for the PLA to go forward with a land-grab against Tibet. For one thing, the communists had already absorbed Amdo. For another thing, they had also secured a solid foothold in eastern Kham. More than that, the Kham citizenry was far from united. Though intensely devout toward Tibet's religious hierarchy on a spiritual level, most Khampas were prone to interclan rivalries and were loyal to only their families or villages. A sense of binding nationalist affinity toward the Tibetan leaders in Lhasa was usually lacking—in no way helped by the ill-concealed chauvinism on the part of many central Tibetans. Khampas, as a result, were apt to fall behind whichever side — Lhasa or Beijing — offered the most attractive terms for absentee rule.

None of this was lost on the PRC. By the beginning of 1950, the PLA had secretly charged its Southwest Military Command with the task of consolidating control across Kham. After massing east of the Yangtze early that spring, patrols crossed the river in late May. Apparently intent only on testing Tibetan resolve, the Chinese soon halted the probes and resumed a riverside stare-down.

In Lhasa, the Chinese incursion shook Tibet's authorities to the core. Although vastly outnumbered, the Tibetan army theoretically could have exploited Kham's rugged topography to force a protracted guerrilla campaign. Squandering this advantage, it chose instead a strategy that hinged on the conventional goal of defending the town of Chamdo. On 19 October, after a pathetic defensive showing by the local garrison, Chamdo surrendered to Chinese control. Once the Tibetan commissioner-general was taken prisoner, he promptly signed over the rest of Kham to the PRC.

While China could take satisfaction in how easily it had taken Kham, the expanding conflict on the Korean peninsula had forced the PRC to push forward its timetable and initiate the Tibet operation before adequate preparations were complete. After all, it was late in the season, and the combination of snow and altitude would work against the PLA's unacclimated troops. For the interim, then, Beijing's rule hinged on co-opting Tibet's existing monastic structure. In particular, it needed to secure support from the kingdom's most powerful figure, the Dalai Lama.

If religion is the lifeblood of Tibet, the Dalai Lama is its heart. A title bestowed by the Tibetan people to the reincarnated leader from the most dominant of the four major schools of Tibetan Buddhism, the Dalai Lama was in his 14th incarnation by the time of Beijing's 1950 invasion of Kham. He was also just 15 years old, still three years shy of completing his intensive monastic studies.

Though bright and energetic, Tibet's youthful leader was initially confused as to how he would handle China's advances. His own inner circle of advisors was split, with some favouring accommodation and others far less willing to concede their freedoms.

As this was taking place, American diplomats in neighbouring India did what they could to monitor the Dalai Lama's movements. In the second quarter of 1951, after a Tibetan delegation to China folded to Chinese strongarming and indicated they would support a 17-point accord that signed away most of Tibet's autonomy, thought was given to offering the Dalai Lama asylum in the US or a third country. The Dalai Lama, in fact, had already taken a caravan across the border to India. He also indicated his intent to send his eldest brother, Thubten Norbu, for an extended stay in the US.

At that point, the US Central Intelligence Agency (CIA) stepped forward to help. By coincidence only weeks earlier the Agency had inaugurated the perfect vehicle for discreetly channelling financial support to persons like the Dalai Lama's brother. On 18 May, the San Francisco-based Committee for a Free Asia (CFA) had been formally unveiled to the public as a means to "render effective assistance to Asians in advancing personal and national liberty throughout their homelands." The committee's charter further declared its mandate to assist non-communist travellers, refugees, and exiles in order to "strengthen Asian resistance to communism." Left unsaid was the fact that the committee was made possible by financial assistance from the CIA.

The plight of Thubten Norbu meshed perfectly with the committee's goals. On 18 June, the US embassy in New Delhi was informed that full sponsorship of Norbu's US visit would be assumed by the CFA. If quizzed by the press, Norbu would allegedly be seeking medical treatment for rheumatism of the legs and might also use the opportunity to take English language classes at the University of California at Berkeley, near the committee's headquarters.

Arriving in New York, Norbu got a night's rest at the posh Waldorf-Astoria. Reporters curious about the new arrival were fed the bromide about his rheumatism and intended study at Berkeley. In reality, he was whisked the following day to Washington for meetings with State Department and CIA officials.

Shortly thereafter, the Dalai Lama in July 1951 heeded advice channelled under trance by the state oracle and departed India on a slow caravan back to the Tibetan capital. He arrived in Lhasa during mid-August, and PLA troops were sighted in the capital by early the following month. On 28 September, the Tibetan national assembly convened to debate the 17-point accord raised the previous May. Less than one month later, confirmation was sent to Mao that the kingdom accepted the agreement. Tibet was now officially part of the People's Republic of China.

2
TIGHTROPE

As 1951 gave way to 1952, Thubten Norbu remained in the US and had sporadic contact with officials in Washington. Also during this period, the Dalai Lama was smuggling out secret letters to his eldest brother, some of which betrayed the pressure he was feeling from China. Looking to put a positive spin on all this, Norbu insisted his sibling was placating the Chinese with apparent cooperation, but was secretly planning an underground resistance.

Given the difficult logistics in following Tibetan developments from afar, the US began to make use of a unique window provided by the Princely State of Sikkim. A sparsely populated cluster of mountains roughly half the size of Connecticut, Sikkim appeared to be an unlikely font of information. But squeezed among India to the south, Nepal to the west, Tibet to the north, and Bhutan to the southeast, it sat at the crossroads of the Himalayas. Sikkim also possessed several key mountain passes linking the Indian lowlands to the Tibetan plateau. These features attracted the attention of the British, who absorbed the territory in 1817 as an appendage to their vast Indian holdings.

Over the next 130 years, the British afforded Sikkim semi-autonomous status and allowed its royals to remain in effective control. Devotees of the same stylised form of Buddhism practiced in Tibet, Sikkimese kings presided over an elite caste with its share of palace intrigue — some of it deadly. In the eighteenth century, for example, a female royal helped assassinate the king by opening an artery as he rested in a hot tub; she was later strangled with a scarf for her treachery.

It was with this traditional system of leadership intact that Sikkim approached the mid-twentieth century. By 1947, however, its future was suddenly in doubt. The British were gone, and a new set of Indian authorities had come to power in New Delhi. Although the Princely States were theoretically entitled to declare their independence, in reality, the Indian leadership was making every attempt to entice them into a federal republic. The result of prolonged negotiations was a December 1950 agreement that gave the protectorate of Sikkim the right to manage domestic affairs, while India regulated its foreign affairs, trade, and defence.

The Sikkimese royals saw leeway in this pact. Though prohibited from making independent foreign policy, they believed that it was still within their right to retain a degree of international personality. This held obvious appeal for the US, which appreciated Sikkim's unique perspective on Himalayan events on account of its royals being related by blood and marriage to the elite in neighbouring Bhutan and Tibet. But it also meant walking a fine diplomatic tightrope, as American contact with the Sikkimese ran the risk of agitating India.

In the spring of 1951, the US consulate in Calcutta gingerly tested these waters. The Chinese had already invaded Kham, and Larry Dalley, a young CIA officer who had arrived in the city the previous fall under cover of vice consul, was eager to collect good intelligence on events across the border. He knew that two members of Sikkim's royal family frequented Calcutta and surmised they would be good sources of information.

The first, Pema Tseudeun, was the older sister of Crown Prince Palden Thondup Namgyal. Popularly known by the name Kukula, she was the stunning, urbane archetype of a Himalayan princess. Married into an influential Tibetan family (her father-in-law was a cabinet official), she once had considerable land holdings in Lhasa. After the Chinese invasion of Kham, however, all was in jeopardy. Leaving many of her possessions back in Tibet, she fled to the safety of Sikkim.

The second royal in Calcutta, Pema Choki, was Kukula's younger sister. Better known as Princess Kula, she was every bit as beautiful and sophisticated as her sibling. Kula was also married to a Tibetan of high status; her father-in-law had been a ranking official at the trade mission in Kalimpong.

In short order, CIA officer Dalley began regular contact with the Sikkimese princesses. At one point he discussed with Kulula plans to send ammunition to Tibet via trade caravans; this was never approved by Washington.

Later in the spring of 1951, the US consulate in Calcutta again turned to the Sikkimese royals for help. At the time the Dalai Lama was still holed up along the Indian frontier, and CIA officer Robert Linn was brainstorming ways of facilitating indirect contact with

Sikkimese Princess Kukula, who acted as a conduit for intelligence about Tibet during the 1950s. (Photo courtesy The Tibet Museum)

the monarch. Two of those he asked to assist in passing notes were Kukula and Kula. Although the Tibetan leader ultimately elected to return to Tibet, it was not for want of trying on the part of the princesses.

One year later, Sikkim's royals once more proved their willingness to help. In June 1952, Kukula approached the US consulate with an oral message from the Dalai Lama. She had just returned from a visit to her in-laws in Lhasa, and although she had not personally seen the Dalai Lama, she had been given information from Kula's father-in-law, who had been in Lhasa circulating among senior government circles. Kukula quoted the Dalai Lama as saying that when the time was propitious for liberation, he hoped the US would give material aid and moral support. Kukula also passed observations about food shortages in Lhasa and about the desperate conditions of the vast majority of Chinese troops in that city.

To maintain the flow of such useful information, the consulate — including its small CIA base — continued its discreet courtship of the Sikkimese sisters. Kenneth Millian, who replaced Larry Dalley in October 1952 under cover as vice consul, counted the Sikkimese as one of his primary targets. By that time, however, the Indians were doing everything in their power to obstruct contact. On one of the rare occasions when he got permission to visit the Sikkimese capital of Gangtok, for example, New Delhi leaked a false report to the press that the American vice president — not vice consul — was scheduled to make an appearance. As a result, entire villages turned out expecting to see Richard Nixon. "Discreet contact," lamented Millian, "became all but impossible."

Occasional trysts with the Sikkimese were conducted by another CIA officer in Calcutta, John Turner. Born of American parents in India, Turner spent his formative years attending school in Darjeeling. He then went to college in the US, followed by a stint in the army and induction into the Agency in 1948. For his first overseas CIA assignment, he was chosen in May 1952 to succeed Robert Linn as the senior CIA officer in Calcutta. Given his cultural background and fluency in Hindi, Turner was well suited for the job. "I felt very much at home," he later commented.

The Sikkimese, Turner found, needed no prompting to maintain contact "They offered us tidbits of intelligence to try and influence US policy," he concluded. "They were never on the payroll; they were not that sort of people." Some of the best tidbits came from the Crown Prince himself. "He was not the kind of person comfortable in dark alleys," quipped Turner. "He would make open, official visits to the consulate, and was the guest of honor with the consul general."

As an aside to these overt visits, the prince would discretely pass Turner relevant information about Tibet. One such meeting took place in the spring of 1954 immediately after the Crown Prince's return from a trip to Lhasa. While in the Tibetan capital, the prince had spoken with the Dalai Lama, whom he found unhappy but resigned to his fate. Even more revealing, the Chinese had feted their Sikkimese guest by showing off their new Damshung airfield north of Lhasa and had motored him along a fresh stretch of road leading into Kham. Turner found the debriefing so informative that he recorded the entire session and sent a voluminous report back to Washington.

Just weeks after the Crown Prince's 1954 visit, the Dalai Lama was invited to the Chinese capital, ostensibly to lead the Tibetan delegation to the inauguration ceremonies for the PRC's new constitution. Though many members of his inner circle were suspicious of Chinese intentions, the young monarch — still determined to work within the system — had little choice but to heed the call. He even made it a family affair, bringing along his mother, three siblings, and a brother-in-law.

On 11 July 1954, the Dalai Lama and his 500-person entourage departed Lhasa. Where possible, they took stretches of the partially finished road that wove east through Kham. Once in Beijing, the visit started out well. Partial to socialist precepts, the Dalai Lama had few qualms with China's economic direction; he had already voiced support for radical land reforms at home, although the landed aristocracy and religious elite had successfully thwarted implementation. The Dalai Lama was also treated with respect by the upper echelons of China's communist hierarchy; Mao, in particular, doted on the teenaged monarch.

But it was Mao who made a major gaff that would cloud the entire trip. Taking the Dalai Lama aside to impart a bit of fatherly wisdom, the chairman likened religion to poison. To a person who devoted his life to cultivating his spiritual side — and whose people believed he had one foot firmly in the celestial world — this was blasphemy of the highest order.

Worse was to come. By the time the Dalai Lama headed home in the spring of 1955, the road leading from Kham to Lhasa was fully finished. A second route from Amdo to the capital was also complete. No longer feeling the need to be tolerant, the Chinese introduced atheist doctrine in Tibetan schools. The PLA also started disarming villagers in eastern Tibet prior to the implementation of harsh agrarian collectivisation; as firearms were a cultural fixture in Kham and Amdo, their removal struck at a tenet of Tibetan tradition. As the Dalai Lama wove his way west, several Khampa leaders presented his entourage with petitions complaining of Beijing's heavy-handed ways.

Indian Prime Minister Jawaharlal Nehru (front seat, right) with Brigadier S.S. Uban visits Chakrata, 14 November 1963. (Photo via Jamyang Norbu)

During that same time frame, a hint of the dissatisfaction brewing in Kham reached the US consulate in Calcutta via a different channel. John Turner, the CIA base chief, had been approached by George Patterson for an urgent meeting in the Indian hill town of Kalimpong. Patterson, the Scottish missionary who had volunteered his services to the consulate in the past, was making the pitch on behalf of Ragpa Pandatsang, a member of a wealthy Kham trading family who had been alternately flirting with Lhasa and Beijing since 1950. Ragpa had done reasonably well for himself under the Chinese, but in a characteristic twist, he was now venturing to India to quietly sound out non-communist options.

Based on middleman Patterson's request, Turner made his way to Kalimpong. Arriving at a house owned by the Pandatsang family, Turner waited outside. Perfectly timed, Ragpa materialised from out of the dawn mist on the back of a Tibetan pony. "He was apparently on his morning gallop," recalls Turner, "and he cut quite a figure." Dismounting, the Khampa greeted the CIA case officer. Patterson, who had befriended the Pandatsang family during his missionary days in Kham, was on hand to act as translator. After brief pleasantries, Ragpa touched lightly on the fact that the Khampas were looking for assistance in resisting the Chinese, including armaments. Without exchanging anything further of substance, he remounted the horse and melted back into the hills. Said Turner, "It was a surreal moment."

Although Ragpa's approach to the CIA went nowhere (as did similar meetings he had with Indian officials and Tibetan trade representatives in Kalimpong), his hint about armed resistance proved prophetic. By the close of 1955, the combination of factors simmering over the previous year — atheist indoctrination, forceful disarming of the population, rapid collectivisation — sparked a wave of violence in eastern Tibet. True to their brigand reputation, nomads from the Golok region of Amdo were the first to unleash their fury on PLA garrisons across that province.

Eastern Kham followed suit in early 1956. Whereas the Amdo revolt was spontaneous and unorganised, the Khampas were more deliberate. With a chieftain from the town of Lithang taking the lead, a coordinated attack was planned for the 18th day of the first lunar phase of the year. Although pre-emptive Chinese arrests threw off that timetable by four days, some 23 clan leaders ultimately responded to the call and laid siege to a string of isolated Chinese posts.

The PLA responded in force. That February, Beijing dispatched several of its massive Tupolev-4 bombers over the Tibetan plateau. Thousands of Khampas and Amdowas reportedly died in the ensuing air campaign, buying time for the PLA to deploy ground reinforcements and retake lost garrisons. Particularly hard hit was Lithang; its grand monastery, home to 5,000 monks, was razed.

With news filtering into the capital of Chinese brutality in the east, the Dalai Lama by mid-1956 was fast reaching his breaking point. Just shy of his 21st birthday, he had already entertained thoughts of withdrawing from all secular life. It was at this critical juncture that his earlier foreign guest, the Crown Prince of Sikkim, made a return visit to Lhasa.

The Crown Prince was on more than a courtesy call. Disturbed by Beijing's apparent lack of restraint, Indian Prime Minister Jawaharlal Nehru was increasingly concerned with events across the border. By coincidence, the 2,500-year anniversary of the birth of Buddha was to be celebrated during the fourth lunar month of 1957.

Special events to mark that date, known as the Buddha Jayanti, were scheduled across India beginning in late 1956. If the Dalai Lama could be enticed to travel to India for the occasion, New Delhi felt that this would symbolically underscore its interest in the well-being of Tibet and its leader. Because he already had good rapport with the Dalai Lama, the Crown Prince was tasked by Nehru to deliver the invitation.

Upon receiving his Sikkimese guest and hearing the news, the Dalai Lama was ecstatic. For a Tibetan, a pilgrimage to India — especially one that coincided with the Buddha Jayanti — had all the connotations of a visit to the holy sites of Rome or Mecca. But more important, it would allow him to air his concerns directly to Nehru and perhaps offset Chinese influence. Perhaps, too, he could finally make good on his earlier contemplation of exile.

Hearing of the Buddha Jayanti invitation, senior Chinese authorities in Lhasa immediately threw water on the plan. Claiming that the Dalai Lama had a tight schedule, they made clear their opposition to any foreign travel.

If the young monarch was frustrated, so too was India's Nehru. On 1 October, Nehru telegraphed an official invitation to the Dalai Lama to supplement the one forwarded earlier by the Crown Prince. Grudgingly, Beijing considered the new appeal from New Delhi, and exactly one month later, the Chinese conceded. Tibet's young leader would be leaving his kingdom.

3
BROTHERS DIVINE

During the second week of September 1956, CIA officer John Hoskins set foot at Calcutta's Dum Dum Airport. At 29, he had already spent two years recruiting agents in Japan and another four shuttling between Washington desk assignments and vigorous tradecraft instruction. Now assigned to the Calcutta consulate, his new post was an experiment of sorts. The CIA's Far East Division had just gotten permission to station its officers at any diplomatic mission where overseas Chinese were found in numbers. This meant superimposing Far East Division personnel outside of their home turf — in this case, in India of the Near East Division.

In Calcutta, Hoskins could choose from a wealth of Chinese targets. Topping the list was the PRC's consulate and a People's Bank of China branch. In addition, some 30,000 Chinese expatriates — three-quarters of all those living in India — made their homes in and around the city.

Hoskins landed the secondary assignment of preening sources in the Himalayan states along the Tibetan border. Just as case officer Kenneth Millian had found out four years earlier, however, the Indians went out of their way to obstruct such efforts. "Overseas Chinese were fair game for penetration," recalls Hoskins, "but the others were considered under Indian hegemony." This was driven home when Mary Hawthorne, a CIA officer assigned to Calcutta, allowed a Bhutanese royal and his family to spend the night at her apartment. When the Indians learned of the incident, their outcry was so shrill that Hawthorne was forbidden by her superiors to attempt any similar invitations.

Mindful of Indian surveillance, Hoskins made plans for an exceedingly discreet approach to establish his own ties with Princess Kukula of Sikkim. As she was known to have an affinity for equestrian events, Hoskins waited until she came to Calcutta for one of the city's thoroughbred competitions. Blending in with the event's large number of Western spectators, he approached the Princess. But Kukula, Hoskins found, had more reservations than in the past. "She wanted to keep contacts strictly social," he concluded.

As things turned out, the services of the Sikkimese royals would soon prove redundant. When the US learned that the Dalai Lama had gotten permission in early November 1956 to attend the Buddha Jayanti celebrations, the CIA scrambled to bypass Sikkim and establish direct links with Tibetan sources close to the monarch.

None were closer than the two of the Dalai Lama's brothers, both of whom were now in exile. The eldest, Thubten Norbu, already had a history of indirect contact with the Agency via the Committee for a Free Asia. After he had been dropped from CFA funding in 1952, both he and his servant, Jentzen Thondup, had for a time become stateless refugees in Japan; in 1955, however, the pair finally get new Indian identity cards and US visas. Settling in New Jersey, Norbu began to earn a modest income teaching Tibetan to a handful of students as part of a non-credited course at Columbia University.

The other brother, Gyalo Thondup, was residing in Darjeeling, India. Six years Norbu's junior, Gyalo was the proverbial prodigal son. The problem was, he was the figurative son to a number of fathers. As a teen, he had befriended members of the Chinese mission in Lhasa and yearned to study in China. Although this was not a popular decision among the more xenophobic members of his family, Gyalo got his wish in 1947 when he and a brother-in-law arrived at the Kuomintang capital of Nanking and enrolled in college.

Two years later, Gyalo, then 21, veered further toward China when he married fellow student Zhu Dan. Not only was his wife ethnic Chinese, but her father, retired General Chu Shi-kuei, had been a key Kuomintang officer during the early days of the republic. Because of both his relationship to General Chu and the fact that he was the Dalai Lama's brother, Gyalo was feted in Nanking by no less than Generalissimo Chiang Kai-shek.

The good times were not to last. With the communists closing in on Nanking during the final months of China's Civil War, Gyalo and his wife fled in mid-1949 to India. Once again because of his relationship to the Dalai Lama, he was added to the invitation list for various diplomatic events and even got an audience with Prime Minister Nehru.

That October, Gyalo briefly ventured to the Tibetan enclave at Kalimpong before settling for seven months in Calcutta. While there, his father-in-law, General Chu, had shifted loyalty to the PRC and attempted to make contact with the Tibetan government. Conversant in Chinese and linked to both the Dalai Lama and General Chu, Gyalo was a logical intermediary. The talks never came to be, however, and ultimately Gyalo decided to head for the US.

Arriving in Washington in September 1951, Gyalo proved to be very restive. Despite State Department efforts to secure him a scholarship at Stanford University, he hurriedly departed the US in February 1952 for the Indian subcontinent. Leaving his wife behind, he then trekked back to Lhasa after a six-year absence. This stay, too, proved short-lived, as he was resettled back in India by the late spring.

Although not exactly endearing himself to anyone with his frequent moves, Gyalo was not burning bridges either. One of the persons he soon came to meet was India's spymaster, Bhola Nath Mullik. As head of the Intelligence Bureau since 1950, the taciturn Mullik was known for his boundless energy (he often worked 16-hour days), close ties to Nehru, healthy suspicion of China, and (rare for a senior Indian official) predisposition against communism. Almost immediately, the Tibetan frontier became his top concern. This followed Beijing's invasion of Kham that October, which meant that India's military planners now had to contend with a hypothetical front besides Pakistan.

Despite Mullik's concerns, Nehru was prone to downplay the potential Chinese threat. Not only did he think it ludicrous to prepare for a full-scale Chinese attack, but he saw real benefits in cultivating Beijing to offset Pakistan's emerging strategy of anti-communist cooperation with the West. "It was Nehru's idealism against hard-headed Chinese realism," said one Intelligence Bureau official. "Mullik injected healthy suspicions."

Astute enough to hedge his bets, Nehru allowed Mullik some leeway in improving security along the border and collecting intelligence on Chinese forces in Tibet. To accomplish this, Mullik expanded the number of Indian frontier posts strung across the Himalayas. In addition, he sought contact with Tibetans living in the Darjeeling and Kalimpong enclaves. Not only could these Tibetans be tapped for information, but a symbolic visit by a senior official like Mullik would lift morale at a time when their homeland was being subjugated. Such contact, moreover, could give New Delhi advance warning of any subversive activity in Tibet being staged from Indian soil.

Of all the Tibetan expatriates, Mullik had his eye on Gyalo Thondup. Besides having an insider's perspective of the high offices in Lhasa, Gyalo had already passed word of his desire for a meeting. Prior to his departure for his first visit to Darjeeling in the spring of 1953, Mullik asked for permission from the Prime Minister to include the Dalai Lama's brother on his itinerary. Their subsequent exchange of views went well, as did their tete-a-tete during Mullik's second visit to Darjeeling in 1954.

Apart from such occasional contact with Indian intelligence, Gyalo spent much of the next two years removed from the tribulations in his homeland. To earn a living, he ironically began exporting Indian tea and whiskey to Chinese troops and administrators in Tibet.

During this period, Gyalo went for several years with virtually no contact between him and American diplomats in India. In particular, he was completely unknown among CIA officers in Calcutta. In 1956, however, this was set to change. Once word reached India in early November that the Dalai Lama would be attending the Buddha Jayanti, John Hoskins got an urgent cable from headquarters. Put aside your efforts against the Chinese community, he was told, and make immediate contact with Gyalo. A quick check indicated Gyalo's predilection for tennis, so Hoskins got a racket and headed north to Darjeeling. After arranging to get paired with Gyalo for a doubles match, the CIA officer wasted no time in quietly introducing himself.

First impressions are lasting ones, and Hoskins was not exactly wowed by Gyalo's persona. "There was a lot of submissiveness rather than dynamism," he noted. At their first meeting, little was discussed apart from reaching an understanding that, to avoid Indian intelligence coverage in Darjeeling, future contact would be made in Calcutta using proper countersurveillance measures.

Later that same month, the Dalai Lama and a 50-strong delegation departed Lhasa by car. Switching to horses at the Sikkimese border, the royal entourage was met on the other side by both Gyalo and Norbu, who had rushed to India from his teaching assignment in New York. The party was whisked through Gangtok and down to the closest Indian airfield near the town of Siliguri, and by 25 November the monarch was being met by Nehru on the tarmac of New Delhi's Palam Airport. During subsequent meetings, the Tibetan leader openly hinted about not going back to Lhasa.

As India's leadership digested these developments, the Dalai Lama departed the capital for an exhausting schedule of Buddha Jayanti festivities. Meantime, Chinese delegations repeatedly visited India through early 1957 in an effort to convince the Tibetan leader to return home.

Despite Beijing's lobbying, Gyalo and Norbu were still insistent that their brother choose exile. Torn over his future, the 21-year-old monarch had already departed Calcutta on 22 January for Kalimpong, which by then was home to a growing number of disaffected Tibetan elite. Once there, he did what Tibet's leaders had done countless other times when confronted with a hard decision: he consulted the state oracle. Two official soothsayers happened to be traveling with his delegation; using time-honoured methods, the pair went into a trance on cue and recited their sagely advice. Return to Lhasa, they channelled.

As far as the Dalai Lama was concerned, the ruling of his oracles was incontrovertible, and the decision was made all the easier by the fact that nobody seemed anxious to give him refuge. Flouting the suggestions of his brothers, he declared his intention to go home. He crossed into Sikkim in early March and was compelled to remain in Gangtok until heavy snows melted from the mountain passes. There, he finalised plans to set out for Lhasa by month's end.

Prior to November 1956, Tibet had never ranged far from the bottom of the priority watch list for those in the Far East Division at CIA headquarters in Washington. The Agency had no officer assigned solely to Tibetan affairs; it, along with Mongolia and other peripheral ethnic regions under PRC control, barely factored as a minor addendum to the activities of William Broe's China Branch.

But as soon as the Dalai Lama received permission to attend the Buddha Jayanti, Broe felt it prudent to show heightened interest. Looking for a junior officer to spare, he soon settled on John Reagan. Twenty-eight years old, Reagan had joined the Agency upon graduation from Boston College in 1951. He was soon in Asia, where he spent the next 24 months working on paramilitary projects in Korea. Switching to China Branch, he served two more years in Japan as part of the CIA's penetration effort against the PRC. Returning to the United States in 1955, Reagan divided the next 12 months between Chinese language training and trips to New York City to practice tradecraft against United Nations delegates.

As the branch's new man on Tibet, Reagan initially did little more than forward instructions for John Hoskins to make contact with Gyalo. He was silent on further guidance, primarily because senior US policy makers had not yet ironed out a coherent framework for dealing with Lhasa. In earlier meetings between CIA and State Department officials during the summer of 1956, there had been those who felt that the Dalai Lama should flee to another Buddhist nation to offer a rallying cry for anti-communist Buddhists across Asia. Others, primarily inside the Agency, believed that he could play a more important role as a rallying symbol in Lhasa among his fellow Tibetans. This was still the CIA's operating assumption in late 1956: once the Dalai Lama was in India, the prevailing mood at Agency headquarters was that he should eventually go home.

Wangdu "Walt" Gyatotsang (right), leader of the Saipan-trained team dropped into Lithang in November 1957, posing with his brothers Kalsang and Thopdu. (Photo courtesy Kalsang Gyatotsang)

Gyalo, meantime, was telling Hoskins that his brother had every intention of seeking asylum. With the Dalai Lama apparently intent on staying away from his homeland — and therefore not conforming to the Agency's preferred scenario of rallying his people from Lhasa — Reagan was largely idle during most of the Dalai Lama's four-month absence from Tibet.

Eventually, however, the CIA looked to hedge its bets. Since the second half of 1956, a band of 27 young Khampa men had been growing restive in the enclave of Kalimpong. Most came from relatively wealthy trading families and had been spirited to India to protect them from the instability in their native province. Full of vigour, the entire group had ventured to New Delhi shortly before the Dalai Lama's Buddha Jayanti pilgrimage to conduct street protests. Once the Dalai Lama arrived, they sought a brief audience to make an impassioned plea for Lhasa's intercession against the Chinese offensive in Kham.

To their disappointment, the Dalai Lama counselled patience. Undaunted, the 27 young men shadowed the monarch during several of the Buddha Jayanti commemorative events. By early January 1957, this took them to Bodh Gaya, the city in eastern India where the historical Buddha was said to have attained enlightenment. While there, the Dalai Lama's older brother, Thubten Norbu, approached the Khampas and asked if he could take their individual photographs as a souvenir. Although it was an odd request, they complied.

For the next few weeks, nothing happened. Frustrated by the Dalai Lama's repeated rebuffs, the Khampas sulked back to Kalimpong. Several Chinese traders were in town, some of whom were rumoured to have links to the Koumintang regime on Taiwan. Desperate, the Khampas sounded them out on the possibility of covert assistance from Taipei. It was at that point that Gyalo Thondup arrived and requested a meeting with all 27. For most of the young Khampas, it was the first time they had spoken with the Dalai Lama's lay brother. As they listened attentively, Gyalo lectured them to steer clear of the Kuomintang. "The United Sates," he told them cryptically, "is a better choice."

Less than a week later, the Dalai Lama arrived in Kalimpong, the oracles had their channelling session, and things changed dramatically. With the monarch's return journey now imminent, John Reagan in Washington scrambled to script a program of action. At its core, the plan called for a unilateral capability to determine how much armed resistance activity really existed in Tibet; further commitments could then be weighed accordingly.

Putting the plan into action, in February 1957 John Hoskins was ordered to immediately identify eight Tibetan candidates for external training as a pilot team that would infiltrate their homeland and assess the state of resistance. Gyalo, who had been in Kalimpong making an 11th-hour bid to convince his brother to seek asylum, was given responsibility for screening candidates among the Tibetan refugees already in India. Although the 27 Khampas did not know it, Gyalo intended to make the selection from their ranks. Using the photographs taken by Norbu at Bodh Gaya, he sought guidance from two senior Khampas in town, both of whom hailed from the extended family of Gompo Tashi Andrugtsang, a prominent trader of Tibetan wool, deer horns, and musk.

With their assistance, Gyalo soon settled on his first pick. Wangdu Gyatotsang, age 27, had been born to an affluent Khampa family from the town of Lithang. He was well connected: Gompo Tashi was his uncle, as was one of the senior Khampas helping Gyalo with the selection. Wangdu also had the right disposition for the task at hand. Despite being schooled at the Lithang monastery from the age of 10, he did not exactly conform to monastic life. "He was hot-tempered from childhood," recalls younger brother Kalsang.

When approached by Gyalo, Wangdu immediately volunteered for the mission. Within days, five other Khampas were singled out (Washington now wanted a total of six trainees, not eight), but only Wangdu was given any hint of the impending assignment. Four were from Lithang; of these, three were Wangdu's close acquaintances, and one was his family servant. The fifth was a friend from the nearby town of Bathang.

Once the Dalai Lama was en route to Lhasa, attention shifted in early March 1957 to smuggling the six Khampas out of India for CIA training. This was easier said than done. Because of Nehru's determination to maintain cordial Sino-Indian ties, New Delhi's complicity remained out of the question. Moreover, the Khampas were refugees without proper identification, discounting overt travel via commercial airliner or boat. Brainstorming covert alternatives, several came to mind. "There was some talk in the Calcutta consulate about floating them off the Indian coast," said Gyalo, "then having them picked up by submarine." Consideration was also given to issuing fake Nepalese passports.

A better option harkened back to a suggestion made by the Crown Prince of Sikkim regarding exfiltration via East Pakistan. At the time, US–Pakistan relations were especially warm. Even before the CIA was sure that the Khampa training was going to proceed, the Agency's station chief in Karachi, L. Eugene Milligan, had broached the exfiltration scheme with senior Pakistani officials. Taking his case directly to President Iskandar Mizra, Milligan asked if — hypothetically speaking — Tibetans might be allowed to cross the northern border of East Pakistan, then be discreetly transported to the abandoned Kurmitola airstrip north of Dacca.

Milligan could make his pitch knowing that the CIA had particularly good relations in East Pakistan. Since mid-1954, the Agency had been allowed to maintain a single case officer at the

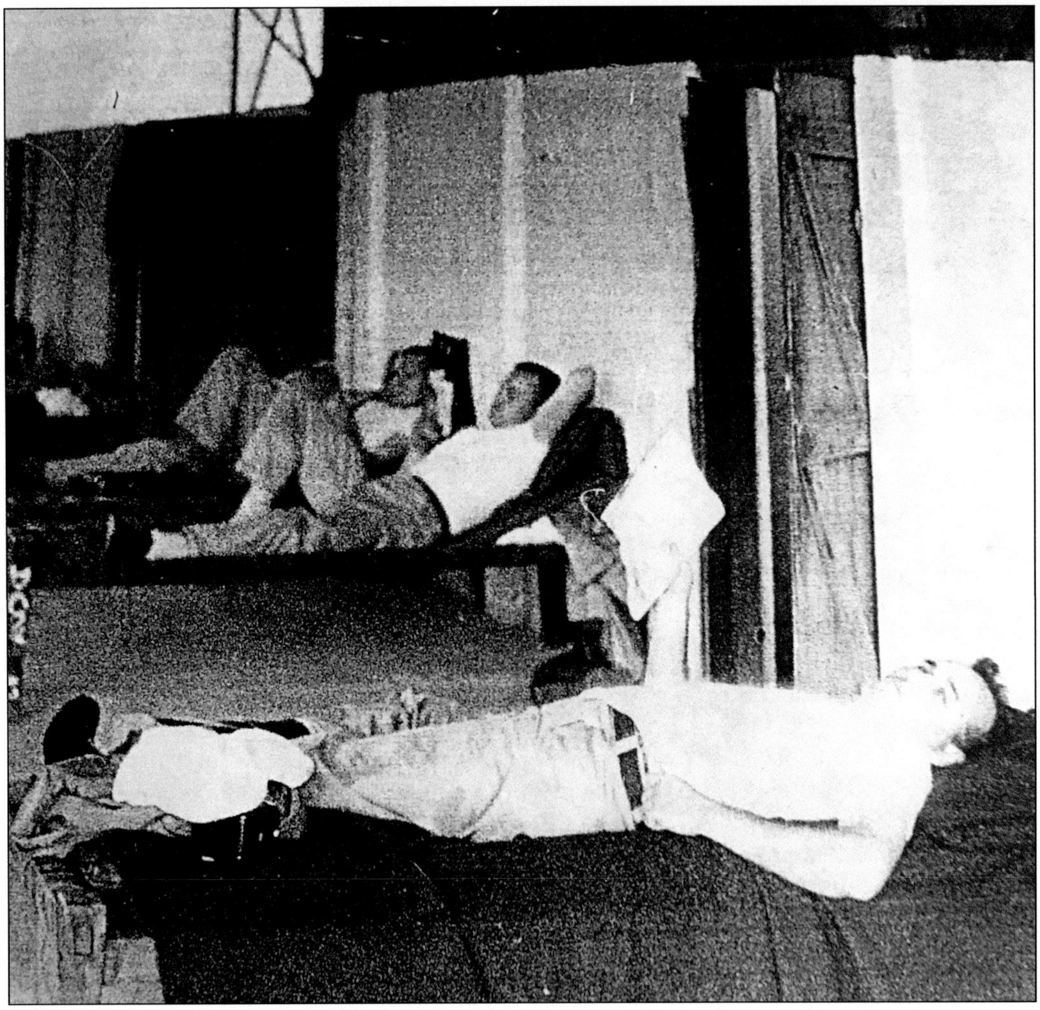

Civil Air Transport crew rests at Kurmitola airfield prior to the first supply drop by a C-118 drop into Tibet, October 1958. (Photo courtesy Gar Thorsrud)

Back in Kalimpong, Wangdu went to the house of 27-year-old Athar and told him they were departing that night for training in a foreign country. Like Wangdu, Athar (many Khampas go by only one name) was an alumnus of the Lithang monastery and had been one of the 27 who lobbied the Dalai Lama during the Buddha Jayanti. A total of six Khampas, he was told, would be making the trip.

Athar's first reaction was shock. To maintain secrecy, none of the trainees (other than Wangdu) had been aware that preparations had reached such an advanced stage. His next reaction was disappointment. "Six was too few," he later recalled. "I thought we needed at least ten of us."

With little time for debate, the six ate and changed into Indian clothes. All identification was left behind. That evening, they gathered on a dark road outside town. Like clockwork, Gyalo arrived at the wheel of a jeep and loaded them into the rear. In the passenger's seat was Gyalo's cook, Gelung, who was designated to escort the group across the Pakistani border. Gelung was a good choice on two counts: not only could he speak Hindi, which might come in handy if they encountered Indian authorities, but he was the only one among them who knew how to read a compass.

In silence, they drove south to the town of Siliguri, then another 20 kilometres to the East Pakistan frontier. As the road narrowed near the entrance to a tea plantation, the jeep ground to a halt and the passengers off-loaded. As Gyalo reversed direction and returned north, Gelung led the Khampas down a foot trail through the plantation. Walking until nearly dawn, they approached a large river. Studying his compass, Gelung calculated that the opposite side was Pakistani territory.

The group found a suitable fording point and waded to the far shore. Moving 45 meters inland, they came across a small road. While they waited without speaking, three soldiers materialised out of the dawn mist. Because they appeared to be armed and dressed like Indian troops, the Khampas began to panic, but Gelung rose and walked forward. Removing a flashlight from his pack, he flicked it on for a moment. Seconds later, the troops returned the signal. Gelung waved at the others to follow, and the Khampas approached the patrol and offered greetings. To their surprise, one of the soldiers was Norbu's servant Jentzen; the rest were Pakistanis. His work done, Gelung bid them farewell and retraced his steps across the river and back to India, while Jentzen, the Pakistanis, and the six Khampas walked a short distance to a covered jeep.

Dacca consulate. That officer, 28-year-old Walter Cox, had nurtured close links with most of East Pakistan's civilian and military authorities, helped in part when he coordinated a generous airlift of US humanitarian assistance following severe floods in August 1954.

Based on this spirit of cooperation, Mizra gave Milligan his consent. When Washington's final approval for the exfiltration came in February 1957, the station chief quickly assigned a Karachi-based case officer, Edward McAllister, to coordinate the operation from Dacca. McAllister was with the Far East Division and — like Hoskins in Calcutta — was posted to Karachi as the division's local representative assigned to penetrate the Chinese community.

Joining McAllister for the assignment in Dacca was John Reagan, who had arrived from Washington for the duration of the exfiltration. One potential hitch remained: although McAllister was fluent in Chinese (and Reagan knew the basics), neither officer shared a common language with the Khampas. They were desperate for an interpreter, but there were few qualified candidates. Gyalo himself was unavailable because he needed to run the operation from the Indian side and could not afford the diplomatic heat if he got caught on the border. Norbu could not risk the embarrassment of exposure either. With little other choice, a call was placed to Norbu's long-time servant Jentzen Thondup, who was patiently awaiting his master's return at their apartment in New Jersey.

"I got on the phone," remembers Jentzen, "with somebody who said he was from the CIA." A quiet, elderly man showed up at the house later that day, and the pair were soon winging their way to South Asia.

After riding for an hour, the group came upon an isolated cottage framed by thickets. Inside, CIA officer McAllister was waiting with hot tea and biscuits. As Jentzen attempted to translate pleasantries in halting English, they finished their refreshments and were directed to a bigger jeep. They rode for the next five hours, not stopping until they reached a railway station. The Tibetans were then hustled aboard a train and seated alone in the first-class compartment.

Heading south, they took the train to the outskirts of Dacca There they were off-loaded to a truck and driven to a safe house near Kurmitola airfield. Unaccustomed to the heat, they spent the next two days hidden away from prying eyes.

For covert airlift needs in Asia, the CIA relied almost exclusively on its proprietary, Civil Air Transport (CAT). A handful of assignments, however, went to a special unit within the US Air Force (USAF). This unit dated back to 1951, when the USAF saw the need to pluck aircrews out of the Soviet countryside after dropping nuclear ordnance and running out of fuel on the way home. Given the innocuous title of Air Resupply and Communications wings, these recovery units were outfitted with an exotic mix of converted bombers, seaplanes, helicopters, and transports.

Almost immediately, the activities of the recovery wings grew beyond their initial role. Their training was expanded to include various aerial aspects of unconventional warfare, and they became fluent in leaflet drops, agent insertions, and the resupply of guerrillas behind communist lines. The Asia-based ARC wing — which in 1954 shifted to Kadena Air Base on the US-controlled island of Okinawa — was especially active, being used on psychological warfare flights over the Korean peninsula, the PRC, and French Indochina.

In September 1956, all Air Resupply and Communications wings were formally disbanded. But electing to keep the Kadena unit intact, the USAF merely changed its name to the equally ambiguous 322nd Troop Carrier Squadron, Medium (Special). In line with the last word of this extended title, the 322nd Squadron continued to focus on unconventional contingencies. A special sub-set of the squadron, equipped with a pair of C-54s and a lone C-118, were given the most sensitive of assignments. Even its pilots were often kept in the dark about their missions.

Such was the case when the detachment had been ordered to dispatch its C-118 to Kurmitola. With perfect timing, a covered truck approached from the rear and stopped at the plane's back door. Six small figures dashed up the stairs, followed by Jentzen and John Reagan. Throttling the engines back up, the crew taxied down the runway and departed East Pakistan as quickly as it had arrived.

4 SAIPAN

After a brief refuelling stop in Bangkok, the Khampas were again aloft and heading over the South China Sea. Curving north, they arrived at Kadena and were taken to the small CIA compound on the airbase for a three-day physical examination.

While still on Okinawa, the group was met by the Dalai Lama's brother Norbu, who joined them on the C-118 as they took to the air and veered southeast. Four hours later, they descended toward a teardrop-shaped island in the middle of the western Pacific. Though the Tibetans were never told the location — some would later speculate it was Guam — they had actually arrived at the US trust territory of Saipan.

Situated on the southern end of the Northern Mariana Islands chain, Saipan had been chosen by the CIA in 1950 as a discreet locale to build a camp to instruct indigenous agents and commandos. Officially known by the cover title Naval Technical Training Unit, the Saipan training station took up much of the island's northern peninsula and featured numerous segregated compounds where groups of Asian trainees from various nations could spend several months in isolation. "We did not even let two classes from the same country know one another," underscored one case officer.

The newly arrived Tibetans presented the training staff with a unique set of challenges. The six recruits were to act as the CIA's eyes and ears back inside Tibet, John Reagan explained to the resident instructor cadre. This necessitated that they absorb not only communications and reporting skills but also a general knowledge of guerrilla warfare techniques, as well as a limited understanding of tradecraft. Although such a broad curriculum would normally require a full year, Saipan station was told to ready the subjects in a quarter of that time.

Under such strict time constraints, three different CIA training teams were assembled to begin instruction. The first team offered the Khampas an extremely rudimentary course on classic espionage tactics. The second started coaching them in Morse communications and use of the RS-1 shortwave radio and its hand-cranked generator. The final team initiated a primer on guerrilla warfare and paramilitary operations.

Very quickly, problems became apparent. Although they had prior experience as traders, many were having trouble quantifying distances and amounts. Precise reporting would be vital once they were back in the field, emphasised one Agency officer, "but too often they tended to use vague descriptions such as 'many' or 'some.'"

To overcome some of these challenges, the CIA instructors had to rely on visual demonstrations. "We had to physically show them," said one trainer, "not simply use a classroom." To clarify the construction of ground signals for an aerial resupply, for example, scaffolding was assembled atop the island's northern cliffs. Below, fire pots were arranged on the beach so the Tibetans could visualise how they would appear from the air.

Communications training proved even more difficult. The main stumbling block: Khampas traditionally received little formal language instruction. The six students, who were barely able to read or write, could hardly be expected to transmit coherent radio messages. Not realising the seriousness of this critical deficiency until nearly halfway through the training cycle, the CIA instructors scrambled to find someone who could teach basic Tibetan grammar. Norbu, who was acting as primary interpreter for the other course work, could not be spared for double duty. Neither could Jentzen, who in any event was weak in language skills.

Enter Geshe Wangyal.

As a result of the unique symbiosis between Tibetan lamas and Mongol khans during centuries past, Tibetan Buddhism had converts spread across the Mongolian steppes of Central Asia. Some of these Mongolians, being a nomadic people, had wandered far with their adopted religion. By the early seventeenth century, one such band had settled in the Kalmykia region of Russia just north of the Caspian Sea.

One especially gifted Mongol monk in Russia was Geshe Wangyal. Born in 1901, he had started monastic life at age six. Known for his ability to memorise several pages of Buddhist text in a single sitting, Wangyal regularly excelled in class.

After being selected to study in Lhasa, Wangyal enrolled at the prestigious Drepung Monastic University. Located on a high ridge eight kilometres west of the capital, Drepung had once been the largest monastery in the world (its population in the seventeenth century was a staggering 10,000 monks), Setting his sights high, the newly arrived Mongolian intended to become *geshe* (doctor of divinity) — a title that can take up to 35 years of study to achieve. In the end, he was bestowed his degree after just nine years.

Unfortunately for Wangyal, China, Tibet, Mongolia, and his native Kalmykia were now all under communist occupation. Exile in India, too, did not appeal to him. There was one attractive alternative, however. In late 1951, the US accepted 800 Kalmyk Mongolians who had been languishing in refugee camps since the end of the Second World War. These refugees were drawn from two waves that had fled the Soviet Union during the preceding decades. Once in the US, one wave of emigres settled around Philadelphia. Another wave — no more than 70 families — established a small but vibrant community near Freewood Acres, New Jersey.

Hearing of this, Geshe Wangyal contemplated a move to the US. Arriving on American soil in February 1955, Geshe Wangyal found that word of his religious accomplishments in Tibet had already made him famous among his fellow Kalmyk Mongolians. With an instant audience, he opened a modest temple in a converted New Jersey garage.

Geshe Wangal's fame was not limited to his ethnic home crowd. As the first qualified scholar of Tibetan Buddhism in the US, he soon came in contact with Norbu, who at the time was also living in New Jersey and teaching Tibetan at Columbia University. Out of mutual respect between *geshe* and incarnation, Norbu was given an honorary chair at the New Jersey temple.

The two cooperated in another way as well. Following Norbu's lead, Geshe Wangyal began teaching languages — first Mongolian, then Tibetan — at Columbia University in 1956. Having dissected Tibetan grammar during years of poring over Buddhist texts, he had a particularly deep appreciation for its written form. The US government, for one, found his linguistic talents more than adequate: among his first Tibetan students at Columbia were two from the US Army.

Given this background, Geshe Wangyal was the perfect choice to instruct the Khampas about their own language. Having already been indirectly exposed to the US government while teaching the army students — and after being informed that Norbu was already involved — the monk offered his cooperation and was soon en route to Saipan.

Beyond the serious language hurdle, the CIA staff on Saipan harboured a more fundamental concern about their Tibetan subjects. The Khampas were Buddhists, and nearly all of them had spent some time as monks. Their instructors wondered whether they would hesitate to kill a fellow human being. Very quickly, however, the CIA came to realise that the Khampas had few reservations about taking the life of a Chinese invader. "Their ideas on what weapons should be dropped were starting to get extravagant," remembers training officer Harry Mustakos. "Machine guns for each of their friends, they said, plus artillery batteries would be nice."

Of the six Khampas, Wangdu — now known as "Walt" — led the cry for more sophisticated weaponry. Partly, this reflected Walt's hot temper. Partly, too, it was a face-saving gesture to compensate for his low scores in Morse training. "He was near the bottom of the class," said fellow trainee Athar, who now went by the name "Tom." "He began complaining that he wanted to train with bigger guns, not waste time on radios."

For the CIA, this posed a dilemma. Walt's demands for heavier firepower conflicted with its need for skilled agents who would observe and report — not rush to attack. Gingerly, the Agency trainers attempted to downplay Tibetan expectations. Said Tom, "They explained that it would be too hard to let us carry artillery pieces into Tibet."

There were health challenges as well. One scare occurred when trainee Tsawang Dorje — now going by the name "Sam" — suffered a ruptured appendix. A few weeks later, the same hapless agent accidentally shot himself in the foot with a pistol. Both incidents required emergency trips to Okinawa, and both resulted in fast recoveries.

On another occasion, Lhotse — his name now Americanized to "Lou" — caught a bad case of dysentery. By chance, CIA Director Allen Dulles was passing through Saipan during a Far East tour and had along his personal physician. From the latter, the local doctor was able to obtain a new drug and get Lou started on a successful course of treatment.

Such medical emergencies aside, the Khampas were shaping up to be model students. "They were new to us," said Mustakos. "Culturally and psychologically, we were learning from them as much as they were learning from us." Sometimes this led to conclusions that bordered on the comical. The Tibetans, for example, saw American omnipotence in seemingly unrelated events. Each night at sundown, the CIA advisors sprayed the compound with an insecticide-dispensing unit mounted on a jeep. This awed the Tibetans, who viewed the routine as proof that the United States was a powerful country. Said case officer Mustakos, "They noted that we had devised ways of killing big things — like people — by using the weapons with which we were training, and even killing little things — like mosquitoes — with the DDT fogger."

Such innocent observations only served to endear the Tibetans to their CIA instructors. One of the most impressed was Roger McCarthy. Thirty years old, the gregarious McCarthy had joined the CIA in 1952 as a communications specialist for its paramilitary cover organisation on Taiwan, Western Enterprises. Promoted to case officer, he arrived in Saipan in 1956 and had just completed a paramilitary training cycle for six members of the Lao intelligence service prior to the arrival of the Tibetans. "The Lao would get frightened during nighttime operations," he recalls, "and hold each other's hands." The Tibetans, by contrast, were of entirely different mettle. "They were brave and honest and strong," said McCarthy. "Basically, everything we respect in a man."

After a month-long extension to allow Geshe Wangyal to complete his language instruction, training for the Khampas was all but finished by mid-September 1957. To properly outfit them for their return, an urgent request had been flashed back to India for six sets of used Tibetan peasant garb, knives, and coins. Once Gyalo gathered the items, he rushed down to Calcutta and notified his case officer, John Hoskins. Smuggled into the consulate, the unwashed, reeking load was divided into half a dozen diplomatic pouches and posted to Saipan.

CIA officers Roger McCarthy (left) and Gar Thorsrud (second from left) while parachuting on the Republic of Taiwan, 1953. Both would play key roles in ST CIRCUS. (Photo courtesy Roger McCarthy)

Other preparations were well under way for insertion of the agents back into Tibet. To save time — and avoid the diplomatic and physical hazards of walking back through Indian territory — the CIA intended to drop them inside their homeland by parachute. As CIA headquarters had given the cryptonym ST CIRCUS to the overall Tibet project, this aerial portion retained the same theme and was code-named ST BARNUM.

Airborne infiltration posed a whole range of difficulties. First, it required a discreet staging base within range of Tibet; just as during exfiltration, East Pakistan was the optimal choice. Second, the flight would necessarily be conducted at night, which meant that the plane needed both clear weather and a full moon to negotiate its way to the drop zone. Fortunately, both weather patterns and moon phases were predictable. In East Pakistan, the annual monsoon season came to a close in October, and over Tibet, the clearest skies could be found in October and November. Factoring in a full moon, this meant that premium conditions were most likely to occur during a six-day window beginning 6 October and during another six-day window starting 5 November.

An even greater challenge was determining where in Tibet the agents would be inserted. From the moment the Khampas arrived in Saipan, part of that station's mandate had been to help select drop zones. During debriefings of the trainees, each was quizzed about his hometown, where he had travelled, what routes he had taken, names of villages along the way, and people he had met. Starting from crude route tracings, the CIA instructors slowly added village names, terrain features, and distance notations.

Concurrently, CIA headquarters assigned the Far East Division's air branch to flesh out the details for ST BARNUM. Heading the task was the branch's deputy, Gar Thorsrud. Although the CIA had a special office for worldwide overhead imagery, Thorsrud found the files on Tibet to be exceedingly thin. Satellites did not yet exist, and the U-2 spy plane — which had been penetrating the Soviet bloc for just a little over a year — had flown only a single Tibet overflight on 21 August 1957. Apart from this, few current photographic and cartographic resources were to be found in the Agency's archives.

Digging deeper, Thorsrud eventually came up with some useful, albeit dated, photographs. These came from a 1904 British military expedition that had pushed its way into Lhasa to seek a trade agreement. The best shot was a photo of the Brahmaputra River, clearly showing the dunes and extensive wash along its northern bank after flood stage. Just 60 kilometres southeast of the Tibetan capital, this sandy expanse was selected as the site for the first drop.

Based on information coming from Saipan, a second drop zone was chosen near Molha Khashar, a tiny village of two dozen families just outside Lithang. Besides being the hometown of Walt's family, Molha Khashar was reputed to be an area of armed Khampa resistance.

With two drop zones selected, Thorsrud now had to decide on planes and crews. He eventually settled on an unlikely source. Back in 1949, the CIA had hired two Czech airmen when it needed a deniable crew to drop Ukrainian agents into their homeland. These Czechs had earlier distinguished themselves while flying for the British during the Battle of Britain and had remained in England after their homeland fell to communism. In a variation on this theme, the CIA and British intelligence had jointly prepared a paramilitary operation the following year to unseat the communist government in Albania.

Roger McCarthy being awarded by CIA Director Allen Dulles for his leadership of the Tibet Task Force, 1961. (Photo courtesy Kevin McCarthy)

Once again looking for foreign aircrews to drop agents, the British had suggested tapping the large pool of Polish veterans in England who had performed brilliantly during the Second World War. Thus, six stateless Poles from within that community had been hired and dispatched to a staging base in Athens, Greece, for the Albanian assignment.

Pleased with the results, the CIA in 1955 again turned to stateless Poles when it needed crews for a covert operation running out of Wiesbaden, Germany. Using modified P2V Neptune anti-submarine aircraft, missions were flown along the Soviet frontier to collect electronic intelligence. Although Americans piloted many of these flights, two of the planes were flown with Polish crews and used for actual penetrations of Soviet airspace.

It was from this seasoned Polish contingent at Wiesbaden — code-named Ostiary — that the Far East Division requested the loan of two five-man crews to perform the Tibetan assignment. The first was to be headed by Captain Franciszek Czekalski, the 36-year-old leader of the Wiesbaden Poles. The second was under Captain Jan Drobny, a former flying sergeant who had flown special wartime drop missions to the anti-Axis resistance movement in Poland.

After gaining approval to use Ostiary personnel, Thorsrud had to decide on an infiltration plane. By 1957, the workhorse for covert China overflights from Taiwan was the B-17. The four-engined Flying Fortress had been a fixture of the European theatre during the Second World War. For the CIA's missions over mainland China its ROC-based bombers had been stripped of all weapons and national markings, painted black, and modified with engine mufflers to shield the exhaust. Given its range and manoeuvrability, it was deemed suitable for ST BARNUM.

In mid-September 1957, the finalised plan was sent to CIA Director Dulles for his signature. Upon his consent, a Taiwan-based B-17 was flown to Clark Air Force Base in the Philippines. Also arriving at Clark were the two Ostiary crews escorted by their Wiesbaden case officer, Monty Ballew. Though none of the Europeans had ever flown a B-17, they were well-qualified in four engines and took to the bomber quickly.

Their pro forma transition complete, the Ostiary contingent loaded into the lone bomber and ferried it to Okinawa. There they married up with the Tibetans, who had arrived to start airborne training. Much preparation and experimentation had gone into this phase of the operation. Leading the effort was James McElroy, head of the CIA's aerial resupply section at Kadena. He oversaw a section of four Americans and 90 Okinawans who were responsible for parachute delivery operations in support of CIA operations across the Far East.

Just prior to the arrival of the Tibetans, McElroy had been contacted by Saipan station with two requests. First, they wanted a parachute with high manoeuvrability. Second, they needed a system to ensure that a large supply bundle would remain with the jumper. McElroy was told that the drop zone was at an elevation of 4,545 meters (15,000 feet) with no elaboration on the destination.

For the manoeuvrable parachute, McElroy took a page from the US Forest Service's smokejumpers. During the early 1940s, the latter had developed a 28-foot flat-surface chute with modified slots and tails that gave them sufficient steering ability to manoeuvre near the edge of firestorms. Inspired by this, McElroy back in 1953 had tried to work similar modifications into the military's standard 35-foot T-10 chute. The results had been disappointing, though in hindsight, he realised that the problem was failure to compensate with sufficiently large slots for the bigger army T-10.

This time, McElroy used the same proportions as the smokejumper prototypes. The new chutes, with bigger slots and longer tails, were tested by McElroy and Saipan training officer Roger McCarthy. After four jumps, they concluded that the modified T-10s had the required steerability.

For the second request — keeping the bundle close to the jumper — McElroy had something much more revolutionary in mind. Harkening back to the end of the Second World War, he recalled seeing a magazine photograph of a row of connected bundles streaming out the door of a C-47. "I wasn't sure if it was ever used in combat," he said, "but I wanted to try something similar." Sketching out his concept, McElroy envisioned a nylon line running from the chest of the jumper to the supply pallet. Static lines would deploy chutes on both the pallet and the parachutist, with a 91-meter line keeping the two connected. If one of the two chutes failed to deploy, the line was designed to break if overstressed. McElroy was confident that the system would work — at least on paper.

Once the Tibetans arrived, they were given a primer on landing techniques and then outfitted with the modified chutes. Fearless of heights after years of peering off tall canyons, they exited the plane without hesitation. Much to the case officer's delight, they even used the steerable rigs to chase one another in the air. Three jumps later, all were declared qualified.

By that time, they were into the first days of October 1957, and optimal moon and weather conditions were set to begin over Tibet. Before leaving Kadena, the resupply section loaded bundles inside the B-17. Each of the two Tibetan teams would get a single bundle weighing no more than 114 kilos (250 pounds). Included inside was radio gear, extra crystals, and personal weapons. To get this bundle off the drop zone as fast as possible, the CIA logisticians had broken the gear down into 36-kilo (80-pound) segments and placed them inside special pouched vests similar to those used by newspaper delivery men.

Once their supplies were secured on board, the Tibetans, along with a handful of CIA case officers and both Ostiary crews, took the B-17 to East Pakistan. As with their earlier C-118 exfiltration, the black, unmarked bomber was cleared to land at the unused airstrip at Kurmitola, 13 kilometres north of Dacca. An Allied runway during the Second World War, the Kurmitola field was 1,060 meters long, 45 meters wide, and almost 2 meters thick — all of hand-laid brick. Adjacent to the strip was a hangar with open ends, some empty brick buildings with tin roofs in bad repair, and little else.

As the B-17 landed and the case officers disembarked, they set about preparing the aircraft for its drop. Captain Czekalski's five-man team was selected to crew the plane; no Americans were to be on board. To minimise exposure over Tibet, the Poles would conduct both drops on the same flight. Because the plane would need to overfly Indian territory without permission, they had to factor in the radar outpost at Calcutta. Gar Thorsrud had already done his homework and knew that the Indian system had no compensation feature and could be defeated if the B-17 used the Himalayan massif as a radar screen. Flying north over Sikkim, the crew would go as far as the Brahmaputra for the first drop, cut east across the Tibetan plateau to Kham for the second drop, then veer southwest through Indian territory back to East Pakistan. "It would be an easy flight for the Poles," concluded Thorsrud.

Inside the B-17, two supply loads were positioned near the 1.4-meter hatch located in the belly of the cabin. The Polish loadmaster for the flight, "Big Mac" Korczowski, reviewed with Roger McCarthy the procedure of placing each bundle over the hole and securing it with restraints.

After a one-day delay (because it was considered inauspicious according to the Tibetan calendar), all six Khampas boarded the aircraft. As Kurmitola had no runway lights, flame pots framed the edges of the runway. Before the plane could take off, however, the weather closed in, and the mission was scrubbed. Three more days of overcast followed, and tension was beginning to mount as the full moon entered its final day.

With just one more chance, the weather finally proved cooperative and the mission was given the green light. As the Tibetans filed inside the plane and their Buddhist prayers echoed through the cabin, they turned one last time to case officer Mustakos and offered up a Christian tradition. "I had taught them the sign of the cross," said Mustakos, "and now they sought a double blessing."

Lifting off from Kurmitola, Czekalski put the B-17 on a northern heading over the Sikkim corridor. With the Himalayas bathed in a celestial glow, the Ostiary crew climbed over the range and negotiated their way onto the Tibetan plateau.

Inside their homeland for the first time in over a year, the agents readied themselves for the first jump. Despite the altitude and unpressurised cabin, the Tibetans were not using oxygen bottles; a lifetime of mountain living had acclimatised them to the thin air.

As moonlight reflected off the distant Brahmaputra, agents Tom and Lou, now given the radio call signs Budwood 1 and Budwood 2, manoeuvred toward the hatch. Selected as the jumper to be connected to the bundle, Tom adjusted a short section of line near his chest; the remaining 91 meters was rolled and covered with elastic loops on the side of the supplies. "I carried a knife at my side," recalled Tom, "just in case something went wrong."

As the B-17 came over the Brahmaputra, the cockpit crew flashed a signal in the cabin. Facing forward with his feet near the hole, Tom watched as Big Mac yanked the restraints on the supplies. Once the load disappeared out the hatch, the line began to play out from the side of the bundle. A second later, Tom dropped into the void.

The sound of the bomber fast receded, followed by the sound of a dog barking. As Tom looked about to get his bearings, he eyed the bundle and its white cargo chute floating before him. The jumper-to-supply line system was working perfectly. Lou, meanwhile, used his steerable T-10 to follow in Tom's wake toward the approaching sandbank.

Inside the B-17, navigator Franciszek Kot wasted no time plotting an eastern course, while Big Mac hauled the second bundle over the hatch. When they came upon Kham, however, they found that clear skies had given way to a solid cloud bank. Without any sophisticated navigational systems aboard, the crew had little choice but to abort the second drop and head back to East Pakistan. By that time, the full moon phase had run its course; any further attempts at infiltration would have to wait until the next lunar cycle.

Back inside Tibet, Lou and Tom landed without incident on the wind-blown dunes north of the Brahmaputra. Freeing themselves from their parachute harnesses, they both unstrapped the 9mm Sten sub machine guns fixed to their chests and peered into the darkness. Although there was a small settlement of three families just 364 meters away, they received no indication that they had been detected.

Turning their attention to the supply bundle, they broke open the load and started removing the prepacked vests. Since the area around the drop zone consisted of soft earth, they decided to dig seven holes and cache most of their supplies in the immediate vicinity. Before doing so, both changed into traditional Tibetan garb and retained one pistol and one grenade apiece. They also kept one RS-1 radio set and buried the spare.

The next morning, Tom and Lou wandered through the nearby village. Because nomads and traders are common throughout Tibet, the sudden appearance of two strangers aroused no undue suspicion. Mingling with the locals, they overheard talk about their plane passing overhead in the night. None of the villagers suspected that any parachutists had landed, so the pair felt safe waiting two days in the vicinity before taking their radio to the top of an adjacent hill. To their dismay, however, they found that the set had sustained damage in the drop. "The light on the transmitter was very faint," recalled Tom, who had graduated as best radioman among the six trainees. "I tapped a few words but had no way of knowing if it was actually sent."

Leaving the malfunctioning set behind, the pair decided to follow the Brahmaputra. After trekking along its bank for a few hours, they eventually came upon a secluded riverside village near Samye. Pivotal in the history of Tibet, Samye was the site of the monastery where Buddhism was officially inaugurated as the state religion. Because it hosted a constant stream of pilgrims, the arrival of the two outsiders again aroused no attention. "I had the grenade and pistol in my pockets just in case," remembers Tom.

After purchasing horses and some food, the agents reversed direction east toward the Woka valley. Riddled with caves and hot springs, Woka was renowned for its shrines and other meditation sites. But before they could reach this area, the agents chanced upon a band of seven Khampa pilgrims heading toward the Tibetan capital. Tom and Lou were in for a shock. Two of the approaching pilgrims were friends from among their own group of young Khampas that had tailed the Dalai Lama during the Buddha Jayanti. Taking the pair aside, the agents swore them to secrecy and asked that they deliver messages to prominent Khampa trader Gompo Tashi Andrugtsang and Lou's own younger brother, both residing in Lhasa.

As the Khampa entourage continued toward the capital, Tom and Lou returned to their drop zone and unearthed the spare RS-1. Finding it in good working order, the pair tapped out several sentences, briefly outlining their activities over the past 10 days.

For Irving "Frank" Holober, 10 days had been a long wait. A 33-year-old Harvard graduate, he had been serving as head of the Tibet Task Force since late July 1957. Like his predecessor John Reagan, Holober was a China specialist: three years at headquarters as a Chinese translator, then a tour with Western Enterprises, where he helped channel support to Muslim rebels in Amdo. Following that had been a three-year sojourn in Indonesia before assuming Reagan's slot.

From the start, Holober had been beset with problems. Reports were coming in from Saipan that the Dalai Lama's brother, Norbu, resented the harsh island conditions, especially being forced to eat the same food as the students. As soon as the training cycle concluded, the incarnation and his servant promptly quit the program.

Of far greater concern was the fate of Lou and Tom. From the moment the two agents jumped from the B-17, the CIA had been straining to hear word from their initial team. After a week had passed, there was growing fear that the pair was lost. With little to do, Geshe Wangyal had been temporarily released from service to return to his New Jersey ministry. As an emergency stopgap, Holober had arranged for help from the National Security Agency (NSA), the US intelligence organisation charged with communications intercepts. Based at Fort Meade, Maryland, the NSA agreed to loan the CIA its sole Tibetan linguist, Stuart Buck.

Buck had his work cut out for him. While on Saipan, Geshe Wangyal had taught his Tibetan students a remedial code in which their native script was roughly adapted to the Roman alphabet. But because the six Khampas were not fluent in their own written language, spelling errors in Tibetan were compounded by an inexact Roman transliteration. This is exactly what happened when Tom's message was flashed to CIA headquarters. Trying to make sense of the poor spelling, Buck threw up his hands. "It basically says, 'I'm alive.'"

That was all Holober needed to know. "The entire Far East Division," he recalls, "was electrified."

At Clark Air Base, the Ostiary crews had also been playing a waiting game. Sitting out the remainder of October 1957 while the moon ran its phases, they married up with the four remaining Tibetans and moved back to Kurmitola during the first week of November. This time the weather was fully cooperative as the B-17 made a moonlit departure for Kham.

Catching sight of the Lithang River — which ran past the town of the same name — the crew dropped low over the hills. As they arrived over what they believed was the vicinity of Molha Khashar, the cockpit flashed a signal to the cabin.

Just as the agents lined up behind the belly hatch, Dick hyperventilated and collapsed on the cabin floor. As the loadmaster pulled him to the side, the other three readied themselves for the jump. Repeating the procedure used in the first drop, restraints were pulled from the supply bundle, and it disappeared through the hatch. On the other end of the belly line went Sam, followed by the remaining two agents in quick succession. Reversing course, the B-17 headed back toward East Pakistan with the unconscious Dick still aboard.

Unlike Tom and Lou — who had landed on a desolate sand flat — the three Kham agents came down in a hillside of conifers. Landing without injury, they cached their supplies and ascended to the top of a nearby mountain under cover of darkness. There they heard gunfire in the distance as the PLA duelled with a band of Khampa guerrillas.

As dawn broke, Walt took his bearings. To his dismay, he found that the plane had overshot their intended drop zone by some 14 kilometres. Walking along the high ground into the afternoon, they spotted a lone Khampa tending to five Tibetan ponies. The herdsman was visibly apprehensive as the agents approached, though he eventually agreed to escort them to a guerrilla encampment on a neighbouring hill.

By nightfall, the three agents had successfully linked up with the rebel band, which coincidentally included Walt's older brother. Together, they headed back to their cache site and retrieved their gear, and just 48 hours after infiltration, they radioed word of their safe arrival. ST CIRCUS was off to a good start.

5
GROWING PAINS

By late 1957, the dusty alleys of Lhasa were crammed with war refugees. As a result of the fierce guerrilla battles waged over the past two years, more than 10,000 displaced Khampas and Amdowas had pitched tents in the hills and plains surrounding the Tibetan capital; many more had fled their villages for sanctuary in the countryside. In a vast country with just around 3 million people — and with the normal population of Lhasa standing at only 10,000 — this was a demographic shift of significant proportions.

Lost among these refugees, Lou and Tom looked like just two more destitute Khampas making their way toward the capital when they departed Woka in November 1957. This was not too far from the truth: on the ground for a month, they had spent nearly all the Tibetan and Chinese coins from their supply bundles. Pausing 60 kilometres east of the capital, the agents were in for a pleasant surprise. Already awaiting them was Lou's younger brother, who had received the earlier message asking for a rendezvous. Better still, he had come with enough Chinese currency to allow Tom and Lou to buy a tent.

As a Lithang Khampa from a reputable family, Lou's younger brother had been living within the vast Lhasa household of Lithang's most accomplished citizen, Gompo Tashi Andrugtsang. The Khampa leader had also received a message from the agents and arrived less than a week later to meet them.

Fifty-two years old, Gompo Tashi was unique among Khampas. Though a native of Lithang, he hailed from a family of savvy businessmen who had made a profound mark in Lhasa due to their generous annual donations to Buddhist causes. Gompo Tashi had followed this example, amassing considerable wealth as a trader and continuing the family tradition of religious largesse. From a young age, he also displayed legendary bravery in confronting the bandit gangs that haunted his district.

Taken together, this put him in a category apart from his peers. Unlike Kham's conservative hereditary chieftains, Gompo Tashi was far more worldly (he had made a pilgrimage to India and Nepal in 1942) and could appreciate the benefits of modernity and the wider implications of Chinese hegemony. And unlike other successful Kham traders, he was less Machiavellian and more principled when it came to support for the central government. This gave him a foot in both camps: his seniority and reputation won respect among the Khampas, while his generosity guaranteed influence within the Lhasa power structure.

There was one sore point, however. As his kinsmen were fighting and dying in Kham, Gompo Tashi rarely strayed far from his comfortable residence in the capital. He was not part of the fledgling Khampa resistance movement, nor did he field any fighters of his own. Not until December 1956, half a year after his native Lithang was struck by PLA bombers, did he begin to test the waters of armed dissent. This he did by proxy: three of his employees were dispatched to Kham, each with a letter signed by Gompo Tashi urging the disparate guerrilla bands to unite in a common struggle against the Chinese.

Apart from this move, Gompo Tashi did little for the next year. Things were complicated by the fact that the Khampas themselves were not all sour toward Beijing. In a classic display of clan rivalry, one prominent chieftain from the town of Bathang visited the capital and lectured his fellow Khampas on the benefits of cooperation with the Chinese authorities; he later made a similar pitch to influential monks in Lhasa's biggest monasteries.

Having suffered some of the PLA's worst excesses, Khampas from Gompo Tashi's Lithang were less inclined to compromise. They assumed that he shared their anti-Chinese sentiment, and it was through him that they funnelled multiple petitions in early 1957 seeking military assistance from Lhasa.

Despite the intense struggle being waged in Kham, Lhasa was not listening. Instead, residents in the capital were fully preoccupied with the Dalai Lama's return from India on 1 April 1957. To affirm their collective support for his leadership, they set about preparing a special offering in the shape of a solid gold throne encrusted with gems. Given his past history of donations, Gompo Tashi was selected as a lead fund-raiser and set out for Kham to solicit contributions.

When the throne was officially presented on 4 July, the celebration was deemed a rousing success. Though this did little to help the guerrillas in eastern Tibet, Gompo Tashi's trip to Kham had given him ample opportunity to discuss resistance activities with his kinsmen. It also afforded him occasional audiences with Thupten Woyden Phala. A tall and dignified monk, Phala had long been a confidant of the Dalai Lama. His official promotion to lord chamberlain — a combination personal secretary and head of the household staff — late the previous year meant that his access to the monarch was without peer.

Not only was Phala a direct conduit to the highest echelon of power; he was also known to have little tolerance for the Chinese. An ardent nationalist, he had been among the most vocal proponents lobbying for the Dalai Lama to seek exile in 1950. And during the early months of 1957, he had strongly sided with brothers Gyalo and Norbu in trying to keep the monarch from returning to Tibet.

By the time Lou and Tom were ready to parachute to the banks of the Brahmaputra, the CIA knew enough about Phala's influence and nationalist disposition to make him a primary target for the two agents. After their rendezvous with Gompo Tashi in November 1957, the agents sought his aid in arranging a meeting with Phala. As that would take time, the Khampa leader suggested that they wait at a location closer to Lhasa. Departing shortly thereafter, he left behind two assistants to help procure supplies.

As suggested, the agents soon moved 26 kilometres northeast of the capital at the village of Pempo. Resuming radio contact from there, Tom was instructed by the CIA to briefly venture farther north into the hills overlooking the Damshung airfield. Once there, he befriended some nomads, determined that the base was rarely used, and returned to Pempo to report his findings over the RS-1.

By the close of 1957, the pair was again on the move. Continuing their counter clockwise trek around the capital, they reached the famed Drepung monastery, where Geshe Wangyal had studied. They stopped there for less than a week and then shifted to the northern city limits of Lhasa near the similarly immense Sera monastery. Pitching a tent among hundreds of others inhabited by student monks, they couriered a coded message into the capital requesting a second meeting with Gompo Tashi.

It did not take long for a response. To avoid possible Chinese surveillance, the Khampa patriarch agreed to a weekend meeting at a park inside Lhasa. Bringing along food, they lost themselves among the throngs of holidaying residents. The agents used the opportunity to again request help in arranging an audience with Phala, and Gompo Tashi promised to pursue the matter.

Their persistence eventually paid off. Two months later, Gompo Tashi sent a messenger to Sera with two sets of monk's robes. The agents were given instructions to proceed to the north gate of the Norbulingka, the walled, 40-hectare enclave on the western outskirts of Lhasa that housed the Dalai Lama's summer palace. Waiting at a cottage inside the gate was Gompo Tashi, who escorted them to Phala's residence.

Sitting in front of the Dalai Lama's confidant, the agents were immediately peppered with questions about their training. Firing back, they quizzed the lord chamberlain about what kind of help Lhasa needed or wanted. They also asked Phala to make an official request for US assistance.

It would prove to be an impossible sell. Whatever Phala's personal views on the subject, the Dalai Lama was determined not to provoke Beijing. This meant restraint from offering the rebels any moral backing, much less material assistance. Echoing his master, Phala kept his distance from any resistance movement. "He was completely noncommittal," recalled Tom. "He also said the Chinese were playing off the Tibetan noblemen and nobody trusted each other anymore."

As they prepared to leave, the agents suggested that Phala might want to provide a written message that could be conveyed to Washington. They also asked to see the Dalai Lama at a future date, noting that his brother Norbu had suggested this during their training on Saipan. Phala promised to do his best on both counts.

Neither proved forthcoming. After two months of waiting at Sera without further contact, it became clear that Phala had gotten cold

The Dalai Lama (seated in dark clothing) with Chushi Gangdruk guards during his flight to India, 1959. (Photo courtesy The Tibet Museum)

feet. "The ClA kept asking for updates, " said Tom, "but there was no news to give."

Worse for the agents, they had no source of income and were constantly living off handouts from family members in Lhasa. (While in Saipan, the CIA had said that it would attempt to smuggle money to them via Phala, but the lord chamberlain truthfully professed that he had not received any such funds.)

Hungry and frustrated, the pair finally received permission for a second meeting with Phala at the Norbulingka in late March 1958. Like the first encounter, they found the lord chamberlain less than warm; he remained silent about providing any written or verbal appeals to the US government. He also rebuffed their second request for a personal blessing from the Dalai Lama, noting that the monarch was surrounded by minders, and secrecy could not be assured. As consolation, he offered some religious relics purportedly from the spiritual leader.

Gompo Tashi, meantime, was growing impatient with Lhasa's waffling. He was especially concerned when the Chinese authorities announced plans to perform a census around the capital and expel any Khampas or Amdowas who had lived there for less than 10 years. Although he did not fall into that category, Gompo Tashi was sufficiently worried to seek advice from the influential state oracle of the Nechung monastery. This particular oracle, say Tibetans, was regularly possessed by one of the more important spirits in their cosmology, and his entranced advice held immense sway over decisions of the Lhasa government.

During his channelling session with Gompo Tashi, the oracle was unequivocal. The Khampa leader should leave Lhasa, he said, no later than the Buddha Jayanti celebrations on the seventh day of the fourth lunar month. When asked what direction Gompo should take, the oracle answered south, toward Drigu Tso lake.

With the decision made for him, Gompo Tashi quietly earmarked pack animals, employees, weapons, and a major slice of his family earnings for the guerrillas in Kham. He also urged the CIA radiomen to remain in Lhasa and stay in contact with one of Phala's assistants. But after a meeting with that assistant who showed no more fortitude than his superior, Tom and Lou elected to join Gompo Tashi in the exodus.

As the date of the Buddha Jayanti approached in mid-April 1958, the Khampa chieftain finalised his departure plans. Knowing that most of the city's residents traditionally made a brief pilgrimage to a monastery across the river from Lhasa on the day after the Buddha Jayanti, he decided to camouflage his exit among those crowds.

So, too, would the CIA's agents. Dressed as monks and with their gear stowed on two mules, they skirted the capital on the prescribed day and waited south of the river. They were met by a band of Gompo Tashi's servants bearing extra horses — but not Gompo Tashi himself — and their small caravan headed south. A day later, the Khampa leader stylishly rendezvoused with them on a motorcycle, which he promptly exchanged for a less flashy equestrian mount.

Continuing south, they made good time to the banks of the Brahmaputra River. They crossed the river on a wooden ferry and then pushed south in the direction of the Drigu Tso. Unfortunately, Gompo Tashi carried a poor map and was taking pains to stay clear of major trails in order to avoid PLA patrols. As a result, when they arrived at a major body of water and made inquiries with the locals, they found that they had inadvertently arrived at Lake Yamdrok, 55 kilometres west of their intended destination.

Pausing for the moment, Gompo Tashi sent a scout party east to reconnoitre the Drigu Tso. The scouts returned with reports that the lake was surrounded by flatland and populated by only a handful of nomads. Satisfied that the oracle had made a good choice, the Khampa leader dispatched his servants across the plateau with a request that resistance members of all Tibetan ethnic persuasions congregate at the Drigu Tso in a month's time. Meanwhile, he took Lou and Tom farther south toward the Bhutanese border to procure adequate grain supplies for the upcoming guerrilla rendezvous.

As this was transpiring, far to the east Walt could speak first-hand about the state of the resistance. From the moment he and his two fellow agents landed in November 1957, they were immersed in the heart of the Kham guerrilla movement. Due to district rivalries, that movement had never developed a unified province-wide command structure. Twenty-three Khampa clans, however, were fighting together under the common title of the Volunteer Army to Defend Buddhism. By early 1958, this functional name had given way to a geographic one: Chushi Gangdruk — "Four Rivers, Six Ranges" — a reference to the major rivers (Mekong, Salween, Yangtze, and Yalung) and mountains that ran across Kham.

In Walt's own band, 500 Chushi Gangdruk rebels were focused on expelling the Chinese around Lithang. Things started out well enough, including the unexpected arrival of the final Saipan-trained student, Dick. After hyperventilating in the rear of the B-17, Dick had been off-loaded in Dacca and smuggled overland back to Darjeeling. Once there, Gyalo Thondup had matched him up with another able-bodied Khampa and sent both on horseback into Tibet via Sikkim.

After making his way to Lithang, Dick presented a letter from Gyalo pledging imminent support. This was welcome news for Walt; almost from the moment he had landed, he had been sending multiple radio requests for weapons and ammunition. Now armed with Gyalo's letter, he generated considerable excitement among the insurgents and succeeded in attracting new recruits.

Walt's ethnic kin were not the only ones taking notice of his recruitment activity. Due to the relatively low altitude and easy access along new roads completed in 1956, the PLA had been able to shift 150,000 soldiers to eastern Tibet by the end of 1957. Specifically targeted against southern Kham were hordes of pro-PRC Muslim cavalrymen, who had already been used to devastating effect against a sister rebellion on the steppes of Amdo.

In the ensuing mismatch of numbers, the fate of Chushi Gangdruk was a foregone conclusion. By mid-1958, Walt's servant Thondup, known as "Dan" while on Saipan, took a bullet to the head. A month later, Sam fell victim to an ambush. Shortly thereafter, Dick was shot. With three of the four Saipan students lost, Walt and the remnants of his band had little choice but to abandon Lithang and begin a fighting withdrawal toward central Tibet.

Walt was not alone. By the summer of 1958, waves of Khampa refugees and defeated rebels were heading west toward Lhasa. Of these, some diverted south to the banks of the Drigu Tso, where on 16 June Gompo Tashi arrived to oversee the inauguration ceremony for a unified resistance movement dubbed the National Volunteer Defense Army (NVDA). With 1,500 guerrillas in attendance and Gompo Tashi named titular head by acclamation, the previous flag of the Chushi Gangdruk (a mythical snow lion on a blue background) was replaced by a new NVDA standard featuring crossed Tibetan swords on a yellow field. Tom was on hand to take photographs of the occasion; the roll of film was then couriered out to Gyalo in India.

The reason for the name change was more than semantic. Although the NVDA was overwhelmingly composed of Khampas, Gompo Tashi intentionally sought to break from the regional overtones of Chushi Gangdruk and present a name and image that would appeal to all Tibetans.

As this was transpiring, Tom and Lou duly radioed updates back to the CIA. Much of their reporting consisted of requests for weapons and ammunition. When none were forthcoming, Gompo Tashi took matters into his own hands and departed NVDA headquarters in August to lead a raid against an isolated Chinese garrison southwest of the capital. There, it was hoped, they could make off with a haul of armaments at little risk.

In the ensuing series of battles, the NVDA was less than successful. Word of its first impending attack had apparently been leaked, and the scout party walked into an ambush. Withdrawing after a three-day fight, they promptly walked into a second ambush. Continuing on a western heading, they next attempted to raid an armoury of the Tibetan army.

There, the NVDA was exposed to the rude ironies of its nationalist struggle. Though it might have shared sympathies with the NVDA, the small Tibetan army, like the central government to which it answered, remained publicly opposed to the anti-Chinese resistance and took pains not to assist the resistance in any way. This was done in part to avoid angering Beijing, which was already pressuring Lhasa to take up arms against the insurgents. In part, too, it was due to lingering ethnic prejudices: the NVDA, like Chushi Gangdruk before it, could not shake the Khampa brigand stereotype held by many central Tibetans. This became painfully apparent when Gompo Tashi and his guerrillas approached the government armoury. Anticipating the raid, Lhasa had secretly ordered the weapons shifted to a nearby monastery. Eventually learning of the ruse, the NVDA leaned on the local monks but found their audience to be less than receptive. Only after many days of cajoling did the religious officials reluctantly open their stores to the resistance fighters.

Back in Washington, updates from their radio operators in Tibet left the CIA far from satiated. Most of the messages were being sent by Tom; although he had been the best Morse code student among the Saipan graduates, his grammatical shortcomings limited most transmissions to only a few clauses. "It was okay from an operational point of view," said Tibet Task Force chief Frank Holober, "but wanting from an intelligence standpoint."

The Agency was particularly reluctant to commit weaponry without a better understanding of the NVDA and where it was headed. Short of visiting Tibet, the only way to get this was to fully debrief one of the agents. For that purpose, word was sent back for Tom to make his way to India. Taking loan of a horse, the agent travelled for 10 days toward the Sikkimese frontier, slipped past a PLA border ambush, and made his way to Darjeeling.

Once there, Tom lost little time locating Gyalo and his personal assistant, Lhamo Tsering. Six years Gyalo's senior, Lhamo was Gyalo's distant relative from Amdo. Lhamo had fought in a Chinese youth militia unit against the Japanese, and shortly after returning to Amdo, Gyalo's mother had tasked him with chaperoning her son while the latter was studying in Nanking. The two had almost been inseparable since.

To assist Tom during the debriefing, Lhamo Tsering accompanied the Kham agent down to Calcutta. There they secretly rendezvoused with CIA officer John Hoskins, who had the pair lie in the back of his car as he drove them to a safe house for a meeting with Frank Holober. Although Lhamo spoke passable English, he and Holober found that they shared more linguistic common ground using Mandarin. Over the ensuing week, the CIA officer translated questions into Chinese for Lhamo, who would pose them to Tom during the afternoon and present his answers the following morning.

Holober also used the opportunity to meet Gyalo. Much like the earlier assessment by Hoskins, Holober was not overly impressed by the Dalai Lama's brother. "I did the briefing," he recalls, "and Gyalo did a lot of nodding."

There were other concerns as well. By that time, the team in Lithang had ceased radio transmissions and been declared missing. The apparent loss of its agents came at a critical juncture, as the CIA did not wish a repeat of the 1956 Hungarian rebellion, when ill-prepared activists proved easy fodder for Soviet cannons. "We wanted to create cells like the Communist Party," said Holober, "not a full-blown resistance that would be snuffed."

But it was too late for that. Based on Tom's observations, the resistance was up and running and would continue with or without CIA support. Despite the Hungarian precedent, the Agency concluded that the Tibetan rebels were one of the best things it had going behind communist lines. Accordingly, a decision was made in the late summer of 1958 to proceed with limited material support. The Agency also decided in principle to train a second group of Tibetans. Unlike the first contingent — which was theoretically to act as eyes and ears — the second wave would be coached as guerrilla instructors to help the resistance multiply exponentially.

To provide material assistance to the NVDA, aerial methods were the Agency's only viable option. Just as during the ST BARNUM insertions the previous year, range dictated that their plane stage from East Pakistan, and the same meteorological considerations called for the supply drop to coincide with the clear skies and full moon of mid-October 1958.

There would also be significant differences from the earlier missions. Although the stateless Poles had performed exceptionally well during the first two Tibetan flights, they had suffered fatalities during a subsequent CIA operation in Indonesia and lobbied to permanently leave Asia for their previous posting in Germany.

With Ostiary out of the running, the officers at the Far East Division's air branch proposed the use of Americans. The idea held more risk than ever. During the Indonesia operation in May 1958, a CAT pilot had been downed and captured — a fiasco that helped end the Agency's entire paramilitary operation in that country. The following month, a USAF C-118 had been brought down by MiG fighters along the Soviet border during an attempted reconnaissance flight, heaping yet more egg on Washington's face.

Despite these embarrassments, the ST BARNUM planners persisted and won permission to use a CAT aircrew for Tibet. Given the depth of multi-engine experience in the CAT ranks, this opened up the possibility of flying a larger plane with more cargo capability than the B-17. They eventually settled on the sanitised USAF C-118 that had been handling covert flights out of Okinawa.

Once this choice was approved, the aircraft was outfitted with a set of rollers curving out its oversized rear door. This allowed for a much larger bundle than could be squeezed through the belly hatch of the B-17. This also meant that the mission would need a larger complement of crewmen to disgorge the load over the drop zone. Searching for suitable candidates, the CIA soon discovered that cargo handlers had become a rare commodity in Asia.

With time pressing, the CIA turned to the smokejumper community. By coincidence, the September rains had brought an abrupt end to the summer fire season in the western United States, and many were readily available. In short order, three were selected and sent to Washington for a security check and briefing.

As the three smokejumpers subsequently made their way to Okinawa, the head of the CIA air operations office in Tokyo, Colonel William Weltman, was informed of the selection of a CAT aircrew. The pilot and co-pilot were to be Merrill "Doc" Johnson and William Welk. Both these aviators had been among a small group of CAT pilots who had performed with distinction during deep mainland penetrations in 1952. Chosen as flight engineer was Bill Lively, the navigator slot went to James Keck, and the radioman was Bob Aubrey.

Waiting at Okinawa until the full moon phase in mid-October 1958, Weltman personally entered the cockpit to ferry the C-118 down to Clark Air Base in the Philippines. Pausing long enough for Weltman to make a symbolic transfer to Doc Johnson, they then proceeded toward East Pakistan. As had been the case during the B-17 flights, the CAT crew found that Kurmitola airfield held few amenities. "We spent the night on cots in an open hangar," recalls Gar Thorsrud, who had arrived from Washington to oversee the mission. Several crew members sighted snakes in the rafters, and local guards repeated apocryphal tales of a man-eating tiger outside the base perimeter.

All of this paled next to the dangers associated with the C-118 itself. Because it was not designed to open inward during flight, the rear door was temporarily removed at Kurmitola. The plane, as a result, would be flying unpressurised for the duration of the mission. Not only did this mean an uncomfortably cold cockpit and cabin, but the crew would need to use oxygen masks to keep from passing out in the thin air over the Tibetan plateau. Worse, the C-118's four engines barely had enough power to clear the Himalayas; if one engine shut down en route, they had little hope of getting home.

The challenges continued to mount once they got airborne the next morning. Following the same route taken during the first Ostiary mission, navigator Keck was shocked by the poor Second World War-era maps they had been given. "Once over the Himalayas," he said, "the charts just showed big sections of brown and tan with no data."

To compensate, Keck climbed into the plane's glass dome atop the fuselage to take a celestial reading. While he was there, disaster nearly struck. To facilitate movement, he and the rest of the crew had been outfitted with walk-around oxygen bottles. As he ascended into the dome, however, the bottle's three-meter tube was accidentally pinched. Unaware of the blockage and slowly lapsing into unconsciousness, Keck nonchalantly told the cockpit that he was going to take a nap. Only through the fast action of the flight engineer was the tube unkinked and Keck's senses restored.

Once the plane approached the Drigu Tso drop zone, Keck, Aubrey, and Lively all converged in the cabin to offer assistance manhandling the loads down the rollers. As instructed by Lou (Tom was still en route from India), local guerrillas had lit a huge flaming cross on the ground. This had been done with a unique Tibetan twist: instead of wood — a precious commodity at high altitudes — the signal had been constructed from more plentiful horse and yak dung.

Sighting the fire, Johnson activated a green light in the cabin. As the plane nosed upward, this was the cue for the cargo handlers to remove the final stops on the pallets and give them a gravity-assisted push. With static lines connected to a beam fitted to the ceiling, the supplies thundered down the conveyor and out the door. Olive canopies blossomed in the plane's wake, and the bundles floated toward the waiting guerrillas.

Converging on the pallets, the Tibetans broke them open to find two-hundred .303 Lee-Enfield rifles and ammunition. A bolt-action rifle that had seen heavy action during the First World War, the vintage Lee-Enfield had two advantages. First, it had been a staple of the Tibetan army since 1914. It could therefore be assumed that the Tibetans had mastered its use and maintenance. Second, it was of British origin and had been liberally supplied to regional armies such as those of India and Pakistan; the US, as a result, was afforded plausible deniability.

Although the guerrillas had no qualms about the choice of weapon, they did question the quantities provided. Almost immediately, they leaned on Tom (who had just completed his return trek from India) to radio an appeal for a second drop.

Elsewhere in the field, not all was going well for the NVDA. After strongarming weapons from the monastery in August, Gompo Tashi and his guerrillas now wielded a mixed selection of mortars, machine guns, and rifles. Working their way clockwise around Lhasa, they eventually approached the PLA's Damshung airfield north of the capital. Despite a string of tactical wins along the way — a truck ambushed here, an outpost overrun there — the Khampa tactics were generally not working. Part of this was due to the fact that Gompo Tashi was manoeuvring his rebels by the hundreds, nearly all of them on horseback. Although it might have been possible to conceal these numbers in the conifer forests of southern Kham, it was not feasible in the barren hills of central Tibet.

The Chinese, as a result, almost always knew where the NVDA was and when it would be coming. Theoretically, the guerrillas should have been able to set the pace of battle and dictate their targets; instead, they were almost always on the run and being corralled by their opponents in a very conventional manner. Bringing spotter planes and field artillery into play, the PLA outnumbered and outgunned the main rebel concentration as it neared Damshung. Peppered with shrapnel, a wounded Gompo Tashi soon ordered a retreat to the east.

Part of the NVDA's problem, too, was the collective cold shoulder offered by the local population. As Mao had preached during the Chinese Civil War, revolutionary guerrillas were akin to fish thriving in the water of the community. Without water, went the metaphor, the fish could not survive. Given Tibet's sparse population, the Khampa guerrillas rarely encountered such figurative water. And when they did, central Tibetans — influenced by anti-rebel proclamations from Lhasa and generations of prejudice — saw them as less than brothers in arms.

Facing these obstacles, Gompo Tashi in September 1958 ordered his task force on a long march out of central Tibet. By October, just as the first supply drop was landing at Drigu Tso, they arrived at the western edge of Kham. Cold and hungry after their trek through knee-deep snow, they hoped for a more friendly reception among their kin. Unfortunately for the NVDA, some of their number chose the opportunity to split from the cause and revert to banditry. Realising that this would undercut any attempt at winning the locals' hearts and minds, Gompo Tashi had no choice but to put the anti-Chinese struggle on hold and instead spend time bringing his rogue members to justice.

In southern Tibet, meantime, the NVDA was also in a state of flux. The guerrillas soon determined why so few people lived around the Drigu Tso: the winds coming off the lake were frigid during winter, and the soil did not support any agriculture. Looking for a more hospitable venue, the headquarters of the resistance shifted north to the more fertile Yarlung valley near the Brahmaputra.

Lou, meanwhile, ventured with a rebel contingent to the village of Lhagyari, 40 kilometres east of Yarlung. Tom briefly joined him there after his return from India, but the two soon relocated far south to an NVDA rear base at the village of Lhuntse Dzong, just 45 kilometres from the Indian border.

While at Lhuntse Dzong, the pair got word in November 1958 that a second supply drop was in the works. Though otherwise inhospitable, the barren plains near Drigu Tso had worked perfectly as a drop zone the first time. Looking to repeat this success, the two agents agreed to take a reception committee to that area to greet the second flight.

For this ST BARNUM reprise, the same C-118 and crew departed Kurmitola on an identical flight path. Without complications, olive-drab parachutes mushroomed in the plane's wake, and the supplies floated down to the waiting rebels.

With the October and November drops, the guerrillas had now been provided with 18,000 pounds of weapons, ammunition, and communications gear. Although this should have been reason for cheer, their attention was instead fixated on a single yellow parachute used during the November shipment. Quickly appropriated by Tom and Lou, the bundle attached to this chute contained additional radios and a satchel of 300,000 Indian rupees to pay message couriers. Always game for a good conspiracy, the Tibetan rebels began bickering that the radio operators had actually received a small fortune in gold ingots — hence the colour of the chute — and were not willing to share their bounty.

Such self-destructive sniping was compounded by the arrival in December of Walt and a handful of stragglers from Lithang. He had been out of radio contact for half a year, and his sudden appearance was an intelligence windfall for the CIA. Walt, however, did not see it that way and had Tom relay his intense frustration over the radio. Infuriated with Washington's refusal to conduct an arms drop for Lithang, the fiery Khampa reported that the resistance in that locale was crushed and his three Saipan-trained colleagues missing (only Dan was a known fatality; the fate of the other two was still unconfirmed at the time). "The CIA asked if he would return to Kham to verify their fate," recalls his brother, "but he said there was no hope and refused."

It was on that sour note — with Walt sulking at Lhuntse Dzong and Gompo Tashi wrestling with the NVDA's self-inflicted wounds — that 1958 drew to an inauspicious close.

6
THE FARM

Returning from his debriefing of Tom in the late summer of 1958, Frank Holober was still far from satisfied with the Tibet Task Force's communications arrangement. Exfiltrating an agent to India had worked once, but it was hardly a practical solution. A big part of the problem was rooted in the complexity of the Tibetan language. Consisting of 30 consonants and five vowels, it had been set down in a Sanskrit script with a less than perfect arrangement. Several symbols were often used for virtually identical sounds, resulting in numerous homophones: different spellings, different meanings, same pronunciation.

Given the poor educational background of the Khampa students, homophones were just one reason they were having such difficulty composing coherent radio messages. To help overcome this, the CIA's instructors on Saipan had developed a telecode booklet listing common Tibetan words and phrases, each transliterated into the Roman alphabet and assigned a five-digit number group. For words that did not exist in Tibetan — like "bazooka " — English was used. All that remained was for the Khampa radiomen to encrypt the number groups with a one-time pad and transmit.

Geshe Wangyal, the CIA's Mongolian translator. (Photo courtesy Joshua Cutler)

Although the telecode booklet was a good start, problems persisted. Not knowing how much radio traffic it would receive, the CIA had included only the most basic vocabulary. When they needed to express words not contained in the book, the agents usually picked the wrong spelling.

Each time one of the resultant garbled messages was received at the Agency's communications facility on Okinawa and relayed to Washington, Holober was faced with the frustrating process of deciphering its meaning. In need of a native speaker to interpret on a phonetic basis, he frequently solicited assistance from the venerable Geshe Wangyal. But even with Geshe Wangyal's linguistic skills, second-guessing the Khampa messages was a trying art.

Looking ahead, Holober recognised that one way to reduce such problems in the future would be to have a telecode list with more words. To accomplish this, both he and Geshe Wangyal patiently expanded the booklet over the course of 1958. By fall, it was starting to approximate a full-fledged book.

That same autumn, Holober's task force was augmented by a pair of officers. One of them, Thomas Fosmire, was a 28-year-old former sergeant in the 82nd Airborne Division who had made his CIA debut launching sabotage and agent teams from small boats during the Korean War.

Following the Korean armistice, Fosmire served in Thailand as an advisor to the Thai border police at four different training camps stretched across the kingdom. In February 1958, he received an emergency call to act as a cargo handler during a covert airdrop in neighbouring Indonesia. Continuing on with the Indonesia assignment, he was secretly posted to the island of Sulawesi, where he advised anti-government rebels through late spring.

When the Indonesia operation was forced to close prematurely — in large part because a CAT pilot had been shot down and captured — Fosmire went to Saipan as the escort officer for a Filipino counterinsurgency team in training. By the late summer of 1958, he was back in Washington and landed a slot on Holober's task force. For the first few weeks, he shuttled around the capital to elicit help in refining the Tibetan radio code.

Not long after, the task force received a visit from the CIA's Far East Division chief, Desmond FitzGerald. A strong supporter of the Tibet project, FitzGerald gave his approval to proceed with training for the second Tibetan contingent. This time, however, it was decided to offer instruction at a location more similar to their home environment than the tropical climes of Saipan. The closest elevation to Tibet in the continental United States is in the Rocky Mountains of central Colorado. That same state hosts the country's highest incorporated city, Leadville, at 3,162 meters. Once bloated with 40,000 residents during the silver boom of the late nineteenth century, Leadville's population in 1958 barely exceeded 4,000. While such tranquillity held appeal for the CIA, of even greater interest was the secluded valley 32 kilometres to its west. There, strung along a 10-kilometre stretch of the Eagle River, stood Camp Hale.

Much like Leadville, Camp Hale was a shadow of its former self. Activated in 1942, the camp at its peak had 1,022 buildings in support of 15,000 troops. On the surrounding slopes, the US Army's 10th Mountain Division learned skiing, rock climbing, and cold weather survival skills — often in temperatures that dipped to 30 degrees below zero.

Despite its contribution to the war effort, Hale was destined to be a peace-time casualty. Nazi prisoners (400 of the most incorrigible members of Rommel's Afrika Korps had been confined at Hale) were assigned to dismantle the camp shortly after the war, and they nearly succeeded. Only a handful of buildings was left standing, and they were used periodically through the early 1950s to train ski troops. By the middle of the decade, however, the Pentagon saw little need to maintain specialist ski formations. The camp — what was left of it — was shuttered and abandoned.

All of this suited the CIA perfectly. In the early fall of 1958, the job of reconnoitring the Hale facilities was given to the task force's second new officer, John Greaney. Given a plane ticket to Colorado and armed with the highest-level government permission, he received excellent cooperation from the US Army officers at Fort Carson in Colorado Springs, which retained administrative control over Hale. Unfortunately for the CIA, the camp's best remaining buildings were within sight of the Denver and Rio Grande Western Railroad. From a security point of view, there was a better area further down the valley, but that would entail laying sewage and water pipes for several kilometres. Since Hale was already frozen under early snows, construction of the pipes promised to be slow. The Agency, Greaney concluded, would need an alternative site for the interim.

The task of finding an alternative fell to Tom Fosmire. Shopping around for an existing facility, he took a trip in September 1958 to the CIA's expansive training base at Camp Peary near Williamsburg, Virginia — nicknamed "The Farm." He presented the camp personnel with a request for temporary use of a remote locale within the grounds.

Eyeing Fosmire's youth — and perceived lack of clout — the staff could barely conceal their boredom. Stalking out, he promised to report their lack of cooperation directly to Des FitzGerald. The threat worked. "A lanky, enthusiastic young officer caught up with me," recalls Fosmire, "and said he had a friend at Fort Eustis that could scrounge up some spare Quonset huts." Assembled in a desolate, wooded corner of Peary, the Tibet Task Force soon had its temporary training site in place.

Task accomplished, Fosmire returned to Washington and was on hand when the first C-118 supply drop was performed near the Drigu Tso. Taking leave of the capital, Fosmire next rushed to Kurmitola for the arrival of the second Tibetan contingent. Like the first group, these trainees had crossed the border with Gyalo's cook and rendezvoused with a train bound for Dacca. Also like the first group, they consisted of Lithang Khampas — 10, this time — recruited from the Kalimpong refugee community. The leader of the 10, Ngawang Phunjung, was a nephew of Gompo Tashi (as was Walt from the first group). Because the first two translators — Norbu and Jentzen — had quit the program, Gyalo dispatched his own assistant, Lhamo Tsering, to act in that capacity.

As the Tibetans filed aboard the C-118, the plane was quickly on its way to Okinawa. Once at Kadena, they were hustled aboard a bus with blackened windows and taken to a three-bedroom safe house within the CIA compound.

The next morning, all 10 students began a battery of medical tests. Two of the Khampas were found to have tuberculosis and ordered to remain at the safe house. The remaining eight, plus Lhamo Tsering, reboarded the C-118 and, several refuelling stops later, got off at a strip inside the confines of The Farm.

By that time, a November dusting had left Peary under a veil of snow. With the weather to their liking, the Tibetans faced a tough schedule of class and field work. Fosmire was to personally oversee the cycle. He would be assisted by a new arrival to the project, William "Billy the Kid" Smith. The nickname was apropos: the cherubic Smith was fresh out of the US Army and on his first Agency assignment.

Together, Fosmire and Smith began teaching seven days a week. Their initial focus was on classroom drills, especially map reading. Additional specialist instructors came to the site as needed. These included several radio experts, the longest serving of whom was Ray Stark.

By February 1959, a third paramilitary officer joined Fosmire and Smith. That officer, Anthony "Tony Poe" Poshepny, age 34, knew his material. A US Marine in the Second World War, he had received a string of Purple Hearts from Iwo Jima and other Pacific battles. Joining the CIA in 1951, over the ensuing seven years his career spanned Asia: running maritime operations in Korea, police paramilitary training in Thailand, assisting anti-communist rebels in Indonesia. After a daring submarine escape from the Indonesian island of Sumatra, he had spent the second half of 1958 giving guerrilla instruction to Chinese Nationalist teams on Taiwan and Saipan.

Poe left the Far East for Peary and was on hand as the Tibetans were being readied for a series of field exercises. For one of these, the instructor cadre prevailed on the Peary staff to give permission to use a secure lake area. Wielding an assortment of British weapons ("The Tibetans loved the Bren and Lee-Enfield," recalls Fosmire), the students infiltrated by night and liberally doused the vicinity with explosive charges, accidentally damaging several boats in the process. As the camp's fire department rushed to the scene, the Tibetans raced away in the opposite direction inside a blacked-out van.

By March 1959, the exercises were over and the training cycle was fast drawing to a close. Already, spring weather had turned parts of Peary into a swamp and unleashed hordes of mosquitoes. Work at Camp Hale had been completed, and the Tibetans warmly welcomed the news that they would soon be switching to a new, colder locale for what was supposed to be just a few weeks, according to their original schedule, before proceeding back to their homeland.

Tom Fosmire, the first training chief at Camp Hale. (Photo courtesy Thomas Fosmire)

Although the Tibetans at Peary did not know it yet, their final days at Williamsburg coincided with monumental changes in Lhasa as the Tibetan government and their Chinese overlords manoeuvred toward a painful showdown. The catalyst for this came in January 1959 as the NVDA re-instilled discipline in its ranks and began gearing up for renewed operations around the headwaters of the Salween in western Kham. For the previous month, Gompo Tashi had been lobbying local chieftains and was pleased with their professed support. Emboldened, he planned twin strikes on PLA strongholds sitting astride the Chinese-built road leading to Lhasa. Each assault would involve multiple prongs, including the participation of 800 horsemen from the NVDA headquarters in Yarlung. Gyalo Thondup had even dispatched two Khampas from India with a movie camera to make a propaganda film of the operation.

In planning such coordinated pincers, however, Gompo Tashi was expecting far too much of his guerrilla army. His own forces had no radio, limiting communications with Yarlung to the occasional message courier. And even if the Yarlung horsemen were intent on joining the battle, it entailed an extended winter trek across the heart of the Tibetan plateau.

Perhaps not surprisingly, when Gompo Tashi ultimately launched his raids, the Yarlung column never materialised. Worse from the NVDA's perspective, the PLA rushed in reinforcements along the road to both locales. Although the Chinese absorbed heavy casualties, neither site fell to the Tibetans.

Overview of Camp Hale. (Photo courtesy Roger McCarthy)

The NVDA had far better luck with its subsequent recruitment drives in Kham. Some 7,000 prospects joined its cause, and a personal appeal from Gompo Tashi to the local governor enabled his insurgents to walk away with nearly the entire inventory of a government armoury. On a roll, 130 guerrillas headed north and laid siege to a PLA outpost near the headwaters of the Mekong. Fighting raged for a month, and it was only after Chinese airpower bloodied the rebels in late February that the NVDA was forced to withdraw and nurse its wounds.

In the immediate aftermath of this last battle, Gompo Tashi huddled with his lieutenants for a war council. Although the Tibetans had inflicted more casualties than they had received, this was not particularly problematic for the PLA, given China's enormous reservoir of manpower. Anticipating the arrival of major Chinese reinforcements come spring, the council made the strategic decision to temporarily abandon Kham and begin shifting the majority of its troops toward Yarlung.

In Lhasa, meanwhile, the PLA's top representatives were fuming. Not only was rebel activity on the rise in Kham, but when the Dalai Lama returned to his summer palace on 5 March 1959 (he had been studying in nearby monasteries since mid-1958 for an exhaustive battery of religious exams), thousands of Tibetan citizens spontaneously formed a protective cordon around the Norbulingka. They had taken this measure because word had leaked that the Chinese were insisting that the Dalai Lama attend a performance by a visiting dance troupe at their military compound in Lhasa — but without his normal contingent of bodyguards. Convinced that this was a ploy to kidnap their leader, the masses had formed a human shield around his palace.

For the 23-year-old Dalai Lama, the situation had an air of the absurd. Rebels were roaming the countryside, the capital was a tinderbox, and the Chinese were irate over his non-attendance at a cultural show. Sensing that the end was drawing near, on 12 March he called for the Nechung oracle to determine whether he should stay in Lhasa. While in a trance, the medium replied in the affirmative. This was not exactly the answer the Dalai Lama wanted, so another form of divination — a roll of the dice, literally — was sought. As luck would have it, the results were the same.

Over the next four days, the crowds kept their raucous vigil around the Norbulingka while the Chinese, not humoured by the Dalai Lama's procrastination over the dance troupe invitation, were insisting that he commit to a date. The oracle was again summoned; apparently of a conservative bent, the entranced medium would not budge from his earlier ruling.

Not until 17 March, during the third channelling session in a week, did the oracle buckle. "Leave tonight," was his entranced message. The dice, too, cooperated, giving identical advice.

The Dalai Lama hardly needed prompting. At nightfall, he stole out of Lhasa on the back of a pony while disguised as a peasant. With him were his mother, younger brother, sister, and a coterie of tutors and counsels. Just prior to this, the lord chamberlain had composed a message for the Indian consul general broaching the possibility of exile. He also dispatched a courier to Yarlung with a note for the NVDA to prepare a reception committee. Although that message had yet to reach Yarlung, Phala had arranged for a small band of rebel escorts to wait on the riverbank opposite Lhasa as the Dalai Lama's party crossed in a yak-skin coracle. Pausing briefly for a final glimpse of the lights flickering in his capital, the Tibetan leader pressed south.

Back in Lhasa, neither the Chinese nor the crowds outside the Norbulingka were yet aware of the Dalai Lama's flight. His departure proved timely, for within a day after his departure, the citizenry broke into full-scale rioting. In this they were supported by the Tibetan army, which had belatedly thrown off its gloves and was attempting to seize strategic points around the capital. Responding in kind, the PLA dropped the last vestiges of restraint and on 20 March started shelling the Norbulingka. Just four days later, the resisters were in full flight from the city.

For the better part of a week, the location of the Dalai Lama and his escape party was a mystery to the outside world. The first to get a hint of his fate was the CIA; this came after the lord chamberlain's message to Yarlung was forwarded by courier on horseback to Tom and Lou at the NVDA rear base in Lhuntse Dzong. Upon reading this, Tom took his radio set and, together with a small band of guerrillas, sprinted to intercept the Dalai Lama near the Chongye valley, 30 kilometres north of the Drigu Tso. Lou followed in his wake with another group hauling the bulk of the weapons received during the second weapons drop.

On 25 March, eight days after he departed Lhasa, the Dalai Lama and his followers arrived at Chongye and linked up with Tom's advance NVDA party. While there, the Tibetan leader was enlightened about the CIA supply drops and the RS-1 radio, which was kept hidden. Discreetly taking his leave, Tom returned to the radio and keyed a message to Okinawa. Tibet's god-king, he informed the Agency, was alive and well.

Back in the US, Geshe Wangyal was summoned from New Jersey to the capital to help the CIA stay abreast of the Dalai Lama's movements. As each of Tom's transmissions arrived via Okinawa, strings of number groups were carried over to the safe house for the sagely monk to extract meanings both stated and implied. For the next week, Tom's brief updates were at the top of Eisenhower's daily Current Intelligence Bulletin. "He was the best-informed person in the world," said CIA officer John Greaney.

By 27 March, Washington time, the US president knew that the Dalai Lama had already reached the NVDA rear base at Lhuntse Dzong. The monarch initially intended to wait there and negotiate his return to Lhasa, just as he had done from Yatung in 1951. But when he turned on his transistor that morning and heard that Beijing had formally dissolved the Tibetan government, chances for a temporary in-country exile began wafting away.

Defiant, the Dalai Lama gathered his entourage inside the village's hilltop fort and issued a defiant statement. With his bridges figuratively burned, he knew that it was only a matter of time before the PLA closed on his position. Unfortunately for him, his counsellors were offering little coherent advice. During the hours that followed, Phala approached the CIA radio-agents and groped for options, including a request to have the US dispatch a plane to Lhuntse Dzong. Remembering Phala's past indecision, the agents asked that he commit himself on paper to a single plan before radioing Okinawa.

As it turned out, Phala's hand was forced that very night. Radio reports indicated that there was heavy fighting in Lhasa, and an NVDA courier arrived at the camp with news that the PLA was massing for a push across southern Tibet. Unable to sleep, the lord chamberlain woke the agents at 2:00 the next morning, 29 March, and asked that they forward an immediate plea for Indian asylum. Returning to their set, the agents lit a butter lamp, cranked up the generator, and relayed the message. "If India refused," Tom summed up, "we were in a bad position."

It was Saturday night, 28 March, when John Greaney was summoned from a downtown restaurant to the safe house on Wisconsin Avenue. He waited at Geshe Wangyal's side as the monk translated the appeal. Realising the gravity of this development, Greaney telephoned his boss.

The Dalai Lama's move was not unexpected, and the Agency already had an inkling that India would give its nod. Two days earlier, CIA Director Dulles had informed the National Security Council that Prime Minister Nehru had privately hinted his support of asylum for the Dalai Lama, but not for the fleeing armed rebels, for fear of provoking incursions by the PLA.

At the same time, policy makers in Washington had come to the conclusion that the Dalai Lama's exile was in the United States' interest. Given its radio link at the scene, the CIA was the logical intermediary to facilitate Indian approval. No time was wasted; at 1:00 in the morning on Sunday, 29 March, a message was sent from Washington to the CIA's New Delhi station asking that it relay the plea directly to Nehru.

Back in Tibet, the Dalai Lama and his entourage had not waited for an answer. Leaving Lhuntse Dzong and riding for a day, they reached a village just four hours from the Indian frontier. Huddling that night inside their tent during a torrential downpour, the CIA agents turned on their radio and learned of New Delhi's official consent via Washington.

Tom and Lou waited until early the next morning for the rains to lighten and then made a dash to Phala's tent and passed on the news. For the first time, they saw the lord chamberlain break into a wide smile.

The Dalai Lama, though haggard after almost two weeks on the road and weakened by a bout of dysentery, was visibly elated. Finally granted a special audience with their leader, the two agents were given a blessing. With little on hand to give as mementos, the god-king offered each a single red coral bead and a braided necklace fashioned, ironically, out of strips of silk salvaged from parachutes from the second supply drop.

The following day, 31 March, some of the fittest members of the Dalai Lama's party went forward toward the border. In one of his last acts on Tibetan soil, the monarch penned a document conveying the rank of general to Gompo Tashi. The next morning, after bidding farewell to his NVDA escorts and the CIA radiomen, he and the rest of his 80-person entourage worked their way south over the final stretch to India's lush, steaming Assam lowlands.

Watching their leader depart, Tom and Lou broke out their radio set and tapped an impassioned update. "The Dalai Lama and his officials arrived safely at the Indian border," they told their CIA handlers. "You must help us as soon as possible," they added, "and send us weapons for 30,000 men by airplane."

7
WHALE

In 1955, John Waller had been posted as the CIA's deputy station chief in New Delhi. While Tibet had been a long-time personal obsession, he spent his first year in India focused on domestic targets. That changed the next year, when the Dalai Lama began his India pilgrimage and Waller was able to attend a diplomatic roast in his honour thrown by the Indian government. Perhaps appropriately, when the Tibetan leader headed home the following spring, Waller, too, took his leave of India and returned to Washington for a headquarters assignment.

Not until March 1959, after receiving word that the Dalai Lama was stealing toward the Indian border for apparent exile, did Waller get emergency orders to rush back to the subcontinent. Once in India, he wasted no time making his way to Calcutta and linking up with fellow CIA officer John Hoskins. Together they drove to Darjeeling.

By that time, word had already leaked that Tibet's monarch was en route to the Northeast Frontier Agency (NEFA; India's euphemism for the rugged buffer it administered along the Tibetan frontier between Bhutan and Burma) and from there would presumably make his way down to the tropical lowlands of Assam state. The story had more than its share of drama, and nearly 200 press representatives descended on Tezpur, a normally sleepy tea planters' town in Assam that was along the Dalai Lama's likely egress.

"It was a media circus at Tezpur," recalled Waller. He knew several of the journalists from his New Delhi assignment, and discretely tapped a few for information.

An even better channel was the Dalai Lama's own brother, Gyalo Thondup. From Darjeeling, Gyalo had made contact with Hoskins before racing east to intercept the monarch's entourage. On 18 April, the siblings met in a village 48 kilometres north of Tezpur. It was there during private conversation that the Dalai Lama passed his brother a verbal message to the US government, reaffirming his determination to support the resistance of his people and asking Washington to recognise his exiled government and supply those who were continuing the resistance.

Together, the siblings made their way down to Tezpur, where the Dalai Lama was briefly overwhelmed by the flood of journalists. By 23 April, Gyalo was able to quietly pass a detailed update to Hoskins and Waller, including a paraphrased account of the Dalai Lama's request.

Suddenly showing more backbone than any time in the past, the 23-year-old Tibetan leader was upsetting apple-carts all over. India, in particular, was in a fix. On the one hand, New Delhi hinted at its sympathy for the rebels inside Tibet. On the other hand, India had long seen an advantage in its delicate dance with China vis-a-vis Tibet. As recently as 30 March 1959 — just a day before the Dalai Lama crossed into India — Nehru had reaffirmed his desire for good relations with Beijing. Now that Tibet's exiled leader was speaking in terms of independence instead of autonomy — and with rumours of thousands of guerrillas fleeing for sanctuary in India — the earlier status quo was no longer viable.

The Dalai Lama's assertive posturing also had Washington scrambling for an appropriate response. Throughout the month of April, the US government took pains to ensure that it did not appear to be instigating or exploiting the revolt for cold war profit. If such a perception arose, there was fear that Nehru might lash out against both the US and the Tibetans.

Behind the scenes, however, some US policy makers were chafing to do more. On 1 April, President Eisenhower had given his approval for continued paramilitary action in support of the Tibetan resistance. CIA Director Dulles assured the president that such action fell within existing policy authorisations and that the US was not exposing itself to an open-ended commitment.

The trouble was, any commitment — much less an open-ended one — was becoming all but impossible to plan. After seeing the Dalai Lama off at the border, the CIA's pair of radio agents — Tom and Lou — had headed north to seek out Gompo Tashi. They had not yet reached Lhuntse Dzong when the Khampa chieftain found them. Notified of his promotion to general, Gompo Tashi hardly had time to celebrate. With PLA forces closing for a two-pronged attack, and guerrilla morale low, Tom and Lou took to the radio to relay desperate pleas for food and ammunition.

Responding, the CIA loaded a C-118 with supply pallets and rushed it to Kurmitola during mid-April. By that time, however, the area around Lhuntse Dzong was on the verge of collapse. With the plane still on the tarmac, Tom and Lou broke for the border. Gompo Tashi and a band of Khampa guerrillas had preceded them by a few days, handing in their weapons to Indian guards on 29 April and crossing into the sanctuary of NEFA.

With the NVDA in southern Tibet in full disarray and having lost its radio link on the scene, the CIA took two interim measures. First, it delayed plans to infiltrate the team of Lithang Khampas that had been training in the US since the fall of 1958. As of the close of April 1959, that team (now attrited to six members; two others had washed out because of poor mental aptitude) was on the verge of shifting to new quarters at Colorado's Camp Hale. The Khampas had originally been scheduled to parachute into their homeland by late May, but plans for the drop were now on hold, pending more information on the disposition of the resistance.

As a second measure, yet another contingent of Tibetans was to be selected by Gyalo from among the refugee community for training in the United States. The recruitment pool was now far larger than at any time in the past. By early April 1959, the number of displaced Tibetans reaching India had grown from a trickle to a steady stream; 6,000 of the new arrivals were crowded inside hastily constructed bamboo huts near Bomdila, and another 1,000 lived in similar arrangements at a transit camp close to Sikkim. From these, 18 young men (15 Khampas and three Amdowas) made the cut. Joining them as translators were three Tibetans Gyalo had sponsored for English lessons over the previous three years.

This group of 21 men made their way toward East Pakistan. Before reaching the border, however, they were caught by an Indian border patrol and sent back to Darjeeling with a reprimand.

Several weeks later, in mid-May, the group again set out for East Pakistan. They now consisted of 23 members: the 18 young recruits and three translators, plus two older Khampas in their mid-40s. This time they managed to evade border guards and slip across the frontier, whereupon they took a train down to Dacca. Switching to a bus with black curtains on the windows, the Tibetans were deposited at the rear door of the USAF's unmarked C-118. Inside to greet them was Tony Poe. "My first impression was that the Americans were so big," recalled one of the interpreters, Tashi Choedak. "I was stunned by his height."

After a refuelling stop at Clark Air Base, Poe took the Tibetans to Okinawa. There they were crowded inside a safe house and taken away in trios for the standard battery of physical exams and aptitude tests. Because the two older Khampas were deemed unfit to undergo the rigors of paramilitary training, they were ordered to remain behind on Okinawa. One of the younger Khampas was belatedly rejected as too frail for parachute infiltration. For the remaining 20, Camp Hale awaited.

With two Tibetan contingents in the US by late May 1959, the Tibet Task Force was making headway in developing a trained cadre that would have a multiplier effect for an active resistance movement. But with the CIA's sketchy intelligence indicating that the NVDA had been soundly thrashed, there was a good chance that there might not be much resistance for them to multiply. Part of the problem was that the PLA was making good use of veterans from the Korean War and combat aircraft. Another part of the problem was that the Tibetan guerrillas were fighting in large concentrations using complex manoeuvres — thus forfeiting their unconventional advantages.

Particularly frustrating from the US perspective was the relative ease with which the PLA was overcoming the serious logistical challenges of feeding and arming thousands of Chinese infantrymen pushing across the Tibetan plateau. It took 22 trucks of equipment, fuel, and other essentials, the Pentagon estimated, for every one truck that reached PLA fighting forces close to the Indian border.

The cost to Beijing, reasoned the policy makers in Washington, could be substantially increased if the supply flow was disrupted. In theory, this was not all that difficult to plan as there were only three drivable roads leading to the plateau. Of the three, the favoured route extended from the city of Xining diagonally across Amdo (now officially known as Tsinghai Province) before plunging south toward Lhasa.

On 1 May 1959, the Amdo road had been the subject of discussion during a closed-door session between State Department officials and the Joint Chiefs of Staff. After initially considering airpower to close the corridor, this option was rejected for fear it could spark a wider war with Beijing.

Instead of using jets, a more palatable solution was to have an indigenous sabotage team parachute in near the target. There were several options to consider. For one, the CIA already had the Lithang Khampas waiting patiently at Camp Hale, all of whom were versed in demolitions. However, these agents would have been ethnically out of place in the Amdo outback, and in any event, they were being held in reserve for a mission alongside the NVDA resistance.

A second option involved the considerable resources found in the Republic of China (ROC) on Taiwan. For several years, the CIA had been helping the ROC turn out a modest number of airborne teams drawn from the various ethnic groups that fled the mainland. These operations had been less than successful, with most teams apparently killed or captured in a matter of days.

All this must have frustrated Generalissimo Chiang, especially given the mounting evidence of genuine, even spreading, dissent on the mainland. The majority of this activity was concentrated along the PRC's periphery, where ethnic minorities were revolting against things such as economic collectivisation and Beijing's campaign to have Mandarin replace local languages. Besides Tibetans, the disaffected included Mongolians, Turkic Muslims, and Hui Muslims.

Beijing viewed the Hui with particular concern. Unlike the Turkic minority in Xinjiang, who saw themselves as a separate people who happened to live within the PRC's borders, the Hui thought of themselves as Chinese who happened to be Muslims. They were heavily represented across the north-central provinces, including the eastern half of Amdo.

Dissent among the Hui was not exactly a new phenomenon. They had launched four minor rebellions between 1950 and the summer of 1958. Learning of the 1958 uprising, the ROC had made a concerted effort to exploit the Hui dissent by including Muslim guerrillas among the teams being trained on Taiwan by the CIA. Tony Poe, later of the Tibet program, was one of their training officers. His assessment of the Muslim guerrillas was not particularly positive, however, as they had made clear to him that they would kill the non-Muslim members of their team immediately upon infiltration.

After Poe was transferred to the Tibet project, the Hui agents remained on Taiwan through the spring of 1959. By that time, events in Tibet were creating unforeseen opportunities in the minds of the ROC leadership. While the CIA had no intention of bringing the ROC into ST CIRCUS, they did see merit in expanding bilateral covert operations on the mainland. In particular, the Agency saw a convergence of interests in closing the logistical corridor across Amdo, which led in May 1959 to a joint project code-named ST WHALE.

The agents for ST WHALE would be drawn from the contingent of Hui Muslims trained earlier by Tony Poe. Four were selected as a pilot team, which was scheduled to drop near the Qaidam Basin in the central part of Amdo. Although none of the Tibet Task Force's guerrilla assets would be exposed to Taiwan, the CIA arranged to lend ST WHALE some of the aerial delivery methods it had used for ST BARNUM. Just as with the cargo drops to the NVDA, the Hui would jump from the same CAT-piloted C-118 (which had now been modified with pressurised doors). As during the Tibet missions, the aircraft would stage through Kurmitola, putting it within closer range of Amdo and allowing the aircraft to circumvent the PRC's concentrated defences along the coast.

Because the team would be left to its own devices on the ground, it was important that it bring adequate supplies. The problem was turned over to the CIA's logistical guru on Okinawa, Jim McElroy. He intended to use the jumper to-bundle system perfected during the 1957 jumps into Tibet. This time around the lead parachutist would be connected to 5,000 pounds of supplies lashed to a plywood pallet.

To study the topography around the target area, the CIA was granted presidential approval for two U-2 overflights of Tibet and China on 12 and 14 May 1959. Shortly thereafter, the C-118 headed for Kurmitola. Most of the crew — Doc Johnson at the controls, Jim Keck as navigator, Bob Aubrey at the radio, and Bill Lively as flight mechanic — had experience on the supply drops the previous fall. In the co-pilot's seat was Truman "Barney" Barnes, a Second World War ace with five confirmed Japanese kills in his P-38. In the rear, Richard "Paper Legs" Peterson was assigned as the cargo handler.

Upon arrival at Kurmitola, the crew and agents waited at the austere base for the order to launch. As soon as the weather and lunar conditions proved cooperative, the C-118 was airborne and heading northeast over NEFA, Kham, and the Amdo steppes. The drop zone, which had been identified in overhead imagery, proved difficult to pinpoint from the cockpit. "There were two forks in a river," recalls Barnes. "We thought we were at the right one and gave the signal."

In the cabin, Peterson, Keck, and Lively were all waiting near the bundle. As Peterson manoeuvred the pallet along the rollers toward the door, one of the packing straps caught on a piece of steel. With it hopelessly stuck and time pressing, he pulled out a knife and sliced off the tie. "In the back of my mind," he remembers, "I became concerned the bundle would not deploy its chute properly."

The jumper connected to the pallet, meanwhile, was also having ill-timed second thoughts. As the supplies roared out of the cabin and the cord started to play out from his chest, he stood firm. Reaching forward, Peterson grabbed the reluctant agent by the chute and heaved him out the door. "I'll never forget the look of raw terror," said Keck, "in the brief second before he disappeared into the dark." With no further hesitation, the other three Muslims leaped from the plane. The plane then turned south and reached Kurmitola without incident.

Within a week, the four Hui made brief radio contact with Taiwan. Encouraged, the same C-118 crew was summoned the next month for a repeat performance. This time around, they were to drop only supplies; McElroy had rigged almost 8,000 pounds on a single pallet.

Heading north from Kurmitola during the full moon phase, Doc Johnson came upon a ground signal and activated the green light in the cabin. Like clockwork, the bundle roared out the side, and the C-118 returned to East Pakistan once more without incident.

The ST WHALE agents, it seems, were not nearly as lucky. When their handlers raised them over the radio and asked if they had received the supplies, the Hui claimed that no cargo had come. Livid, the CIA case officers grilled the C-118 crew over the accuracy of the drop. Very quickly, however, doubt fell on the team itself. Communications intercepts later indicated that the agents had been captured early on, and the radio operator doubled. ST WHALE was quietly shelved, and no additional Hui saboteurs were dropped inside Amdo. The PLA truck convoys to the Tibetan front, meantime, remained on schedule.

8
CAMP HALE

The unmarked C-118 materialised out of the western skies and landed at Peterson Field well after nightfall. This allowed for the discreet transfer of 20 Tibetans from their plane to a bus with covered windows. Two hundred and eight kilometres later, they were at the gates of Camp Hale. Stepping out in the predawn chill, the Tibetans were at home. Even in late May, the temperature dipped below freezing at night, and snow capped the surrounding mountains. "It looked and felt like Tibet," remarked interpreter Tashi Choedak.

On hand to greet the new arrivals were CIA paramilitary instructors Fosmire, Poe, and Smith. Also present were the six Lithang Khampas who had shifted from Peary to Hale less than two weeks earlier. These six holdovers were combined with the 17 new students, and a training cycle for all 23 began the following day. Each Tibetan was given an American first name to ease identification. American names were also assigned to each of the three Tibetan translators: Tashi Choedak now went by "Mark"; Tamding Tsephel, a former medical student and the nephew of Gompo Tashi, became "Bill"; and the short, expressive Pema Wangdu was dubbed "Pete."

The interpreting skills of the three immediately came into play during an opening phase in radio operations. Ray Stark, one of two Agency communications instructors assigned to Hale, discovered the Tibetans to be surprisingly astute. "Maybe it was the memorization and meditation associated with their Buddhist training," he later speculated. "They picked up codes fast and were a lot sharper than most people gave them credit."

After two weeks, the seven best students from among the newcomers continued with an advanced radio class. For the remainder, intensive physical conditioning began. Given their mountain upbringing, the Tibetans already had tremendous lower body strength, but their upper body strength lagged behind. CIA officer Jack Wall was charged with correcting this physical shortcoming. A former smokejumper, Wall had been working on CIA paramilitary operations in Asia since the Korean War. Initiating a comprehensive exercise and self-defence regimen for the Tibetans, he and the other instructors found them to be a competitive bunch. During a class on pistol disarming techniques, for example, the star student from the Peary contingent — a spirited Khampa named "Donald" — took on a newly arrived Amdowa. "Donald had a certain devilment in his eyes," recalls lead instructor Fosmire, "and he began striking his opponent with the pistol butt and cut his forehead." Fosmire promptly halted the class to let tempers settle.

Weaponry training followed. Significantly, the CIA had decided that the element of plausible deniability was now less important than improved firepower. This meant that students could now be provided with the US-made M1 Garand in lieu of the earlier British selection. Honing their skills on a makeshift range, all the Tibetans soon became proficient shooters.

As on Saipan, the CIA instructors found that they were learning from the Tibetans as much as they were imparting. Particularly remarkable about the Tibetans was their lack of fear of heights. "They would nonchalantly step off the sides of a ravine with barely a thought, " said Stark. On one occasion when a Khampa stumbled and came within a step of falling to his death, his countrymen reacted not with horror but with shrieks of laughter over the embarrassing faux pas.

Such light-hearted innocence remained the hallmark of the Tibetans throughout the weeks of tough instruction. Not once did they register anger; indeed, the students considered it humorous when the Americans displayed emotion. Continued Stark, "They would intentionally leave doors open to get a rise out of me. I told them that when I visited them in a free Tibet, I was going to rip their tent flaps off. They thought this was hysterical."

By late June 1959, the project also got a fourth paramilitary instructor. Albert "Zeke" Zilaitis, the son of Lithuanian immigrants, had had his heart set on a career in professional football after playing for Saint Francis College in Pennsylvania. But when he did not make the cut at rookie camp for the Pittsburgh Steelers, he opted for the CIA. The choice turned out to be a good one, as he proved himself an able advisor in Thailand alongside Fosmire and Poe.

Zilaitis's arrival coincided with the start of heavy weapons instruction. Among the systems introduced to the Tibetans were bazookas, mortars, recoilless rifles, and .30-calibre light machine guns. Also making a debut at Hale was a consignment of five-inch rockets, courtesy of the US Navy. Intrigued by their possible use for

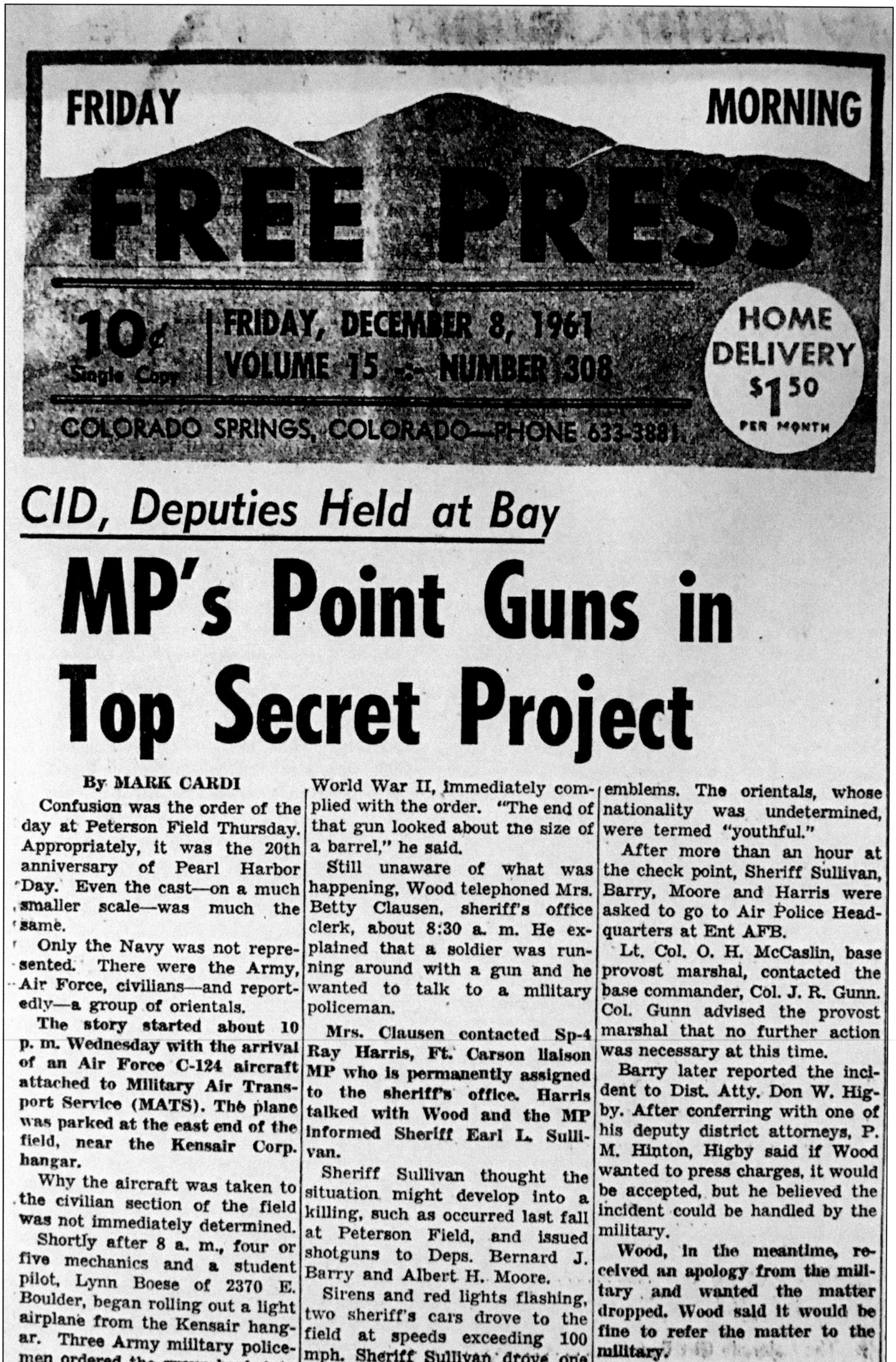

FRIDAY MORNING

FREE PRESS

10¢ Single Copy | FRIDAY, DECEMBER 8, 1961 VOLUME 15 — NUMBER 308

COLORADO SPRINGS, COLORADO—PHONE 633-3881

HOME DELIVERY $1.50 PER MONTH

CID, Deputies Held at Bay

MP's Point Guns in Top Secret Project

By MARK CARDI

Confusion was the order of the day at Peterson Field Thursday. Appropriately, it was the 20th anniversary of Pearl Harbor Day. Even the cast—on a much smaller scale—was much the same.

Only the Navy was not represented. There were the Army, Air Force, civilians—and reportedly—a group of orientals.

The story started about 10 p. m. Wednesday with the arrival of an Air Force C-124 aircraft attached to Military Air Transport Service (MATS). The plane was parked at the east end of the field, near the Kensair Corp. hangar.

Why the aircraft was taken to the civilian section of the field was not immediately determined.

Shortly after 8 a. m., four or five mechanics and a student pilot, Lynn Boese of 2370 E. Boulder, began rolling out a light airplane from the Kensair hangar. Three Army military policemen ordered the group back into

World War II, immediately complied with the order. "The end of that gun looked about the size of a barrel," he said.

Still unaware of what was happening, Wood telephoned Mrs. Betty Clausen, sheriff's office clerk, about 8:30 a. m. He explained that a soldier was running around with a gun and he wanted to talk to a military policeman.

Mrs. Clausen contacted Sp-4 Ray Harris, Ft. Carson liaison MP who is permanently assigned to the sheriff's office. Harris talked with Wood and the MP informed Sheriff Earl L. Sullivan.

Sheriff Sullivan thought the situation might develop into a killing, such as occurred last fall at Peterson Field, and issued shotguns to Deps. Bernard J. Barry and Albert H. Moore.

Sirens and red lights flashing, two sheriff's cars drove to the field at speeds exceeding 100 mph. Sheriff Sullivan drove one

emblems. The orientals, whose nationality was undetermined, were termed "youthful."

After more than an hour at the check point, Sheriff Sullivan, Barry, Moore and Harris were asked to go to Air Police Headquarters at Ent AFB.

Lt. Col. O. H. McCaslin, base provost marshal, contacted the base commander, Col. J. R. Gunn. Col. Gunn advised the provost marshal that no further action was necessary at this time.

Barry later reported the incident to Dist. Atty. Don W. Higby. After conferring with one of his deputy district attorneys, P. M. Hinton, Higby said if Wood wanted to press charges, it would be accepted, but he believed the incident could be handled by the military.

Wood, in the meantime, received an apology from the military and wanted the matter dropped. Wood said it would be fine to refer the matter to the military.

Sheriff Sullivan spoke with

In December 1961, a contingent of Tibetans from Camp Hale transiting through Peterson Field in Colorado were nearly exposed to the public. This headline from a local newspaper hints at the mysterious activity in the vicinity. (Author's collection) long-distance harassment, Zilaitis promptly loaded the rocket noses with high explosives, fitted wires to a car battery, and began firing them from a makeshift trough. Although the rocket trajectory could be slightly altered by bending the rear fins, accuracy was almost nil. Predictably, one veered off course and struck a transcontinental telegraph cable hanging across the valley, causing significant monetary loss and a flurry of angry messages from headquarters. Earning the name "Werner von Zilaitis" for the mishap, he quietly retired the remainder of the projectiles.

Elsewhere within the CIA, the debate on how to return the Tibetans to their homeland had been raging for weeks. Following the earlier ST WHALE flights, the Agency had firmly concluded that its C-118 was in need of replacement. "It might have been good for Pan Am," one CAT pilot later commented, "but it was not a war bird."

Beyond this general consensus, however, there had been considerable disagreement over the C-118's replacement. Gar Thorsrud had his eye on the C-130 Hercules, which in late 1956 had been introduced to USAF squadrons to rave reviews. The problem, however, was that the Hercules had been in exclusive service with the USAF for less than three years and could not be mistaken for anything other than an American military aircraft. If one were ever lost over unfriendly territory, plausible deniability would be impossible. But following the earlier decision to replace British rifles with American ones, plausible deniability for the Tibet project was now subject to exception.

Thorsrud, for one, thought that the upgrade in aircraft capability outweighed the risk of exposure. The Pentagon agreed and an order was relayed to Sewart Air Force Base in Tennessee (which hosted one of the USAF's original Hercules squadrons), where the local wing commander, Colonel George Norman, was petitioned for loan of a single airframe and volunteer crew. The cover story: aviators were needed in Colorado Springs to give weekend joyrides to the first batch of graduates from the new Air Force Academy.

In short order, six airmen took up the offer. Their assignment, they soon discovered, had nothing to do with an academy boondoggle. Met on the Peterson tarmac by Thorsrud, they were ordered to sign secrecy documents and given a skimpy mission brief. Palleted supply bundles were to be loaded into the back of the C-130, instructed Thorsrud, and then dropped on ground signals in the mountains around Hale.

Over the following week, the Sewart aviators made flights over Colorado to boost their self- confidence. After that, the practice drops began. Jim McElroy, the Agency's logistics chief from Okinawa, was temporarily deployed to Peterson to help rig loads. Once the pallets were packed inside the Hercules, the USAF crew was simply told to drop them to unknown persons setting signal fires near Hale; if they did not see the correct signal, they were to abort.

After several days of this, Thorsrud eagerly lobbied to begin the next phase of Hercules trials. To confirm the suitability of the C-130 for long-distance airdrops, the Agency had mapped out a circuitous route covering 2,419 kilometres (1,500 miles) of mountainous terrain leading to a small ground target at Hale. The entire flight was to be done at low level (much of it at less than 500 feet) with a full cargo load. The idea was to have the terrain mask the aircraft from radar; only if there was trouble would the crew bounce ascend above the highest terrain feature. Further, the CIA planners allowed for just a 10-second variance between flight checkpoints, and a 30-second variance over the drop zone. As if that were not enough, the return journey was to be flown with one of the plane's four engines shut down. Although the C-130 had been placed at its performance limits, the flight went off without a hitch.

Now that the USAF crew had proved the concept, there remained the task of transitioning the CIA's own pilots for the actual mission. Earlier in July 1959, the Agency's Far East proprietary, Civil Air Transport, had changed its corporate identity and been renamed Air America. Despite the name change, its roster still included Doc Johnson, William Welk, and the rest of the team that had performed the initial C-118 drops over Tibet. Called to Colorado on short notice, they were turned over to the USAF crew for instruction.

After nearly a month of Stateside training, Doc Johnson and his men were sent back to the Far East at the beginning of September 1959. The Tibetans at Hale had also graduated, and the skies over their homeland were clearing. Thus, the race was on to perform the first C-130 parachute infiltration as soon as the weather and lunar conditions proved cooperative. According to the CIA's original plan, the agents were supposed to link up with the NVDA and provide a multiplier training effect. But having lost its eyes inside Tibet back in April, the Agency had no timely intelligence on the current location of resistance pockets, if any.

An attempt had been made to rectify this shortcoming early that summer. In May, Lhamo Tsering had ventured to the CIA's Okinawa safe house and met with a motley ensemble of seven Tibetans — all medical rejects or academic washouts from the two contingents in the United States. Of these, he selected four and escorted them back to East Pakistan, then across the border to India.

Meeting up with the group in Darjeeling, Gyalo Thondup chose three to conduct an overland infiltration into Tibet to determine the disposition of the NVDA. Because the PLA was believed to be blocking most of the passes along the NEFA and Sikkim frontier, the team was to skirt west of the Kanchenjunga massif and enter Tibet via a trading route in eastern Nepal.

As it turned out, the mission did not last long. They had barely crossed the border when the agents ran headlong into a PLA patrol. Two of the three were killed instantly; the third went on the run and did not make it back to Darjeeling for several months.

Still without eyes, the CIA had little recourse but to sift through the rumours circulating among Tibetan refugee camps in India. From these sources came apocryphal tales of an isolated NVDA band 190 kilometres north of Lhasa near the shores of the Nam Tso, Tibet's second largest saltwater lake. If true, the stories were dated by at least several weeks. But they reflected a certain logic: just as the lake's serenity had long made it a favourite destination for religious pilgrims, that same isolation made Nam Tso a good pick for a guerrilla redoubt.

With no better options coming to the fore, the CIA on 3 and 4 September 1959 directed its U-2 spy planes to make a pair of high-altitude passes over the Nam Tso; a third overflight was conducted on 9 September. Air America's Hercules crew was then summoned to Kadena to view the photographs and pinpoint a drop zone. Pending good weather, the mission was set for the full moon cycle during the third week of the month.

Back at Hale, the CIA instructors had taken aside the original Lithang Khampas — who by that time had been training for more than 10 months — and briefed them on their impending Nam Tso mission. As their number had been attrited down to six, the decision was made to augment them with a single commando from the follow-on contingent. Before departing Colorado, all were coached in the use of the "L-Pill," an innocuously titled cyanide ampoule cushioned inside a small sawdust-filled box. In the event of severe injury during the parachute jump, or some other dire contingency, the agent merely had to place the pill in his mouth and bite; death was guaranteed within seconds.

At the beginning of the third week of September 1959, Fosmire loaded the seven Tibetans into Hale's shielded bus and ferried them to Colorado Springs in the dead of night. A USAF crew and Gar Thorsrud were waiting on the Peterson tarmac as the bus pulled close to the C-130's rear ramp. With the Tibetans, Fosmire, and Thorsrud filing into the back, the Hercules lifted off and headed west for McClelland Air Force Base near Sacramento, California. Pausing just long enough to take on more fuel, they were back in the air and en route to Hickam Air Force Base on the Hawaiian island of Oahu for another refuel.

What had been a clockwork operation to that point quickly ground to a halt as the Hercules blew an engine shortly after take-off from Hawaii. Making an emergency return to Hickam, the crew was informed that repairs promised to be extensive and lengthy. The ST BARNUM team was now in a bind: not only would the delay make them miss their lunar window of opportunity, but it would be hard to conceal seven Tibetans on base for any length of time without risk of exposure.

Thinking quickly, Thorsrud relayed a call to the Pentagon's Office of Special Operations. A new C-130 from Hickam's own inventory was quickly substituted for the stricken Sewart airframe, and the mission was again underway.

Upon reaching Okinawa, the C-130 was joined by Doc Johnson and his Air America crew, who took their places behind the USAF aviators. Boarding, too, were smokejumpers William Demmons, Andy Andersen, and Art Jukkala, all assigned as cargo handlers on this maiden Hercules flight. Squeezed in among the passengers was 13,500 pounds of palleted supplies; though far short of the C-130's full potential, this was still an increase over the C-118.

Two others joined the flight as well. Baba Lekshi and Temba Tileh, both Khampas from the contingent that had exfiltrated to Hale in May, had been deemed too old to endure the stress of paramilitary training. Left behind at the Kadena safe house for the previous four months, they were now ordered to join the Nam Tso team as its eighth and ninth members.

On 18 September 1959, the crowded Hercules proceeded southeast to Thailand and landed at Takhli Royal Thai Air Force Base, 130 kilometres north of Bangkok. Instead of Kurmitola, the CIA intended to stage all future Tibet infiltrations from Takhli, an option made possible by the C-130's extended range. Primitive, remote, and backed by a supportive government in Bangkok, Takhli had all the necessary ingredients for a discreet launch site. Moreover, Tibet flights launching from Takhli entailed a less risky overflight of Burma rather than India. East Pakistan's Kurmitola would still be available, but only for emergency diverts.

Shortly before midnight, Fosmire, Thorsrud, and the USAF crew stood on the Takhli runway to bid farewell. With Doc Johnson at the controls, the C-130 roared down the airstrip and disappeared into the northern sky.

Staring at the radar console, navigator Jim Keck called course corrections as the C-130 took a direct bearing up Burma's Salween valley. Leaving Burmese airspace and skirting easternmost India, the Hercules arced west toward the southern extreme of the Tibetan plateau. The flight to the drop zone promised to be a trying seven hours each way.

Without incident, Keck directed the plane around Lhasa and north toward the Nam Tso. Before long, the surface of the lake could be seen reflecting moonlight in the distance. Already, the nine agents had taken up positions in front of the right door, while a string of table-sized pallets was manoeuvred along rollers leading out the left.

In the final minutes before the drop, the three cargo handlers put on oxygen masks and pulled open the doors. Cold air sliced through the cabin as the airplane slowed to 120 knots with flaps down. With the plane's nose edging skyward and the green light flashing, Tibetans and cargo exited without incident. Cutting a tight circle over the Nam Tso, the Hercules was quickly winging its way back to Takhli.

Remaining in Thailand, Tom Fosmire ventured down to the CIA station in Bangkok to await initial radio contact from his agents. Team leader Ngawang Phunjung, who had gone by the call sign "Nathan" while in the United States, had consistently impressed the Agency instructors during training. "He had a good sense about him," opined Fosmire.

But good sense or not, the days ticked by without Nathan coming on the air. After a week of fruitless waiting — and amid speculation that the team might have accidentally landed in the lake and drowned — a dejected Fosmire headed back toward the mountains of Colorado.

9
HITTING THEIR STRIDE

Nathan and his eight teammates hit the ground running — literally. The C-130 had landed them nearly a day's march from the planned drop zone and dangerously close to a PLA encampment. Frightened of detection, they immediately fled toward their intended target without pausing to recover any supply bundles, including the radio.

Over the ensuing days, their comedy of errors continued. Chancing upon some locals, Nathan learned that the resistance they sought had dispersed half a year earlier. Then when they tried to enter a village for refuge, the residents eyed their light complexions (the result of frequent classroom sessions over the previous 10 months) and suspected them of being Chinese provocateurs. On the run from their own countrymen, the tired and hungry agents feared thick PLA defences farther south near Lhasa so they instead headed west toward the Nepal border, some 500 kilometres away.

None of this was known to the CIA's planners, who were busy preparing for the next round of airborne infiltrations. Once again, they had to generate a list of potential drop zones without the benefit of current intelligence inside the country. One possibility had surfaced back in early June 1959 when the head of the Tibet Task Force, Roger McCarthy, had ventured to Darjeeling to debrief NVDA chief Gompo Tashi. The same officer who had trained the first Tibetan agents on Saipan in 1957, McCarthy had assumed command of the Tibet Task Force from Frank Holober in March 1959.

Arriving in Darjeeling by way of Calcutta, McCarthy debriefed Gompo Tashi at a safe house over the course of three days. The chieftain was honest about the resistance's shortcomings — including bad behaviour and defeats — but overall, he thought the NVDA had done well.

In the end, Gompo Tashi had no ready answer about the future course of the resistance. Losses were costly, he conceded, and replacements were not readily available. Given the PLA's air capabilities, it was impossible to do much more than ambushes and interdiction of convoys and perhaps some sabotage. He was optimistic about running such missions from enclaves in Nepal, but more guarded about similar strikes staged out of NEFA.

Gompo Tashi let something else slip as well. In his detailed recitation of NVDA activities, he recounted how he had operated with success along the westernmost edge of Kham in December 1958. Particularly around the town of Pembar, a supportive Khampa populace had allowed the resistance to keep the area free of Chinese. Though this information was dated, the location appealed to the CIA on another count: situated near the south bank of the Salween, Pembar was within striking distance of the drivable road the Chinese had constructed between Chamdo and Lhasa. Cutting traffic there would accomplish the same goals as the earlier stillborn effort, ST WHALE.

Brainstorming further leads, the CIA came up with two other drop zone candidates. The first of these, deeper in Kham, was chosen in order to better exploit the ethnic background of most of the Hale students. Using the same logic, a third target was selected in southern Amdo in order to milk value from the three Amdowas in the contingent. To map out the exact routes to and from these locations, a U-2 overflight was sanctioned on 4 November to cover Tibet, China, and Burma.

Back at Hale, the 16 remaining graduates were briefed on their upcoming mission. Six would be dropped at Pembar, the CIA told them, five would land farther east in Kham, and another five would parachute inside Amdo. With the full moon falling at mid-month, the agents were rushed through Okinawa late in the second week of November on their way to Thailand. Escorting them this time was Zeke Zilaitis. Special permission had also been extended for Ray Stark to make the trip. Failure to contact the Nam Tso team, and a lingering suspicion that the Agency's Thai-based communications officers might not have been sufficiently attentive to pick up a faint transmission out of Tibet, led Stark to vow to stay in Bangkok and personally "guarantee" to raise this latest wave of agents over the airwaves.

Once at Takhli, the Tibetans waited until last light on the day before the full moon. At that point, they were then given an 11th-hour change of plans: all three teams would jump at Pembar from a single plane, the CIA had decided, rather than using three separate drop zones; the Amdo and Kham teams would then travel to their final destinations from Pembar on foot. This brightened the agents considerably, as they appreciated the psychological security of infiltrating as one. Waving good-bye to Zilaitis on the tarmac, they boarded a lone C-130 and disappeared toward the Burmese frontier.

Inside the Hercules, 21-year-old Donyo Pandatsang adjusted the cyanide ampoule encased in fine wire mesh that was strapped to his forearm. Answering to the name "Bruce" while at Hale, he had spoken no English when he arrived in Colorado but showed great natural aptitude and went on to advanced radio training. He was selected as team leader for the six men designated to remain at Pembar.

Now lined up in front of the right cabin door, Bruce was apprehensive. But to his own surprise, as soon as he launched himself into the slipstream, all fear vanished. With the sound of the plane fast receding, Bruce was overwhelmed by the prospect of being home. Dangling from the risers, he could clearly see that he was heading for a valley with snow-caps glistening on either side. Though he was told they would land in a forest, they landed among rocks.

Working in the moonlight, Bruce and his colleagues quickly located their supply pallets, including one that had to be fished from a river. Later that same night, they encountered locals from a small nearby village who had come to investigate the noise. Not only did the locals appear friendly, but they said that many Khampas were still living in the area.

With this positive news, Bruce assembled his radio the following morning and tapped out a short message. His handlers at the Tibet Task Force now knew that the team was alive.

It did not take long for word to spread around Pembar about the arrival of the CIA-trained cadre. As guerrilla recruits flocked to the scene, the agents knew that this rousing reception was a double-edged sword. Just as when Wangdu had landed in Kham in 1957, some of the Khampas came with no weapons; others came with an assortment of rifles but no bullets. Three different calibres of ammunition were in heavy demand, and expectations were high for the CIA to deliver.

Back in Washington, the Tibet Task Force weighed the radioed requests for supplies. Approval was quickly secured for a single Hercules to be packed with pallets at Kadena and staged through Takhli during the next full moon in mid-December 1959. Unlike the two earlier drops, the C-130's expansive rear ramp would be used instead of the smaller side doors; this would allow more supplies to be dispatched in less time.

On the ground, the Tibetan agents had assembled a veritable fleet of mules at the designated drop zone. Six enormous dung bonfires were lit in an enormous "L" shape and, like clockwork, the C-130 materialised overhead. Moments later, bundles hit earth. Inside each were stacks of cardboard boxes with four rifles apiece. As per their training at Hale, the agents had affixed ropes to the mule saddles, allowing two boxes to be quickly secured to each animal. Within two hours, the entire drop zone had been cleared.

Nearly all the 200-plus Garand rifles were distributed to local guerrilla volunteers. Fifty rifles, however, were earmarked for a band of Khampas selected to escort the five agents destined to shift from Pembar to Amdo. As planned, those five crossed the Salween at year's end and proceeded 150 kilometres northwest. Still 80 kilometres short of Amdo's Jyekundo district, the team came upon a resistance presence and decided to go no further.

With this second guerrilla network running by the start of 1960, at long last the task force was beginning to hit its stride. Seeing this, the task force decided to ratchet up its resupply operations. Through December 1959, these had been limited to one Air America aircrew flying a single mission during each full moon phase. Since the lunar window of opportunity could not be expanded, the only other option was to increase the number of sorties flown. In anticipation of this, Air America in early December allocated additional personnel for C-130 operations.

More C-130 flights also meant the need for more cargo handlers. By the full moon cycle of January 1960, nearly a dozen smokejumpers, many of them newcomers to the Tibet project, were assembled on Okinawa. Four were selected to go on that month's maiden flight: two from the new contingent, and two veterans from earlier flights. The mission took place as scheduled and without complications, prompting the ST BARNUM planners to reduce the number of kickers to two for the month's second resupply flight.

During this encore, a single Tibetan agent was scheduled to jump along with the supplies. That agent, a 28-year-old Khampa monk named Kalden, had been one of the academic washouts from the

Lithang contingent that had parachuted at Nam Tso. Kalden had been sitting idle at the Kadena safe house for the past 16 months while the CIA debated what to do with him. That decision: drop him at Pembar.

As the Hercules made its final approach toward the drop zone, Kalden got a tap on his shoulder as the signal to leap off the ramp. For the first time, a Tibetan balked. Turning his back on the black void, the monk grabbed one of the cargo handlers in an unwelcome embrace. All too aware of his precarious position, the handler spun the agent around and heaved him ahead of the exiting cargo. Reaching backward in a final act of desperation, the Tibetan snatched the radio headset off the handlers' head. Trailing a 30-foot cord in hand, he disappeared into the night sky.

Down at the drop zone, Kalden landed to a reception committee of 11 fellow agents and hundreds of Khampa guerrillas. He came with orders to join the five agents meant to shift farther east into Kham, though plans for that movement were now on hold. Remaining at Pembar, the 12 took stock of their growing inventory. Included in the pallets were a pair of machine guns on anti-aircraft mounts and a large stock of TNT. None of these items were rated as particularly relevant by the Tibetans, though they did go out of their way to use the explosives to down a nearby bridge.

Sensing that it had arrived at a winning formula, the Tibet Task Force planned more of the same for February 1960. By the March full moon, the C-130 crews had amassed sufficient Tibet experience to begin staging two aircraft per night.

The news got even better when the Nam Tso team — on the run since September 1959 — reached the Nepalese border and couriered word to Darjeeling that it wanted a resupply. Lhamo Tsering, who had been deputised by Gyalo Thondup to manage agent operations from India on a daily basis, quickly relayed the request to the Tibet Task Force. Rejecting the plea, the CIA instead ordered the team to exfiltrate via East Pakistan to Okinawa. Re-armed with carbines and recoilless rifles, Nathan and six of his men (due to failing physical health, the two older agents remained behind at Kadena) were loaded back aboard a Hercules and dropped during the March full moon to augment the five-man Amdo team that had shifted from Pembar.

Not until the next month, April 1960, did the CIA's luck finally run out. It started out well enough, with two Hercules flights set for the beginning of the lunar cycle. The first plane departed without incident at last light. The second left Takhli 15 minutes later. Halfway to the target, things turned sour. Hitting an unexpectedly heavy head wind, the lead plane took a radar fix and determined that they were more than 45 minutes behind schedule. Hearing this, the pilot added power; by the time they approached the drop zone, they were only four minutes late.

Head winds, however, were just part of their problem. Although April is traditionally rain free in Tibet, 1960 proved the exception to the rule. As the Hercules overflew the location where bonfires should have been, all the crew saw was a thick blanket of clouds. Circling once in frustration, the pilot made the decision to return home. As they had burned an inordinate amount of fuel to make up for lost time on the way into Tibet, his colleagues in the cockpit were keen to dump their cargo to lighten the plane for the remainder of the journey. But reasoning that the same strong head winds would provide equally strong tailwinds, the pilot insisted on keeping the payload aboard.

That decision was nearly fatal. By the time they arrived near Takhli at 5:30 the next morning, their fuel supply was almost exhausted. Worse, April is the hottest month in Thailand, coming

Roger McCarthy, head of the Tibet Task Force. (Photo courtesy Roger McCarthy)

less than two months before the summer monsoon; farmers in the central part of the kingdom traditionally slash and burn their fields during that time, prior to planting a new crop. This throws into the sky a layer of haze the colour and consistency of chocolate milk, which is exactly what the crew saw as they searched frantically for the lights of Takhli. As the plane turned for a second pass, two of the engines immediately begin to sputter, then coughed back to life as the Hercules rolled out. The engines started to die again during a third pass.

Listening from the tarmac, a USAF support officer acted in desperation. Locating a flare gun, he began firing red star clusters into the sky. The idea worked: spotting a red glow lighting the bottom of the haze, the crew took the plunge and emerged in clear skies near the airfield. Only one engine was still running by the time they taxied to the end of the runway.

Hard luck, too, plagued the second flight of the night. The pilot also hit a head wind and found the drop zone covered with clouds. Like the first plane, he elected to return with his payload aboard. Unlike the first plane, however, he believed that the emergency facilities at Kurmitola were closer. The CIA retained a skeleton technical crew in East Pakistan for just such contingencies and had even erected a non-directional beacon to help pilots vector toward the strip. Normally, this would have been sufficient, since April in East Pakistan is generally a month with humid temperatures but clear skies. But in yet another exception to the rule, Kurmitola that night was hit by an unseasonably early thunderstorm. Captain Al Judkins was at the controls, and as he dipped the Hercules for a landing, there was almost zero visibility. At the last moment, the hangar flashed in the windshield, prompting Judkins to reflexively jerk back on the controls to avoid a collision. Doing what it could to help, the CIA team rushed several jeeps out onto the tarmac, their headlights barely cutting into the pounding rain.

As Judkins nosed downward for a second attempt, cargo handlers Miles Johnson and Richard "Paper Legs" Peterson braced for the worst. After a night of jinxes, they finally got a break. As a bolt of lightning flashed across the sky, the crew got a clear glimpse of the airstrip ahead and aligned the plane. Landing hard, they taxied to the hangar with little more than fumes left in the gas tanks.

Though it had nearly lost two aircraft, ST BARNUM barely flinched. On the following night, the same Takhli crew was rescheduled to deliver its payload. Fearful of again running into meteorological complications, the airmen brainstormed ways of carrying more fuel as an emergency reserve. Besides the internal wing tanks, they were already slinging two extra pontoon tanks, as well as a special 2,000-gallon bladder inside the cabin itself. But even with these, the crew could not fly an evasive route to the target, could not loiter, and, as the previous flights had dramatically proved, could not afford to hit a strong head wind.

Showing some lateral thinking, they came up with an offbeat solution. Reasoning that fuel is denser when chilled, the Air America crew topped its tanks on the night of the mission and circled Takhli at 9,091 meters (30,000) feet. After determining that the gas was sufficiently cold — and dense — they landed and began packing more fuel into the extra tank space. Wet burlap was draped across the wings to keep the tanks cool. Whether because of this or because the crew did not encounter another head wind, the mission made it to Tibet and back with fuel to spare.

On the other side of the world, a key link in the CIA's Tibet supply program was a modest Washington safe house where radio messages from the teams were translated. By that time, the venerable Geshe Wangyal, eager to spend more time with his Buddhist disciples, gracefully exited the program for a permanent return to New Jersey. Replacing him was Tsing-po Yu, a recent Chinese immigrant who had lived part of his life in Tibet and spoke the language like a native.

As luck would have it, Yu had been granted leave during April 1960 when the two Tibet overflights had their near brushes with disaster. Filling in as his temporary replacement was Mark, one of the three Tibetans serving as translators at Hale. Alongside Mark was case officer John Gilhooley. Having recently come off a tour in Burma, Gilhooley was holding the headquarters job with the Tibet Task Force between field assignments.

Each morning, the young Tibetan would begin the process of converting incoming number groups into coherent messages, which Gilhooley would then convey to task force chief Roger McCarthy. Return messages would go through the same process in reverse. Mark enjoyed the work but could feel the growing sense of urgency among all those involved. There was good reason for this: the approaching May rains on the Tibetan plateau would make further resupply flights all but impossible until autumn. In order to deliver as much equipment as possible before the weather proved prohibitive, three C-130 flights were launched on two consecutive nights at the end of the April lunar cycle.

In the end, even this proved insufficient. Over the previous two months, Pembar had been experiencing frequent probes by PLA infantry. Just as the April full moon was waning, Beijing got serious. Pamphlets were dropped from aircraft warning the rebels to cease contact with the foreign reactionaries. After that, groups of five aircraft began bombing runs while long-range artillery was brought forward. The guerrillas — conservatively estimated at a couple of thousand — suffered horrific casualties.

The PLA was not finished. Placing blocking forces on three sides of the guerrilla concentration, the Chinese set the forests on fire to flush out the remaining partisans. Keeping together, the 12 CIA-trained agents made an escape bid. Rather than running south toward India, they attempted to evade north across the Salween. "We thought it might be colder near Amdo," said Bruce, "and the Chinese would not be able to tolerate the cold."

But as they approached the river, its swift waters proved too hard to ford. Complicating matters, their horses were growing weak from insufficient food and were hobbled by broken horseshoes. Abandoning their steeds, the dozen decided to reverse direction and weave their way toward the southern border on foot. After a month of harrowing encounters with the PLA, only five survivors reached Indian soil.

The losses were even more horrific for the Amdo contingent. After overrunning Pembar, the PLA shifted its full attention northwest near the end of April. Under withering fire, Nathan, leader of the Amdo augmentation team, radioed frantic messages that tank-led columns were closing on their position.

With few options available, the Tibet Task Force sanctioned an emergency C-130 drop for the evening of 1 May. This promised to be doubly risky: not only was the PLA massing in the area around the drop zone, but the moonless night would make navigation much more complicated. Knowing that they might again need to divert to East Pakistan, a CIA technical team went to Kurmitola to man the emergency recovery site. While there, 30-year-old communications officer Stephen "Gip" Kasarda scaled a shed to scout locations to place an antenna. While doing so, he was electrocuted on the metal roof, which unknowingly had a current from an improperly grounded wire.

In the end, the C-130 flight was scrubbed at the last moment. The reason was a mishap in yet another CIA operation. That morning, a U-2 spy plane had departed from an airfield in Pakistan for an overflight of the Soviet Union. En route, Soviet air defence batteries had fired multiple surface-to-air missiles in a shotgun configuration, disabling the aircraft with one of the concussion blasts. Although the exact fate of the plane and its pilot was not yet known to the CIA (it was several days before Moscow revealed that the crewman, Francis Gary Powers, had been captured alive), Washington quickly flashed a blanket prohibition against all further aerial penetrations of the communist bloc.

With its hands tied by the senior policy makers in the Eisenhower administration, the Tibet Task Force was powerless to help its Tibetans in their greatest hour of need. The radio near Amdo soon fell silent; none of the 12 agents ever reached India. Years later, it was learned that 10 of the 12 were killed in action; the last two were sent to prison, where one died in a hunger strike and the last, Choni Yeshi, was finally released in November 1978.

10
MARKHAM

Back on 4 February 1960, just as the Tibet Task Force thought it had settled on a winning formula, CIA Director Dulles ventured to the White House to brief top administration officials on the Agency's Tibet operation to date. He closed with an appeal for continuation of the project. His audience was complicit in its silence, with only President Eisenhower wondering aloud if the net results merited the effort involved. Might not stoking the resistance, he posed, only invite greater Chinese repression? Des FitzGerald, who had joined Dulles for the briefing, spoke directly to the president's concern.

There could be no greater brutality, he assured those at the table, than that already inflicted on the Tibetans.

Still playing devil's advocate, Eisenhower turned to Secretary of State Christian Herter and asked if his department held any reservations. Far from it, responded Herter. Not only could the Tibetans offer "serious harassment" of the Chinese, but a successful resistance would keep "the spark alive in the entire area." Suitably convinced, Eisenhower granted his consent for continuation of the Tibet operation.

On the heels of the president's approval, Lhamo Tsering began canvassing Darjeeling for a new batch of recruits. In short order, he assembled half a dozen suitable Khampas. Departing India on 22 March, the candidates followed the well-worn route through East Pakistan, pausing in Kadena for thorough physical exams. By 2 April, they were in Colorado, joining 15 of their countrymen who had arrived at Hale the previous November just days after the departure of the Pembar contingent.

Hale had changed little over the previous year of training. Still in charge was Tom Fosmire. Zeke Zilaitis, back to experimenting with rockets, had been promoted to his deputy. In the field, Tony Poe and Billy Smith remained as tactical instructors. Joining them was Don Cesare, a former Marine captain who had previously served as a security officer for the U-2 spy plane program.

Making the occasional appearance was a logistical assistant on the Tibet Task Force, Harry Archer. A Virginia Military Institute graduate and former Marine, Archer lobbied for the Tibetans to be rotated from Hale to the Marine Corps School at Quantico, Virginia, for a change of pace. There was sound logic behind Archer's proposal: Quantico at the time had a special cell that trained various foreign groups in guerrilla warfare and small-unit tactics. The school also had a pack-mule course where the Marine instructors could teach slinging a 75mm recoilless rifle, one of the more cumbersome weapons being dropped inside Tibet.

Escorted by Roger McCarthy, an initial group of 12 Tibetans was flown directly to the airstrip at Quantico in early 1960. There a five-man Marine team — which was not privy to the students' nationality — put them through two weeks of instruction on everything from caches to camouflage. Mark and Pete were on hand to provide translations.

Impressed by the training at Quantico, McCarthy sent a request up the chain of command for the loan of two instructors. The Marine Corps was agreeable, releasing both Sergeant Willard "Sam" Poss and Staff Sergeant Robert Laber that spring for temporary duty in Colorado. A Korean War veteran, Laber had been involved in the final combat actions of that conflict; he had since served as a heavy machine gun instructor before joining Quantico's special training cell.

Initially, Poss focused on map reading. Since the Tibetans were weak in mathematics, special maps were adapted from dated World Airway charts. Printed on cloth, they were simplified for the Tibetans by making both magnetic north and true north the same.

Laber, meanwhile, spent his time at the rifle range. As both a former machine gun instructor and a mortar section leader, he focused on developing skills with both these weapons. Because Fosmire and Zilaitis insisted on keeping the training as authentic as possible, blanks were never used. This resulted in an embarrassing breach of security midway through the dry summer. As Laber watched the Tibetans blaze away one afternoon with white phosphorus rounds, one ricocheted into the tress. In minutes, an entire hillside was in flames.

The CIA staff was now in a quandary. They could not cope with the fire themselves, but inviting the Forest Service into the camp could expose the project. There was really no choice. The Tibetans were rushed back to their quarters and quarantined before the gates were opened to allow in the fire trucks. It eventually took an entire week to bring the blaze under control. The firefighters were instructed not to ask too many questions, though they did remark that "strange inscriptions" in a foreign language had been carved into some rocks.

That incident aside, the Tibetans made good progress through the late summer of 1960. As graduation approached, the Tibetans were scheduled to showcase their skills to a headquarters delegation led by Des FitzGerald. Joining him was Gyalo Thondup, who was in the United States for what was becoming an annual tour for consultations and to bolster international support at the United Nations. The Hale staff had assembled some stands for their guests and spent days rehearsing their demonstration. Recalls Fosmire: "It ended with a mad minute attack on a 'Chinese' camp. All of the weapons were used, even mortars. One camouflaged Tibetan with a Bren was hiding near the reviewing stand and surprised everyone. When the last mortar round landed, they looted the camp."

FitzGerald was delighted with the performance of what was widely recognised as his favourite project.

Although FitzGerald might have been deeply committed to it, trouble loomed for the Tibet project. For one thing, all the airborne teams operating inside Tibet during the first quarter of 1960 were wiped out by late spring; sending more agents according to the same

Training officer Willard "Sam" Poss, on loan from the USMC, stands over the burned wreck of the administration building at Camp Hale following an electrical short circuit, 1960. (Photo courtesy Sam Poss)

script no longer seemed an enlightened idea. For another thing, the Eisenhower administration was dragging its feet on lifting the prohibition against overflights put in place after the downing of the U-2 in May. Not only was Eisenhower still smarting from the diplomatic fallout from that incident, but Washington was now backdrop to a tight presidential race between Vice President Richard Nixon and Democratic Senator John Kennedy. Political prudence dictated that potentially embarrassing covert action — particularly overflights — be put on hold until after the November election.

The delay came at a bad time for the Tibet Task Force. The late fall was good parachuting weather over Tibet. Moreover, there was concern that morale among the Tibetans at Hale might fray if they got stranded for an extended period. To keep them occupied, US Army engineers were dispatched to build a gymnasium alongside their Quonset huts. The CIA also procured reels of television westerns and showed them every night.

The CIA instructors, too, were growing bored with the tedious weeks of waiting. Billy Smith had already taken an opportunity for reassignment. A gruff Tony Poe, who was losing patience with some of his fellow officers, and disappointed that many of the Tibetans had taken up the habit of cigarette smoking, left near year's end. The two Marines also made plans for a return to Quantico.

But the biggest blow came when Tom Fosmire elected to join McCarthy back at the task force desk in Washington. As the figurative heart of the training project since its inception, he had connected with the Tibetans more than any other CIA officer. Much of this had come about while sitting around the campfire at night swapping tales and bonding with his students.

On the night before Fosmire was set to leave, he assembled all the Tibetans and made the announcement. Instantly, tears began to flow. Even when he tried to assure them that he would be working on the program from Washington, it did no good. "We were all crying like babies," said translator Mark. Choked with emotion, Fosmire took a 20-minute walk to clear his head. "We made a note never to tell them again when one of us was leaving."

With morale already low following Fosmire's departure, the project took another hit in early November 1960. By one of the closest margins in recent presidential history, John Kennedy came out the winner. Although he had been given a pair of confidential CIA briefings by CIA Director Dulles prior to the election, Tibet had not been broached with the youthful nominee. "I'll brief Nixon," Eisenhower was rumoured to have told top Agency officials regarding Tibet, "but if the other guy wins, you've got to do it."

When Dulles again got a chance to speak with President-Elect Kennedy on 18 November, 10 days after the vote, Tibet was pencilled on the agenda, but it never came up in conversation. Even after Kennedy was inaugurated in early January 1961, other foreign policy items grabbed the early spotlight. Besides Cuba, the deteriorating situations in Laos and South Vietnam were making headlines, relegating Tibet far down the priorities list.

Not until a snowy day in mid-February 1961 did things begin to change. Fosmire, who had been minding the quiet Tibet desk through the winter, remembers: "Bill Broe, the deputy chief of the Far East Division, stormed into the office with ice in his hair. He took off his jacket and waved a slip of paper. It was our permission to resume."

That permission followed from a 14 February decision by Kennedy's top foreign policy advisors — his so-called Special Group — to continue the covert Tibet operation started under the previous administration.

It had been almost a year since the last agent drop. With clear skies over Tibet, the task force moved to seize the moment. Even though the earlier airborne teams had met with only limited success, plans were drawn up for yet another parachute infiltration. This team would be led by a young Khampa named Yeshi Wangyal, who was easily among the most capable Tibetans to pass through Hale training. Known as "Tim" during his tenure in Colorado, he hailed from the town of Markham. Located between the Mekong and Yangtze Rivers, Markham was reputed to host an active guerrilla presence (where one of the chieftains was Tim's fathers). Moreover, it sat at the terminus of a second drivable road the Chinese were building across Kham, and the CIA remained committed to disrupting Beijing's logistical flow.

To increase Tim's chances of success, he was allowed to pick his own teammates from among the candidates at Hale. Selected as deputy team leader was Bhusang, a 32-year-old former medical student from Lhasa who went by the call sign "Ken." Five others — Aaron, Collin, Duke, Luke, and Phillip — also made the cut.

During the last week of March 1961, the seven began their long return journey from Colorado. Escorting them was translator Mark and CIA officer Zilaitis, who had been promoted to training chief following Fosmire's departure. After a three-night delay at Takhli due to unseasonably bad weather, the team boarded a C-130 as the sun set on 31 March.

Inside the cockpit, the Air America crew re-familiarised themselves with the controls. It had been nearly a year since they flew the last Hercules drop, and the company had few aviators to spare, given its busy flying schedule for the rapidly expanding CIA operation in nearby Laos. Cargo handlers, too, were at a premium, with only Miles Johnson and Paper Legs Peterson assigned to Asia in early 1961; all their fellow smokejumpers-cum-cargo handlers were in Latin America working on the imminent CIA paramilitary invasion of Cuba.

Roaring down the runway, the aircraft rose slowly on its journey toward Kham. At 2300 hours, under a full moon, the green light flashed in the cabin. Seven men and cargo exited the side doors. Assembling on the ground undetected, the agents had no problem locating their supplies. Though this might have been cause for celebration, Tim was far from happy. Landing among rocks, one of his teammates, Aaron, was cringing in pain with a dislocated shoulder. Worse, by sunrise he made the unwelcome discovery that the Hercules had significantly overshot the intended drop zone. Their current position, he calculated, was due west of the town of Gonjo — which in turn was 100 kilometres north of their intended drop zone, Markham.

Resting through the afternoon of the second day, the team prepared for the long walk south. Given Aaron's shoulder, their supplies were divided among the six healthy members. The remaining evidence of their drop — parachutes and rigging materials — was placed atop a pyre of wood and brush. They struck a match to the tinder and then set off at dusk up the first mountain between them and Markham.

By dawn on the third day, the team had reached the summit. Looking back, they could still see smoke hanging in the air from their bonfire. It was not until the next morning, after putting sufficient space between themselves and the drop zone, that the agents paused to send an initial radio message back to the Tibet Task Force, reporting the navigational error and their intended movement.

Even though the agents were tired and hungry, their journey over the first five days was trouble free. On day six, things started to change. Pausing near sunset, they spied 10 PLA soldiers and a Khampa guide in the process of concealing an observation post near

CIA officer Roger McCarthy after completing 150 parachute jumps, mid-1950s. McCarthy trained Tibetans on Saipan and later commanded the Tibet Task Force from March 1959 to December 1961. (Photo courtesy Barbara McCarthy)

The communications shed at Kurmitola airfield, East Pakistan; the lightning rod at right is where CIA technician Stephen "Gip" Kasarda was electrocuted in May 1960. (Photo courtesy Walter Cox)

CIA airborne advisor Thomas "T.J." Thompson touring the mountains around Chakrata, 1964. (Photo courtesy Thomas Thompson)

CIA airborne advisor Thomas "T.J." Thompson during a farewell ceremony with Tibetan riggers at Agra airbase, 1964. (Photo courtesy Thomas Thompson)

A Helio 500 Twin Courier with US registration N8745R transits through Sharjah Royal Air Force Base, Dubai, while en route to India on 16 March 1966. This was one of five Twin Couriers turned over to the ARC in the spring of 1966. (Photo courtesy John Phillips)

A Helio 500 Twin Courier with US registration N10037 transits Sharjah, Dubai, enroute to India on 6 April 1966. This was one of five Twin Couriers turned over to the ARC in the spring of 1966. (Photo courtesy John Phillips)

CIA Director Richard Helms in 1969 presents the Intelligence Medal of Merit to Sam Currie, the case officer during the successful mission in 1967 to place a sensor atop Nanda Kot in order to intercept Chinese missile telemetry. The SFF provided critical logistical support throughout this project. (Photo courtesy Sam Currie)

The ARC memorial at Charbatia for those killed in action. During the second half of the 1960s, two ARC C-46 transports crashed with the loss of crews. In addition, one ARC Helio Courier ditched into the Mahanadi River near Charbatia in May 1964, resulting in the drowning of co-pilot Benjamin Collins. (Photo courtesy Mohinder Kumar Anand)

RAW chief R.N. Kao and his daughter Achala visit the SFF at Chakrata during Tibet New Year celebrations in December 1974. They pose with senior political leaders Jamba Kalden (standing left) and Ratuk Ngawang (standing right). The plume of coloured feathers on the beret was unique to the female members of the force. (Photo courtesy Tenzin Yeshi)

The Annapurna Guest House in Pokhara, Nepal, built with CIA rehabilitation funds for demobilised Mustang guerrillas. (Author's collection)

Jamba Kalden (centre), the original dapon in the SFF, who was succeeded by Amdo Thondup (left). Penpa Tsering (right) was the first Tibetan to reach the rank of colonel in the SFF. In the 1980s, the Indian Army began commissioning young, educated Tibetans and enabled them to reach the rank of colonel in the SFF; the program was cancelled by the end of that decade. (Photo courtesy Kaydor Aukatsang)

Insignia of Establishment 22/SFF. Top row (left): beret badge worn on a maroon beret from 1963 through present. Top row (right): SFF formation insignia worn on the left shoulder from 1963 through present. Second row (left): jump status indicator worn on the right shoulder from mid-1960s through 1977. Second row (right): jump status indicator worn on right breast pocket, circa 2000-present. Third row: Indian Air Force freefall badge, awarded by ARC to SFF freefall parachutists in 1976. Fourth row (left): SFF freefall badge used in the late 1970s and based on commercial skydiving design; sewn in silk thread by Tibetan seamstresses and worn on the right breast pocket. Fourth row (right): current badge worn over left breast by members of 1 Archers; note the kukri knife associated with the Gurkhas. (Author's collection)

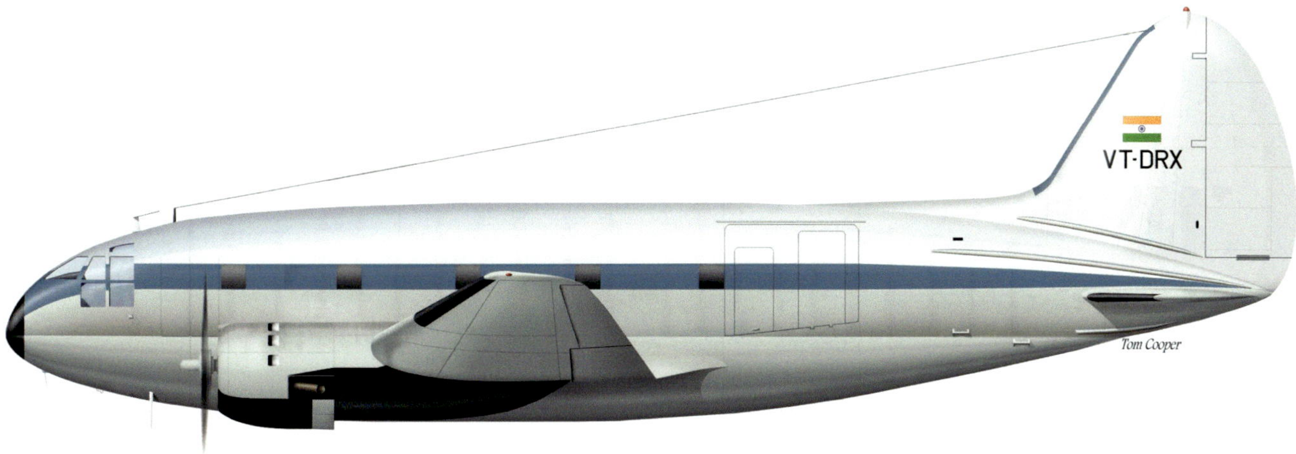

In late 1963, Air America temporarily dispatched three C-46Ds with crews to India to assist with Tibetan parachute training. During 1964-65, ten C-46s were delivered to the ARC. Of this total, two crashed with complete loss of life. This included a fatal incident during a resupply flight along the northeast frontier; among those killed was Captain Srivastava, an Intelligence Bureau pilot who was among the original ARC cadre trained at Camp Peary in 1963. (Artwork by Tom Cooper)

In late 1964, two Helio 500 Twin Couriers were delivered to the ARC. These did not receive Indian civil registration numbers until October 1965. Five additional Twin Couriers were delivered in the spring of 1966; one of this group is depicted still bearing US registration in blue. (Artwork by Goran Sudar)

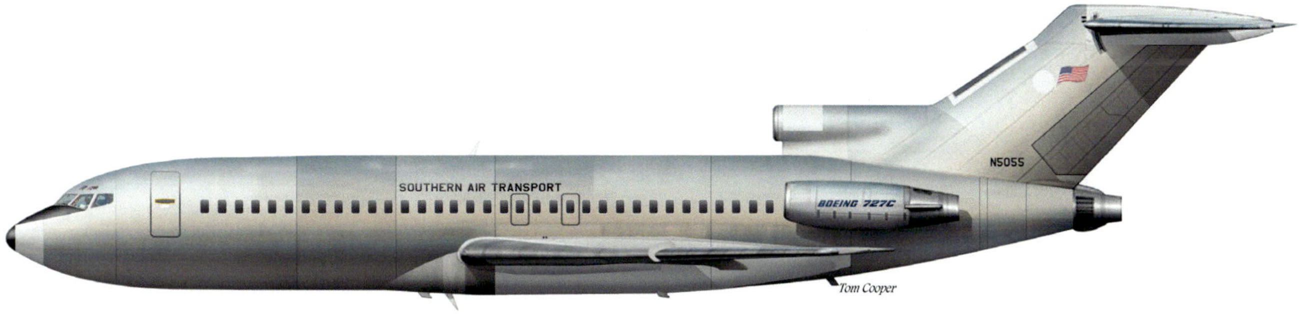

In late 1966, the CIA wanted a faster transport aircraft for Tibetan contingencies and gave three Boeing 727C jets to the proprietary Southern Air Transport. Not until May 1968 was one of these 727s, with its markings removed, sent to Takhli for top secret proof-of-concept trials. The stairs of the rear ventral exit were removed and replaced with sheet metal to make a slide, enabling personnel and bundles to be dropped from high altitude. T.J. Thompson, the airborne instructor at Agra in 1963, was deputy head of the project. Bill Welk, who flew on several Tibetan overflights, was the pilot. The trials were successful but no 727 flights over Tibet were ever undertaken. (Artwork by Tom Cooper)

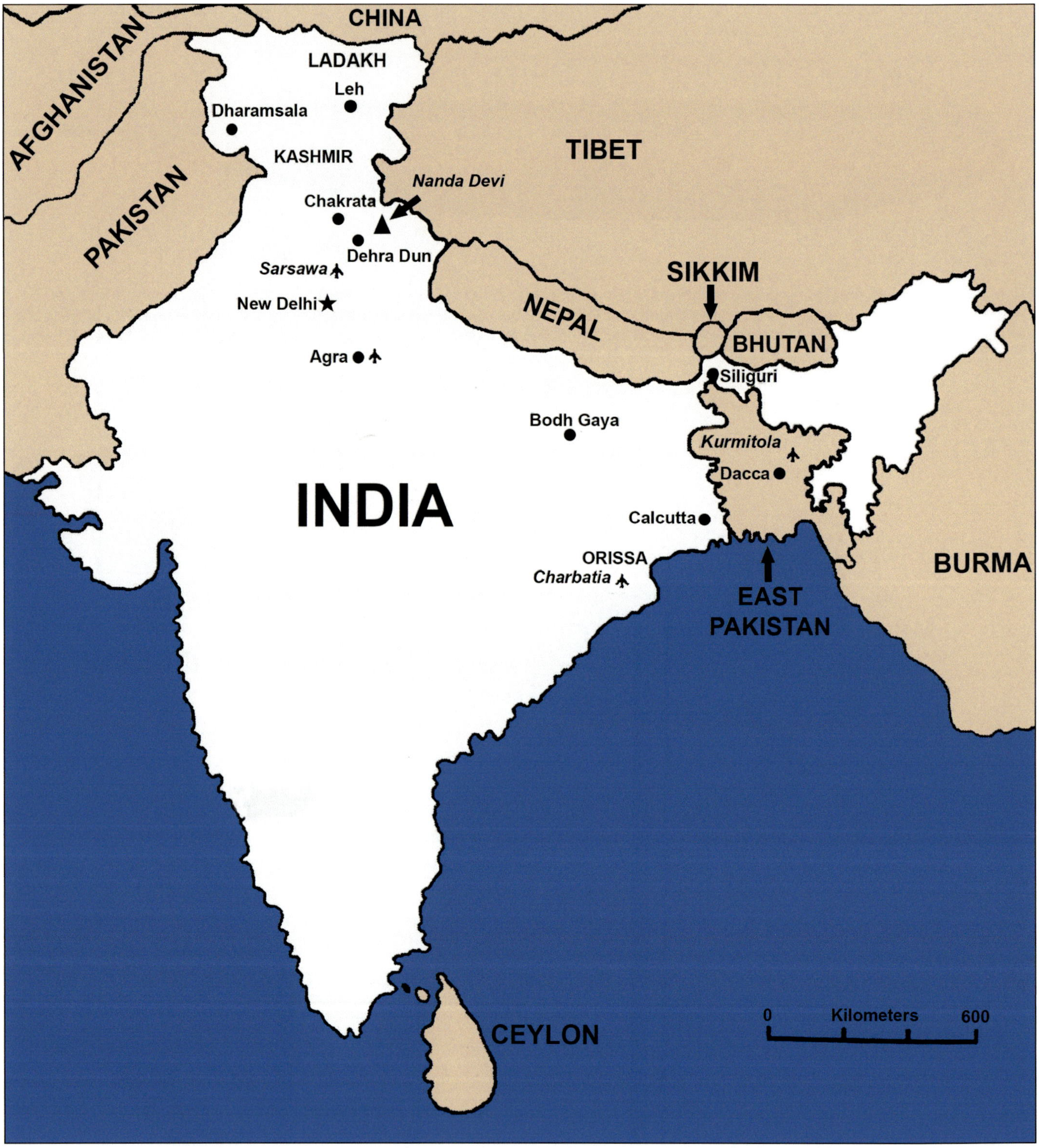

Map of India. (Map by Author)

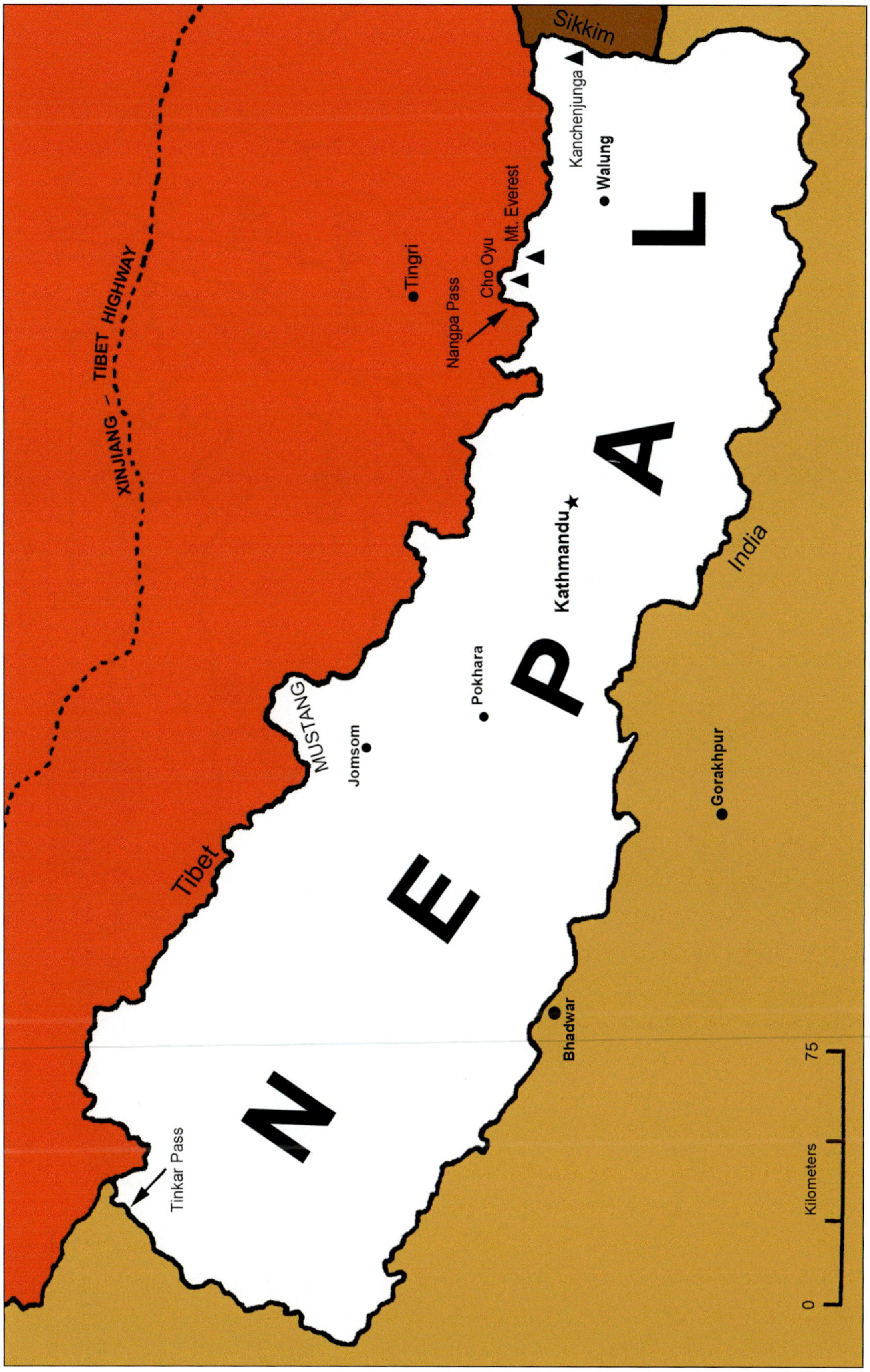

Map of Nepal. (Map by Author)

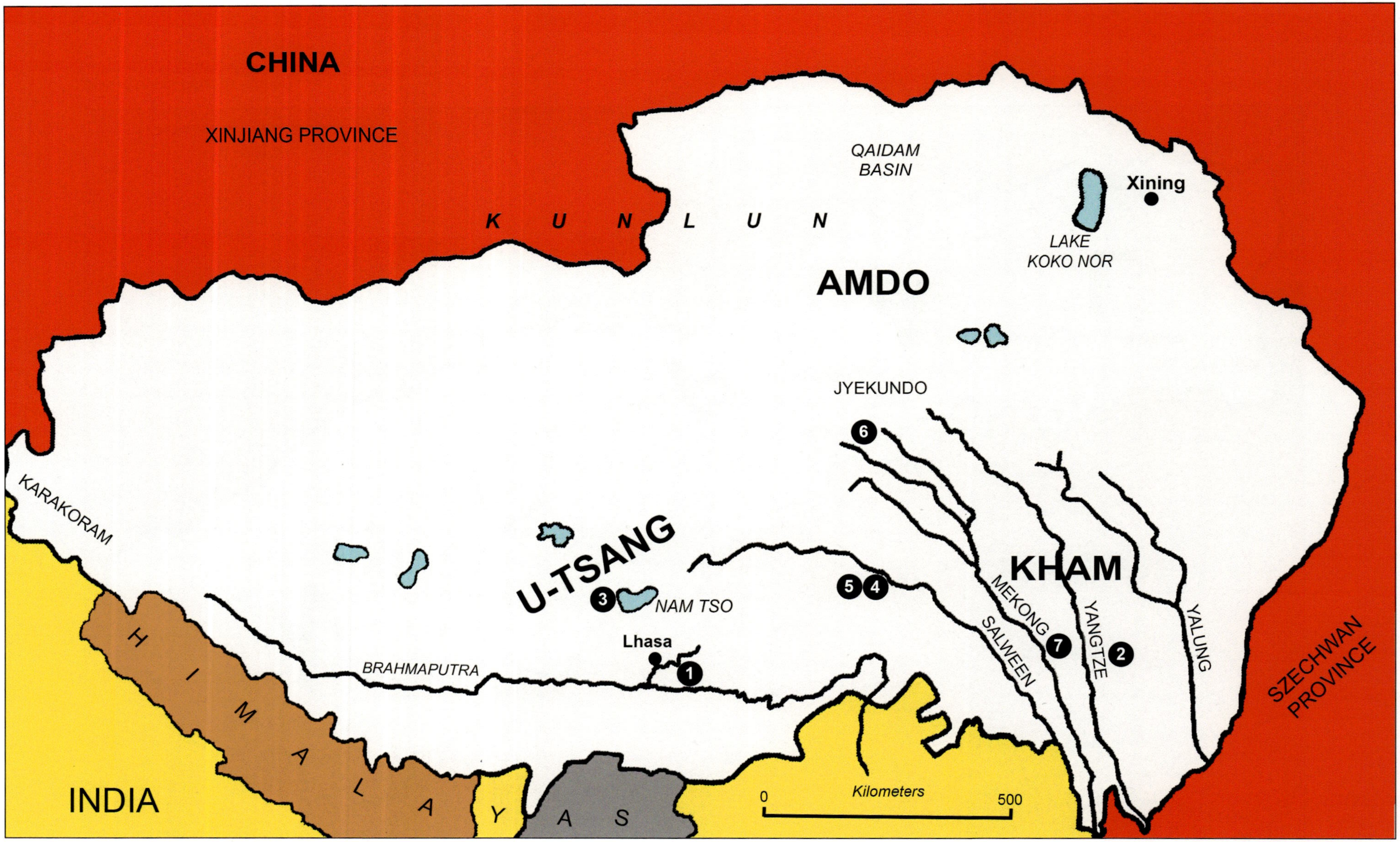

Location of ST CIRCUS agent drops in Tibet:
1. North bank of the Brahmaputra River, October 1957, 2 men.
2. Lithang, November 1957, 3 men.
3. Nam Tso, September 1959, 9 men led by Ngawang "Nathan" Phunjung.
4. Pembar, November 1959, 16 men.
5. Pembar, January 1960, 1 man.
6. Amdo, March 1960, 7 men led by Ngawang "Nathan" Phunjung.
7. Markham, March 1961, 7 men led by Yeshi "Tim" Wangyal.
(Map by Author)

Bhonshod "Ken" Bhusang, the deputy leader of the team dropped into Markham in March 1961, photographed prior to parachute insertion. (Photo via Jamyang Norbu)

the crest of a nearby hill. Not knowing if this was a coincidence or if their presence was suspected, Tim ordered the team to detour into the bush and cache those supplies not deemed vital, such as a mimeograph machine and an inflatable rubber raft the CIA had provided for crossing the rivers that bracketed Markham.

Patrolling forward, Tim and Ken made a two-man reconnaissance over the next hill and detected no other Chinese. The team continued its trek under cover of darkness. After one week of slow, careful movement, they could at last see Markham in the distance. Between them was a green valley pockmarked with the black, rounded tents used by herdsmen and traders. Though their goal was almost within reach, by that point, the agents had completely exhausted their rations and were thinking of little other than their stomachs. Leaving four members behind, Tim, Aaron, and Phillip crept toward the nearest tent in a bid to procure food.

At the last moment, Tim called a halt. By sheer coincidence, he recognised the occupant as a servant of his father. Approaching cautiously, Tim offered greetings and asked the servant of his father's whereabouts. The news was heart wrenching: he had been killed during a battle with the Chinese a few months earlier. Two other local chieftains had inherited his command, said the servant, and had continued to resist near Markham until their food stocks were depleted; both were now hiding with their guerrillas in the neighbouring hills. When asked, the servant admitted that locals had heard the aircraft that dropped Tim, and the Chinese had deployed patrols as a result.

Tim knew that he needed to act with discretion, if not suspicion. But still without rations, he imposed on the servant to convey a request for one of the rebel leaders to rendezvous with tea bricks, yak butter, and tsampa (ground roasted barley, a Tibetan staple). This meeting took place as scheduled, and although Tim received warm embraces and the customary deference afforded the son of a martyred chieftain, there was no mistaking an undercurrent of strain.

By day 10, the team arranged for a meeting with another local chief. Again, pleasantries were tempered by palatable tension. It was fast becoming apparent that the agents were seen by some as an invitation for a Chinese crackdown. Persisting, Tim was finally taken to the forest redoubt where the remnants of his father's guerrilla band were holed up. Women and children were among the weary partisans, including Tim's sister. They were a sad sight, with food in short supply and footwear in tatters.

Tim used the opportunity to pass on statements of encouragement from the Dalai Lama, and he tried to breathe life back into his crowd by speaking about the material support he was set to receive from the United States. As proof, he sent four of his agents to the cache site to recover their hidden supplies. On the way back, they left leaflets urging all tsampa-eaters (a euphemism for Tibetans, as opposed to Han rice-eaters) to remain vigilant against Chinese attack.

Over the following week, the rebel chieftains weighed Tim's exhortation back to arms and then called an emergency meeting in his absence. Despite the promise of foreign support, more than five years of fighting had taken a heavy toll. Exile was now utmost on their minds, not ratcheting up the war against China.

Deputy team leader Ken, who was present at the meeting, tried to stem the tide. Their orders, he noted, were to exfiltrate only after exhausting all means of resistance. The rebels were hardly swayed; they were intent on heading for India.

By that time, the team had been on the ground for 24 days. After the conclusion of the emergency session, a radio message was sent notifying the Tibet Task Force about the impending rebel exodus from the hills around Markham. When no immediate reply was forthcoming, the agents saw little choice but to join them.

They did not get far. News of the team had invariably spread across the Markham countryside, and it was only a matter of time before local informants tipped off the PLA. Together with pro-communist Khampa militiamen, Chinese troops closed in on the guerrilla concentration just as they started to move. Nine separate engagements were fought over the course of the first day. The agents sought refuge deeper in the forest, but not before the Chinese onslaught killed Collin and Duke. Cranking up their radio, the survivors had time to tap out a brief message. Recalls Mark, who was helping with translations in Washington at the time, "It was an SOS."

Taking along fewer than two dozen guerrillas and dependents, the remaining team members slipped through the PLA cordon and for a time shook off their pursuers. Over the next three days, they attempted to rest. But again, their hunger pangs were overwhelming. After nearly running into a Chinese patrol the following morning, they left the forest to approach a lone herdsman. Upon seeing the guerrillas, the shepherd turned over a yak and hurried from the scene. Ignoring tradecraft, the famished agents butchered and cooked the animal on the spot.

The PLA was not far behind. Having corralled the rebels toward a mountain, the Chinese looked to flush them out by setting the forest ablaze. With no alternatives, the agents and a handful of partisans left the protection of the trees and scurried up the bare slope in the dark. The Chinese had already circled atop the summit, allowing no escape.

As the sun rose, Ken took account of their bleak situation. "It was like a dream, unreal," he later commented. Squeezed behind boulders, Tim's sister and two other children could be heard weeping loudly. Aaron and Luke were huddled behind another rocky outcropping, Tim and Phillip behind a third. As the Chinese leapfrogged closer, they fired an occasional rifle shot and called for surrender.

By 1000 hours, the Chinese had manoeuvred within a stone's throw. Surging forward, they grabbed the three bawling children. Ken fingered the cyanide ampoule hanging from a necklace around his neck. The previous night, the agents had agreed to commit suicide after firing their last shot. Seeing no movement from Aaron and Luke, Ken assumed that both had already taken their lives. He placed the cyanide ampoule in his cheek, only to be knocked unconscious by a Chinese soldier leaping from behind. Bound and led away to prison, Ken would not see freedom for another 17 years.

Although the CIA did not have immediate confirmation of the Markham team's fate, the desperate tone of their last radio message spoke volumes. It was glaringly apparent: the task force needed a new strategy.

11
MUSTANG

Well before the parachute drop at Markham, the seeds of a new Tibet strategy were germinating. The impetus for this had come from NVDA chief Gompo Tashi and from Lhamo Tsering, Gyalo Thondup's able lieutenant in Darjeeling, who watched with concern as thousands of able-bodied Tibetan men were siphoned from Indian refugee camps and channelled into road construction gangs to help offset mounting aid costs.

Both were receptive to the idea of a reborn NVDA army, though they realised there were serious geopolitical hurdles to overcome. To properly refit any guerrillas, they needed a secure staging area. Given Nehru's continued desire to refrain from provoking the Chinese leadership, use of India for this purpose was out of the question. Similarly, Bhutan and Sikkim were too firmly under India's thumb to consider their territory as host for a significant paramilitary endeavour.

By default, that left the Hindu kingdom of Nepal. While it was true that Nepal was taking pains to remain on good terms with the PRC, one corner of Nepal — the backwater enclave of Mustang — was for all intents and purposes part of Tibet that barely recognised Kathmandu's writ. The highest kingdom in the world, Mustang encompassed 1,943 square kilometres of arid gorges and cliffs centred along Nepal's northern border. Surrounded on three sides by Tibet, it consisted of just 12 large villages and the walled capital of Lo Monthang, where a modest palace was centred in a maze of temples and homes for 800 residents.

Besides its quasi-independence, there were other reasons for Lhamo Tsering and Gompo Tashi to favour Mustang. For one thing, the border between Mustang and Tibet did not have any high passes blocked by snow in winter. For another thing, although its climate was dry and the land largely infertile, there was a handful of valleys with enough tree cover to camouflage a guerrilla encampment during the summer.

Although Gompo Tashi and Lhamo Tsering (who, it was understood, carried Gyalo's consent) were swayed that Mustang was a good bet for a guerrilla sanctuary, the US had to be convinced. Traveling to Calcutta in February 1960 to meet with CIA liaison officers, the two lobbied for support of their Nepal plan. At the time, Washington's relations with Kathmandu could only be described as cool and proper. This was largely due to King Mahendra's engagement policy of playing off the major powers, milking aid from all but not endearing himself to any. Had the US requested permission from Mahendra to use Mustang, it is unlikely that it would have been granted.

But the question was never asked. Just as Gompo Tashi and Lhamo Tsering had calculated, poor transportation and communication networks severely curtailed the Nepalese government's extent of control. Concluded Ralph Redford, the CIA station chief in Kathmandu, "The king's permission was not necessarily required."

Once word of the pitch from the two Tibetans reached Washington, the CIA's task force officers quickly concurred that a modest guerrilla operation staging from Mustang had merit and would not irreparably harm US-Nepal relations. Gompo Tashi was given approval in March 1960 to begin the process of identifying candidates to lead the paramilitary force.

Rushing north to Kalimpong, the ailing chieftain beckoned seven senior NVDA officers for three days of intense discussion. Informed of the pending Mustang operation, they were told to choose a field commander from among their number. Their unanimous decision: 43-year-old Baba Yeshi, a native of the central Kham town of Bathang. A monk and cloth trader prior to 1956, he had also been head of an NVDA sector near Drigu Tso lake. He had subsequently retreated to India and was sitting in a refugee camp when Gompo Tashi called him to Kalimpong.

Upon confirmation of Baba Yeshi as overall leader, Gompo Tashi and Lhamo Tsering made the rounds of the various refugee camps to select another two dozen candidates to serve as a US-trained officer cadre for the guerrilla force. The choice was limited to NVDA veterans without dependents and in good physical condition. To maximise clan coverage, no more than two men were chosen from each large district (such as Lithang), and only one from small districts.

When the final cut was made in May 1960, 27 candidates had assembled in Darjeeling. Reflecting the composition of the NVDA, as well as the makeup of the refugee pool, only two were from Amdo; the rest were from Kham. Most were in their mid-30s, although four were close to 50 years of age.

Before getting to Mustang, there remained the matter of training. Escorted by Lhamo Tsering to the East Pakistan frontier, the 27 approached the river defining the border. One week later, they were in their element among the mountains of Colorado.

As leader of the Mustang force, Baba Yeshi had a whirlwind schedule prior to departure for the front. First was a plane ride to meet CIA representatives in Calcutta, followed by a stop in Darjeeling for an audience with Gyalo Thondup. After that was a trip to Siliguri to rendezvous with two CIA-trained Tibetan radio operators.

Then came the long trek into Nepal. From Siliguri, the monk and two radiomen — plus a Tibetan guide provided by Gyalo — took a train west to the Indian city of Gorakhpur, then a bus north to Kathmandu. For two weeks, they waited in the Nepalese capital. Unknown to the Tibetans, a storm brewing within the CIA was causing delays. So as not to burden Baba Yeshi with heavy equipment during his trip into Nepal, the Tibet Task Force had intended to pass him three radio sets after his arrival in Kathmandu. Kenneth "Clay" Cathey, a CIA officer based in Calcutta, had been charged with overseeing the transfer. Helping him would be Ray Stark, the former Hale radio instructor beckoned from an assignment in Manila.

Unfortunately for Cathey and Stark, the CIA station in Nepal was doing all it could to stymie the transfer plan. Backed by Near East Division colleagues in New Delhi and at headquarters, station chief Redford opposed the scheme because he did not want to risk exposure on his home turf. Only after explicit instructions from the office of Director Dulles did the Nepal embassy reluctantly cooperate. Following this high-level directive, the three radios arrived in Kathmandu in a diplomatic pouch. To make them portable, Stark helped break them into 40 smaller loads. Cathey then procured some burlap and wrapped the equipment.

By that time, Lhamo Tsering and another Tibetan radioman had arrived in Kathmandu to help with the radio delivery. Because it was too risky to have Baba Yeshi come to the embassy, they needed to bring the gear to him. The station chief, still intent on obstructing the plan, insisted on using a taxi, but Cathey eventually persevered in getting loan of an embassy jeep.

That night, Cathey, Lhamo Tsering, and the radioman drove with the dissembled communication equipment to a darkened corner of Kathmandu's Swayambhunath stupa. Baba Yeshi, his two radiomen, and 18 more Khampas that had joined the party made the rendezvous. There they split in two, with a pair of the radiomen and 12 of the Khampas securing the radios on their backs and setting off on foot in the direction of Mustang.

Fifteen days later, Baba Yeshi and his men thought it prudent to leave the Nepalese capital. Making their way back to Gorakhpur, they took a train northeast along the border, then recrossed into Nepal from the frontier town of Bhadwar. From there, it was a five-day trek on foot to Pokhara. Fearful that the Nepalese authorities might have been alerted, they wasted no time walking another four days up narrow paths to the village of Tukuche. By the time Baba Yeshi arrived there, the party that had departed Kathmandu on foot was already waiting in tents and had established radio contact with Darjeeling.

Hearing of the successful rendezvous at Tukuche, Lhamo Tsering assembled the first group of guerrilla prospects from the Indian refugee camps. Earlier, Gompo Tashi had talked in terms of eventually building a 2,100-man force, but the CIA had approved support for only 400. Making the selection at Darjeeling, Lhamo Tsering gave each approved recruit a pair of shoes and a small rupee stipend to pay for food on the trip through Nepal. It was a relatively old crowd, with most close to 40 years of age. Nearly all were Khampas.

Very quickly, word of the recruitment flashed among the refugees. What was supposed to be a clandestine shift of personnel suddenly became a very public one. By early fall, Lhamo Tsering's 400 approved candidates were joined in Nepal by 200 unapproved Tibetans; several hundred others were on the way.

With Tukuche fast growing crowded, Baba Yeshi sent three men north to make a 10-day reconnaissance trek for suitable locations inside Mustang. By October, they had returned with a pair of recommendations. The first was Yara, little more than a cluster of earthen huts in a fertile valley dotted with conifers and tucked under a massive cliff honeycombed with caves. The second, 12 kilometres southwest of Yara, was Tangya. Sited in one of the lowest valleys in Mustang, it was packed with barley fields and, like Yara, was in the shadow of an imposing cliff eroded like the flutes of an organ. Both were east of the Kali Gandaki River and several days' hike from the other major villages in Mustang.

Baba Yeshi started dispatching recruits to the Yara valley. In November, he himself made the shift from Tukuche to Tangya. With no weapons, a handful of tents, and little food, the prospective guerrillas and their leader settled in for the long, cold winter.

On the other side of the world at Camp Hale, the Mustang leadership cadre spent the winter of 1960–1961 training alongside the agent team destined for Markham. Despite the advanced age of several in the group, the 27 were put through all the paramilitary paces. By the spring of 1961 they completed airborne training and were briefed on their impending mission to Mustang. The CIA's task force officers had been particularly impressed by Lobsang Jamba, a 40-year-old Lithang Khampa using the call sign "Sally." According to revised plans, Sally would parachute into Mustang and assume the role of field commander inside Tibet; Baba Yeshi, meanwhile, would be relegated to administrative chief at the Tangya rear base.

Back in Nepal, Baba Yeshi had not yet been informed of this new leadership arrangement. His attention had been fixated on the dire food situation at his guerrilla camp. As long-time Mustang residents well knew, the infertile kingdom could not stockpile enough food to feed all its people through winter. For that reason, just 35 percent of the population of Lo Monthang (primarily the elderly) remained in town year-round; the remainder migrated for the coldest months down to Pokhara.

When Baba Yeshi showed up at Tangya in November 1960, neither he nor his men at Yara had brought any food with them. They also carried little cash to purchase tsampa and other essentials. And even if they had brought money, more than 1,000 would-be guerrillas had assembled at Yara by year's end, far out-stripping the amount of staples that valley could produce. Very quickly, malnutrition reached critical levels. In desperation, more than a few boiled shoe leather for a meal.

Compounding matters, the CIA still did not have permission to make a supply drop, due to the prohibition against overflights following the U-2 affair. And if that were not enough, the new Kennedy administration was divided over whether the Mustang plan should even proceed. Heading the resistance was the new US ambassador to India, John Kenneth Galbraith. Galbraith's seething opposition was apparently grounded in his belief that the Tibet operation's benefits — especially from the Mustang component — did not outweigh the risk of harm to Indo–US relations.

Galbraith was hardly alone. Even within the CIA, opposition to the Tibet project was evident. This had less to do with arguments over the operation's potential yield than turf battles between the Agency's geographic divisions. Heading that list was the CIA station chief in New Delhi, Harry Rositzke. The ambitious Rositzke did not appreciate hosting part of an operation that earned him no credit in Washington but would leave him reaping bad publicity if things went sour. "The Far East Division got all the kudos," said one India case officer, "but the Near East Division risked the potential embarrassment."

Despite simmering opposition from the likes of Rositzke and Galbraith, President Kennedy in the second week of March 1961 approved an initial supply drop to Mustang. It was scheduled for the end of the month during the full moon phase and would total 29,000 pounds of arms and ammunition for 400 men. The bulk of the load was to consist of bolt-action Springfield rifles, plus 40 Bren light machine guns and a mix of 40 M1 Garands and carbines.

Also included in the drop would be seven Hale graduates. Four were from the pool of 27 Mustang leaders, including field commander-designate Sally. The remaining three were radiomen, all ethnic Khampas. They flew to Okinawa on the same plane as the Markham team and then waited a week on the island for weather conditions along the Nepal border to clear. Not until the last day of March did they continue on to Takhli.

Back at Tangya, Baba Yeshi's radiomen had already received word of the impending drop. Eight hundred men, led by Baba Yeshi himself, shifted 15 kilometres northeast to the border, then another 10 kilometres deeper into Tibet. Given the snow and terrain, this translated into a two-day trek. As they had no beasts of burden, 600 of this number were to act as porters; the remaining 200, having borrowed a handful of antiquated rifles from local herders, were to act as a paltry security force in the event of a PLA attack.

Once at the designated drop zone, the reception committee arranged piles of yak dung to serve as fuel for flame signals. Unfortunately for them, atmospheric conditions frustrated further radio contact with Takhli for two days. With the seven agents and supplies grounded in Thailand for an extra 48 hours, dozens among the 800 suffered frostbite.

Not until the evening of 2 April 1961 did the radio prove cooperative, and an all-clear signal was conveyed to the launch site. Due to the large size of the load, supplies had been divided between two Hercules transports. Even then, the seven agents barely had room to sit as they boarded the first aircraft. This, combined with the extreme distance, made for an exhausting albeit uneventful flight. Sighting the flame signals on the ground, the Air America crews continued deeper into Tibet, then circled around for a second pass.

In the rear, a nervous Sally was the first out the door. Landing in snow up to his waist, he worked quickly to get clear of the pallets that followed. Porters soon swarmed over the bundles, securing them on their backs before beginning the arduous journey back to Mustang.

Although the drop was a success — and the Indians had not indicated any knowledge of, much less displeasure with, the brief intrusion into their airspace — Ambassador Galbraith was more determined than ever to close the Mustang project. Traveling to Washington in May, he played on his rapport with Kennedy (who was already incensed with Dulles over the Bay of Pigs fiasco in April) to lobby the president for an end to what he saw as CIA interference. But even though the ambassador was able to stop most of the Agency's covert operations inside India, he failed to put a damper on the Tibet project.

Ironically, Galbraith was about to get an unlikely ally in the form of the Pakistani government. During the course of the Eisenhower presidency, the CIA had enjoyed cordial ties with Karachi. This included permission to use not only East Pakistani territory for the Tibet operation but also an airfield near the city of Peshawar as a U-2 launch site. Even when it was publicly revealed that the U-2 downed in May 1960 had originated from that airfield, Karachi hardly registered any protest over the resultant embarrassment.

But these warm ties looked set to change with the election of Kennedy and the pro-India bias he brought to office. Pakistani concerns seemed confirmed in April 1961 when Washington pledged a staggering $1 billion in economic aid for India's upcoming five-year development plan. Even more troubling for Karachi, the new administration, citing a threat from China, agreed to sell 350 tanks to New Delhi at low rates.

Pakistan wanted to retaliate, but it saw few ready options. It could not slam the door on Washington's military and economic assistance, because there were few alternative sources of aid that matched US largesse. And it would do no good to withhold permission to use the Peshawar air base, because U-2 flights were still suspended. With little other choice, the Pakistanis closed their border for the Tibet project.

For the Tibet Task Force, the timing could not have been worse. Twenty-three Mustang leaders (the four others had jumped on 2 April) were still at Hale awaiting word to return. Because the onset of the monsoon season prevented further parachute drops until late in the year, the CIA had intended to smuggle them through East Pakistan and let them enter Nepal on foot. With Karachi's change of heart, however, they were stranded in Colorado.

As it turned out, the Agency saw a brief window of opportunity midway through summer. Despite his strong leanings toward India, Kennedy was unwilling to completely write off Pakistan. He had invited President Ayub Khan to Washington for a weeklong visit beginning 11 July. On the day of his arrival, the polished Pakistani leader and his daughter were the guests of honour at picturesque Mount Vernon.

Seated between Kennedy and wife Jacqueline, Khan was feted during a spectacular dinner. Afterward, the two leaders took a stroll on the lawns of the estate. Taking advantage of the moment, Kennedy conveyed a personal plea from CIA Director Dulles to reopen the border. Caught up in the atmospherics, Ayub relented and agreed to let 10 more Tibetans pass through his territory.

Wasting little time, the CIA had the Tibetans through East Pakistan and into Mustang by August 1961. There they found that eight companies had been formed in the Yara vicinity, each numbering fewer than 100 men. Half of this number were issued rifles from the first weapons drop; the remainder were designated as support personnel. Eight of the Hale graduates took charge as company commanders; the rest were to act as trainers and headquarters staff.

Despite this promising start, problems quickly ensued. In particular, Baba Yeshi had not responded well to the CIA's plan for him to share authority with Sally. Outmanoeuvring the Hale-trained officer, he made it clear that he was in complete control of both administration and field operations. Not that there were any field operations to command. Despite the influx of 400 weapons and couriered cash from Gyalo Thondup, allowing for the purchase of horses, the guerrillas stood fast inside Mustang. Not until September 1961 did seven guerrillas on horseback head northeast into Tibet. As the Chinese had declared the border area off-limits to herders, they found the region completely devoid of population. Moving over the course of four nights, they eventually came upon a small PLA outpost on the south bank of the Brahmaputra. While two tended to the horses, the remaining five guerrillas ambushed a Chinese patrol and killed several (estimates ranged between eight and 13) before racing back to Nepal.

Upon receiving a radio message with the results of Mustang's baptism by fire, the CIA was less than impressed. No photographs had been taken as proof of the supposed ambush, and no weapons were retrieved. And as this had been the first and only operation in the six months since the weapons drop, the guerrillas were not exactly setting a breakneck pace.

Realising that he had to do better for an encore, Baba Yeshi gathered his officers and outlined plans for a 40-man foray. Their target would be any vehicle plying the trans-Tibet road running between Lhasa and Xinjiang. Completed in 1957, it was the only route connecting PLA border garrisons along a 2,400-kilometre stretch.

Chosen to lead the incursion was 35-year-old Rara, a Lithang native known as "Ross" during his stint at Hale. Since arriving via East Pakistan in August, he had assumed command of a company at Yara. For the road ambush, he assembled a composite unit by soliciting five men and five horses from each of the eight companies.

They were all armed with a mix of Garands and carbines; in addition, Ross took a camera to document their foray.

Heading north from Mustang on 21 October 1961, the guerrillas travelled for three days before crossing the frozen Brahmaputra and coming upon the Xinjiang road. Keeping their horses concealed, the Tibetans deployed in an extended line among the boulders of an adjacent hill. There they sat in the biting cold for an entire day. Not until 1400 hours on 25 October did the sound of a distant vehicle break the silence. From the west, a lone olive-drab truck came into view. Due to encroaching sand dunes, it could manage only a crawl along the clogged roadbed. Ross, who was at the closest end of the ambush, signalled the three guerrillas at his side to hold their fire until the vehicle was within range.

Taking aim with his carbine, Ross initiated the attack. Bullets ripped through the windshield, the driver's head snapped back, and the jeep veered to a halt on the shoulder. Two others in the front seat — one male, one female — slumped as their bodies were riddled by gunfire. Leaving the safety of the boulders, Ross exchanged his weapon for the camera. But as he moved forward to take photographs, gunfire began to pour from the rear of the truck. Ross dived for cover while the three other guerrillas resumed their fusillade toward the back of the vehicle. After a minute, they converged on the now silent target and removed four dead Chinese.

Putting his Hale training into practice, Ross wasted no time recovering three Chinese-made Type 56 carbines and a machine gun. He also took a large leather case from the front seat. The bodies were laid on the ground and stripped of uniforms, shoes, socks, and watches. After setting the jeep on fire, Ross blew a whistle as the signal for the rest of the guerrillas strung along the ridgeline to rendezvous near their horses.

Three days later, the 40 guerrillas were safely back in Mustang. Although photographs of the ambush were a bust (Ross had forgotten to take off the lens cap), the leather case looked promising. Baba Yeshi assigned two couriers to deliver the satchel to Lhamo Tsering in Darjeeling, who then personally carried it to CIA officer Clay Cathey in Calcutta.

When the case was opened, Cathey found himself staring at 1,600 pages of documents. Once Lhamo Tsering began preliminary translations of a sampling, the CIA officer determined that most of the material was classified up to top secret. "I sent a long cable listing some of the report titles," recalls Cathey. "A day later, headquarters sent a message saying it could be a gold mine."

Once the satchel was back in Washington, the CIA quickly realised that its initial assessment was correct. The male passenger in the front seat of the truck, it turned out, had been a PLA regimental commander assigned to Tibet. Among the documents he was carrying were more than two dozen issues of a classified PLA journal entitled *Bulletin of Activities*. In the end, more than 100 CIA reports were generated from these papers. "This single haul became the basic staple of intelligence on the Chinese army," concluded Cathey.

The CIA was ecstatic over its intelligence windfall, but Ambassador Galbraith did not share in the celebration. Persistent in his determination to put a stop to Mustang and further supply overflights, he fired off a series of scathing cables to Washington during November 1961. To add further punch, he made special note of Kennedy's 27 May letter to all American ambassadors charging each with responsibility for operations of the entire US diplomatic mission. Implicit in this was his prerogative to cancel what he deemed an objectionable CIA operation.

Still, Galbraith could barely make headway. With the documents in the truck satchel just beginning to be digested in Washington, the Tibet Task Force now had tangible proof of the operation's benefits. Armed with this, they secured final approval in early December 1961 for another pair of Hercules drops. For the guerrillas at Mustang, the omens were starting to look good.

12
FAVOURED SON

Just days after the CIA received approval for resupply flights, two C-130s lumbered down the Takhli runway. Following the same flight path as the previous Mustang mission, the pair of aircraft skirted the Tibet–Nepal border. From several kilometres away, the pilots could see an enormous blazing "I" not far from the drop zone used seven months earlier.

On the ground, Lobsang Jamba was among the 400-man reception party. Better prepared this time than they had been in April, the Tibetans had brought along 60 mules and horses. As pallets impacted the snow, the guerrillas descended on the bundles and divided them among pack animals and porters.

By week's end, they were back in Mustang and taking inventory. Besides 600 Garands, the load included eight 60mm mortars, eight 75mm recoilless rifles, and some Bren light machine guns. The extra weapons were sorely needed to keep pace with the fast-expanding Mustang force. Doubling on paper, it now counted 16 light companies, nearly all commanded by Hale graduates. From the contents of the first and second drops, half of each company was armed with rifles. Each company, too, received a single Bren and either a mortar or a recoilless rifle. Those not issued rifles or assigned to the 12-man heavy weapons squad were given a single grenade. In that way, each guerrilla was armed in some fashion.

Although these developments gave the CIA cause for cheer, the same could not be said for the situation back in Colorado. With more than a dozen Mustang leaders still languishing at Hale, the Agency had planned to whisk them back to Asia during the first week of December and appeal to Pakistan once more for permission to use its territory as a conduit.

Almost from the start, plans went awry. Leaving Hale on the night of 6 December, the remaining Tibetans narrowly avoided media exposure when their bus arrived at Peterson two hours behind schedule and had to dodge an early-morning crowd. Loading into a C-124 transport, Hale instructor Don Cesare escorted them as far as Okinawa, where what was intended as a brief transit stop extended into days and then weeks. The reason for this was due to India's December 1961 invasion of the small Portuguese enclave of Goa. This had irritated Pakistani leader Ayub Khan, who reasoned that if Washington refused to help when a European ally suffered at India's hand, they certainly would not come to Pakistan's aid in a pinch.

Roger McCarthy visits Camp Hale, 1961. Don Cesare is in the background. (Photo courtesy Barbara McCarthy)

As US–Pakistani relations plunged to a new low, use of East Pakistan for the Tibet project was well and truly out of the cards. Rather than retracing his steps back to vacant Camp Hale, Cesare diverted his Tibetans to a remote corner of the CIA complex on the island of Saipan. With no chance for overland infiltration anytime soon, he stocked up on movies and began looking for ways to keep his students preoccupied for the long wait ahead.

Infiltration of the Mustang leaders was not the only part of the Tibet project on hold. In a concession to Ambassador Galbraith, Kennedy had given the nod to the December supply drop only on the condition that future drops would include the participation of the Indian government. Such support, knew the CIA, was a long shot. Although Indian spymaster Mullik quietly gave his tacit approval of the Agency's efforts in 1961, and had earlier claimed that Nehru held similar beliefs, his influence with the aging Prime Minister was more than offset by India's ambitious and abrasive defence minister, Krishna Menon.

Known for his frequent baiting of the West, Menon was a devout socialist whose take on non-alignment fell decidedly left of centre. As defence minister, he was openly biased toward purchases of Soviet hardware, even when his generals requested Western alternatives. And given his soft stance toward China — as well as his close links with Nehru — Indo-US cooperation on the Tibet front was an impossibility as long as Menon enjoyed his pronounced clout.

Unable to meet Kennedy's requirement for Indian participation, the CIA knew that additional drops to Mustang were out of the question for the time being. The Tibet Task Force, as a result, came to reflect the resupply stand-down. With Hale empty and no new students scheduled for arrival, all the camp's instructors had been reassigned, with the exception of Cesare at Saipan. Roger McCarthy had already left his seat as head of the task force in December 1961 for an assignment on Taiwan, leaving Ken Knaus — who had often made teaching appearances at Hale — to assume command over a shadow of the former program.

Coincidentally, there was also a changing of the guard on the subcontinent. During May 1962, India station chief Harry Rositzke finished his tour and was replaced by David Blee. Arriving along with Blee was a new deputy station chief, William Grimsley. On his second India tour (he had been posted to New Delhi between 1956 and 1958), Grimsley had been given a second hat. Although a residual Tibet Task Force would remain under the Far East Division, Grimsley would be the primary Tibet case officer in India. This move effectively put Tibet operations directly under the control of the Near East Division.

Though largely emasculated, the Tibet Task Force was not yet out. In June 1962, officers from the task force travelled to Darjeeling to rendezvous with Mustang commander Baba Yeshi. To start on a good note, they congratulated the chieftain for the previous year's jeep ambush and offered an Omega chronograph watch in appreciation. But as talk shifted to the future, the secret tryst proved a bust. Speaking for his Tibetans, Baba Yeshi demanded a long list of supplies before his men would shift their action inside Tibet. As far as the CIA was concerned, it wanted the guerrillas to start launching reconnaissance teams north of the Brahmaputra without further preconditions. "It was basically a chicken or the egg scenario " said task force chief Knaus.

With no promises offered by either side, the CIA men returned to Washington with little hope. "Guerrilla harassment continues," read an Agency assessment prepared at month's end, "but poses no serious threat to [Beijing's] control." It even noted signs of reduced popular discontent against the Chinese.

Based on this sentiment and after further consultations at the highest levels of government, the Kennedy administration in the late summer of 1962 decided that the entire future of the Mustang resistance — not merely supply drops — would hinge on the unlikely prospect of active, not tacit, Indian support.

Baba Yeshi, meanwhile, went back to his perch at Mustang. There his men poured their energies into improving their respective tent camps. Eight of the companies had set up quarters in a line along the eastern side of the Kali Gandaki; the remainder ran in a mirror arrangement on the opposite side of the river. Aside from this, they did little else, not launching even a single foray following the previous October's satchel snatch.

For all intents and purposes, the epitaph to the Tibet project was ready to be scripted. It would be China, however, that provided a reprieve. On 8 September 1962, 600 Chinese troops had surrounded a position near Towang, the town where the Dalai Lama had first paused after crossing from Tibet. Cutting bridges and threatening the water supply, they forced the resident Indian garrison to send out a shrill plea for help.

Truth be told, the Chinese incursion into NEFA was not wholly unexpected. Ever since the PLA had invaded Tibet, China and India had been bickering about the delineation of their common border. Basing their claims on a 1914 treaty — of which Tibet was a party — India placed its NEFA boundary generally along the Himalayan watershed. China at times appeared ready to accept this but had most recently produced maps that showed much of NEFA under its control. Complicating matters was a second area of contested territory at the westernmost extreme of the Indo-Tibet border along the desolate Ladakh Range.

Slowly at first, the two sides had resorted to arms to press their conflicting claims. The first known PLA incursion took place in September 1958 when Chinese troops arrested an Indian police patrol in Ladakh. The following year, after the exile of the Dalai Lama, the frontier heated up after the Indians sent soldiers directly up to the Himalayan watershed; previously, they had been bivouacked well behind that line. The Chinese, in return, sent small numbers of troops into both NEFA and Ladakh, including an October 1959 attack in the west that killed nine Indians.

Though the Indian military raised a cry at that time, Defence Minister Menon would hear none of it. Even after the September 1962 report about the attack at Towang, Menon was keen to dismiss the incident as nothing more serious than the minor incursions of previous years.

One month later, there could be no mistaking Chinese intent. On 20 October 1962, PLA troops rolled down from the Himalayas and smashed Indian outposts across a wide front. Better acclimated to the altitude, properly stocked from nearby roads, and outnumbering the Indians eight to one, the PLA held every key advantage and showed it.

As the Indian top brass brainstormed ways of salvaging the desperate situation in the Himalayas, one solution was to create a guerrilla force that could strike behind Chinese lines. Because the Chinese were coming from Tibet, members of that ethnic group were the logical guerrillas of choice. Finding volunteers would not be a problem; there was no shortage of Tibetans on Indian soil, and virtually all were vehemently anti-Chinese and would not hesitate to take up arms for their own patriotic reasons.

But who would lead such a force? There needed to be a senior Indian officer who could win the confidence of the Tibetans, embracing their independent nature and promoting a semblance of discipline without resort to a rigid army code. And he would need to have a bent for the unconventional — something that was in short supply in the Indian military, as the trench mentality in the Himalayas had dramatically proved.

The choice eventually fell upon Brigadier Sujan Singh Uban, until recently the commander of the 26th Artillery Brigade in Kashmir and currently in New Delhi after having just processed his retirement papers. Forty-eight years old, he had been an artilleryman all his career. Normally, this would have provided little room for innovation, but Uban had spent much time with mountain units and was familiar with fighting at high altitudes.

On 26 October, Uban was called to the defence minister's office. With the Chinese still inside Indian territory, Uban was given sketchy details of the proposed behind-the-lines guerrilla mission. As a sweetener, the brigadier was promised a second star in due course. Uban was hooked; he grabbed the assignment without hesitation.

Now that the guerrilla force had a leader, there remained the job of signing on Tibetan volunteers. To help, the Indians sent an emissary from the Intelligence Bureau to Darjeeling to fetch the Dalai Lama's brother, Gyalo Thondup. After years of attempting to court the Indians — who were often sympathetic but never committal — Gyalo relished the moment as he sat in front of a select group of senior intelligence and military officials in the capital. Speaking in theoretical terms, his hosts asked whether he could organise the needed volunteers. Of course, replied Gyalo. When asked how many he could gather, Gyalo conjured a robust, round figure. Five thousand, he said.

Next came a key question. Would Gyalo prefer that the Intelligence Bureau or the Ministry of Defence be involved? Based on his earlier contact with Mullik and his current cooperation with the CIA (through Lhamo Tsering), the decision was easy. "Not Defense," was his indirect response.

In the US, meantime, the Kennedy administration had recently come to the brink of nuclear war when the Soviets looked to station missiles on Cuba. Not until 28 October did the world breathe a sigh of relief when Moscow agreed to withdraw its weaponry. The very next day, Prime Minister Nehru contacted Washington and made an unequivocal request for US military assistance against the Chinese advance.

Immediately, Washington stepped into the fray and responded generously to Nehru's appeal. By 2 November, the USAF was using Europe-based Boeing 707 transports to fly eight missions into India every day for a week. Each plane was packed with basic infantry equipment to refit the Indian soldiers streaming off the Himalayas, who in most cases were outfitted with more primitive gear than had been afforded the CIA's Tibetan guerrillas. These supplies were later ferried by USAF C-130 transports to smaller airfields near the frontier battle lines.

Back on 28 October, America's *bete noire*, the discredited Krishna Menon, had tendered his resignation. With him out of the way and the situation on the frontier critical, Kennedy gathered some of his best and brightest on 19 November to discuss the war in the Himalayas. Broached at the meeting was increased US military assistance to India and options for a show of force in the region. Also mentioned was the possibility of using the CIA's Tibetan guerrillas.

By meeting's end, it was decided to send a high-powered delegation to New Delhi to more fully assess India's needs. From the CIA, Des FitzGerald won a seat on the mission, as did the head of the Tibet Task Force, Ken Knaus.

On 21 November, the entourage departed Andrews Air Force Base in Maryland. Although the Chinese declared a unilateral ceasefire while the group was en route, the situation was still tense when it reached New Delhi the following day. The end results of their discussions were plans for a major three-phase military aid package encompassing material support, help with domestic defence production, and possible assistance with air defences.

As a covert aside, the CIA representatives on the delegation held their own sessions with Indian intelligence czar Mullik. Both the CIA and the Intelligence Bureau were quick to seize the opportunity. Most of their ideas centred around use of the Tibetans. "The Indians were interested in the Tibet program because of its intelligence collection value," said station chief David Blee, who sat in on some of the meetings. "Mullik was particularly interested in paramilitary operations." There was good reason for this: following Menon's resignation, and Gyalo Thondup's stated preference, the Intelligence Bureau had been placed in charge of the 5,000 Tibetan guerrillas forming under Brigadier Uban.

Mullik was cautious as well. Although he was well connected to the Nehru family and had the Prime Minister's full approval to talk with the CIA, he knew that the Indian populace was fickle, and until recently anti-Americanism had been a popular mantra. It was perhaps only a matter of time before the barometer would swing back and make open Indo-US cooperation political suicide. To offer some protection against this, Mullik and one of his close deputies, M. I. Hooja, made a special request during a session with FitzGerald and Blee. "They made us promise that our involvement," said Blee, "would remain secret forever."

By the end of their talks, the CIA and Intelligence Bureau had arrived at a rough division of labour. The Indians, with CIA support from the Near East Division, would work together in developing

Uban's 5,000-strong tactical guerrilla force. The CIA's Far East Division, meantime, would unilaterally create an underground resistance movement inside Tibet. The Mustang contingent would also remain under the CIA's unilateral control.

Meanwhile, the CIA arranged for a sign of good faith. One of the Agency's DC-6 transports was loaded with an assortment of military aid and made three shuttles between Thailand and the Charbatia airfield near the city of Bhubaneswar in India's eastern state of Orissa. A relic of the Second World War, Charbatia had fallen into a severe state of disrepair. More remarkable than its poor condition were the precautions taken to keep the CIA's largesse a secret from die-hard Soviet supporters among New Delhi's political elite. "We flew the last few miles just fifty feet above the ground to avoid radar," said pilot Neese Hicks. "We would land at dawn, eat a fast breakfast, and be back in the air toward Takhli."

By the last week of November 1962, the CIA representatives from the New Delhi talks were back in Washington and making their pitch before top officials of the Kennedy administration. Though they could now count on Indian participation — which had been a prerequisite for future support to the Mustang group — they had a tough sell. CIA Director McCone, for one, was a pronounced sceptic with relatively little interest in covert paramilitary operations. Citing the example of Mustang (which had done precious little over the past year), he was dubious about the utility of developing a tactical guerrilla force that the United States could not ultimately control. And although officials in New Delhi believed that limited war between India and China might continue intermittently over a number of years, he questioned what would happen in the event of Sino–Indian rapprochement. Would the CIA have to cut its support to the guerrillas and the resistance in midstream?

Despite McCone's comments, the chance of making significant inroads with the Indians — and giving a bigger headache to Beijing — was too good to pass up. On 13 December, the Kennedy administration approved training assistance to Uban's guerrilla force. At the same time, the Tibet Task Force drew up plans to reopen Hale and train at least 125 candidates for the resistance movement. Commented task force chief Knaus, "We had suddenly gone from stepchild to favored son."

13
CHAKRATA

Jamba Kalden was a latecomer to the resistance. A successful Khampa trader from Chamdo, he had been present in Lhasa in March 1959 when the PLA began shelling the capital on the day after the Dalai Lama fled for India. Attempting to evade the closing Chinese cordon, Jamba Kalden took a bullet to the thigh and was promptly arrested. He was confined to a small Lhasa cell while he nursed his wound, and not until summer was the injury sufficiently healed for him to be assigned to one of the prison gangs the Chinese had dispatched to various construction sites near the capital.

Jamba Kalden did not take well to forced labour. His once impressive physique turned gaunt from the hard work and meagre rations, and he began planning his escape. This did not come until 17 January 1960, when he slipped away from his minders and headed through blinding winter snowstorms toward the southern border. In May he reached Bhutan; two months later, he crossed into India.

By that time, the Dalai Lama and his entourage had taken up residence in the remote Indian hill town of Dharamsala. There he had set about creating a de facto government-in-exile. Part of this involved reforming the cabinet offices that previously existed in Lhasa. It also involved preparation of a draft constitution. At the same time, a straw vote was held in each of the main refugee camps over the summer. From this rudimentary selection process, 13 representatives were chosen: three from each province, plus one for each of the four Tibetan Buddhist sects.

Jamba Kalden arrived in Dharamsala as the 13 delegates were convening for the first time in September 1960. In deference to his relative wealth and influential position back in Chamdo, he was named as a key advisor to the nascent government. He was still serving in this capacity in late October 1962 when Gyalo Thondup came looking for 5,000 volunteers to fill Brigadier Uban's guerrilla force.

Gyalo's task was not particularly complicated. With word quickly spreading, volunteers by the thousands — mostly Khampas — stepped forward over the ensuing weeks. Gyalo also sought four political leaders who could act as the force's indigenous officer cadre. Given his seniority and ethnicity, Jamba Kalden was an easy first pick.

By early November 1962, an initial contingent of Tibetans, led by Jamba Kalden, was dispatched to the hill town of Dehra Dun. On hand to meet the Tibetans was Brigadier Uban and a skeleton staff of officers on loan from the Indian Army. While a transit tent camp was set up on the edge of town to process the 5,000 promised volunteers, on 14 November the Indian cadre and four political leaders shifted 92 kilometres northwest to the village of Chakrata.

Situated along a ridge and surrounded by forest glades, Chakrata had been chosen for good reason. Home to a thriving population of panthers and bears, it had once boasted two training centres for a pair of Gurkha regiments in the Indian Army. Since 1960, however, both regiments had relocated to more favourable climes. With almost no local residents and a set of vacant cantonments, Chakrata had both the ready facilities and the seclusion needed for the covert Tibetan project. Uban and his team settled in to await the arrival of the rest of the 5,000 volunteers by year's end and began mapping out the process of moulding them into effective guerrillas.

For intelligence chief Mullik, the Chakrata project signalled a new sense of militancy regarding Tibet. This was communicated in strong fashion on 29 December when Mullik — through Gyalo Thondup — told the Dalai Lama that New Delhi had now adopted a covert policy of supporting the eventual liberation of his homeland.

Although the US government did not match this with a similar pledge, the CIA wasted no time making good on its promise to help with the various Tibetan paramilitary schemes. As a start, Jim McElroy — the same logistics expert who had been involved with ST CIRCUS since its inception — was dispatched to India in early January 1963. He was escorted to the Paratroopers Training School at Agra, just a few kilometres from the breath-taking Taj Mahal palace. Because aerial methods would be the likely method of supporting behind-the-lines operations against the PLA, McElroy began an

Charles "Ken" Seifarth with two Tibetan student riggers, Agra airbase, summer 1963. (Photo courtesy Thomas Thompson)

assessment of the school's parachute inventory to fully understand India's air delivery capabilities. He also started preliminary training of some Tibetan riggers drawn from Chakrata.

McElroy's deployment paved the way for more substantial assistance. Stepping forward as liaison in the process was 47-year-old Indian statesman Biju Patnaik. A close ally of spy chief Mullick, Patnaik was the chief minister in his native eastern state of Orissa. He was also well versed in aviation and had earlier founded a charter air company based in Calcutta. He dubbed the venture Kalinga Air Lines, taking its name from an ancient kingdom in Orissa. It was Patnaik, too, who had arranged in November 1962 for the CIA to quietly delver its three planeloads of supplies to Charbatia airfield in Orissa. And in December 1962, after the CIA notified New Delhi of its impending paramilitary support program, he was the one dispatched to Washington on behalf of Nehru and Mullik to negotiate details of the assistance package.

Upon his arrival in the US capital, Patnaik's primary point of contact was Robert "Moose" Marrero. Thirty-two years old, Marrero was aptly nicknamed: like Patnaik, he stood over two meters tall and weighed 102 kilos. He was also an aviator, having flown helicopters for the Marines before leaving military service in 1957 to join the CIA as an air operations specialist.

As the two pilots conversed, they recognised the need for a thorough review of the airlift requirements for warfare in the high Himalayas. They also saw the need to train and equip a covert airlift cell outside of the Indian military chain of command that could operate along the Indo–Tibetan frontier.

While Patnaik was discussing these aviation issues in Washington, the CIA's Near East Division was forging ahead with assistance for the Tibetans at Chakrata. Heading an eight-man CIA paramilitary training team would be 45-year-old Wayne Sanford, a former Marine who was a veteran of CIA operations on Taiwan. He would do so from an office at the US embassy in New Delhi while acting under the official title of Special Assistant to Ambassador Galbraith. As this would be an overt posting with the full knowledge of the Indian government, both he and the seven other paramilitary advisors would remain segregated from David Blee's CIA station.

Back in Washington, the rest of the team took shape. Another former Marine, John Magerowski, was fast to grab a berth. So was Harry Mustakos, who had worked with the Tibetans on Saipan in 1957 and served with Sanford on Taiwan. Former smokejumper Thomas "T. J." Thompson was to replace Jim McElroy at Agra. Two other training officers were selected from the United States, and a third was diverted from an assignment in Turkey. The last slot went to former US Army airborne officer Charles "Ken" Seifarth, who had been in South Vietnam conducting jump class for agents destined to infiltrate the communist north.

By mid-April 1963, the eight had assembled in New Delhi. If they expected warm greetings from their CIA colleagues in the embassy, it did not happen. "We were neither welcomed nor wanted by the station chief," recalls Mustakos. For Sanford, this was eventually seen as a plus. "Blee gave me a free hand," he remembered, "but Galbraith wanted detailed weekly briefings on everything we did."

At the outset, there was little for Sanford to report. Waiting for their gear to arrive (they had ordered plenty of cold weather clothing), the team members spent their first days agreeing on a syllabus for the upcoming six months. One week later, their supplies arrived, and six of the advisors left Sanford in New Delhi for the chilled air of Chakrata. The last member, Thompson, alone went to Agra.

Once the CIA advisors arrived at the mountain training site, Brigadier Uba gave them a fast tour and then introduced them to their guerrilla students. By that time, the Chakrata project had been given an official name. A decade earlier, Brigadier Uban had had a posting in command of the 22nd Mountain Regiment in Assam. Borrowing that number, he gave his Tibetans the ambiguous title of "Establishment 22."

In reviewing Establishment 22, the Americans were immediately struck by the age of the Tibetans. Although there was a sprinkling of younger recruits, nearly half were older than 45; some were even approaching 60. Jamba Kalden, the chief political leader, was practically a child at 43. As had happened with the Mustang guerrillas, the older generation, itching for a final swing at the Chinese, had used its seniority to edge out younger candidates during the recruitment drive in the refugee camps.

With much material to cover, the CIA advisors reviewed what the Indian staff had accomplished over the previous few months. Uban had initially focused his efforts on instilling a modicum of discipline. The Indians had also started a strict regimen of physical exercise, including extended marches across the nearby hills. In addition to exercise, the Indians had offered a sampling of tactical instruction. But most of it, the CIA team found, reflected a conventional mind-set. "We had to unteach quite a bit," said Mustakos.

This combination — strict exercise and a crash course in guerrilla tactics — continued through the first week of May 1963. At that point, classes were put on temporary hold in order to initiate airborne training. Plans called for nearly all members of Establishment 22 to be qualified as paratroopers. This made tactical sense: if the Tibetans were to operate behind Chinese lines, the logical means of infiltrating them to the other side of the Himalayas would be by parachute.

When told of the news, the Tibetans were extremely enthusiastic about the prospect of jumping. There was a major problem, however. Establishment 22 remained a secret not only from the general Indian public but also from the bulk of the Indian military. The Intelligence Bureau arranged for the Tibetans to use crude barracks in a distant corner of Agra airbase, reducing the chance of an encounter with inquisitive army paratroopers.

To oversee the airborne phase of instruction, Ken Seifarth relocated to Agra. Five jumps were planned for each candidate, including one performed at night. Because of the limited size of the barracks at the airbase, the Tibetans would rotate down to the lowlands in 100-man cycles. With up to three jumps conducted each day, the entire qualification process was expected to stretch through the summer.

On 11 May, an Indian Air Force C-119 Flying Boxcar crossed the skies over Agra. As the twin-tailed transport aircraft came over the drop zone, Uban was the first out the door, Seifarth the second. In the weeks that followed, the rest of Establishment 22 clamoured for their opportunity to leap from an aircraft. "Even cooks and drivers demanded to go," recalled Uban. Nobody was rejected for age or health reasons, including one Tibetan who had lost an eye and another who was so small that he had to strap a sandbag to his chest to deploy the chute properly.

Nehru, meanwhile, was receiving regular updates on the progress at Chakrata. During the fall of 1963, with the deployment of the eight-man CIA team almost finished, he was invited to make an inspection visit to the hill camp. The Intelligence Bureau also passed a request asking the Prime Minister to use the opportunity to address the guerrillas directly. Nehru was sympathetic but cautious. The thought of the Prime Minister addressing Tibetan combatants on Indian soil had the makings of a diplomatic disaster if word leaked. Afraid of adverse publicity, he agreed to visit the camp but refused to give a speech.

Hearing this news, Uban had the men of Establishment 22 undergo a fast lesson in parade drill. The effort paid off. Though stiff and formal when he arrived on 14 November, Nehru was visibly moved when he saw the Tibetans in formation. And knowing that the Prime Minister was soft for roses, Uban presented him with a brilliant red blossom plucked from a garden he had planted on the side of his stone bungalow. Nehru buckled. Asking for a microphone, the Prime Minister poured forth some ad hoc and heartfelt comments to the guerrillas. "He said that India backed them," said Uban, "and vowed they would one day return to an independent country."

14
OAK TREE

In mid-March 1963, eight Indians — six from the Indian Air Force, two from the Intelligence Bureau — were sent to Washington as cadre for the covert airlift cell conjured earlier by Biju Patnaik and Bob Marrero. For the first two weeks, Marrero, who was playing host, arranged for briefings at a row of CIA buildings near the Tidal Basin. By the beginning of April, the group was flown to an isolated barracks at Camp Peary for a month of lectures on a range of intelligence and paramilitary topics.

The leader of the eight Indians, Group Captain Lal Singh Grewal, had a decade earlier been in the first class of Indian aviators selected to head to the United States for transition training on the C-119 transport. When the call went out for a dynamic air force officer to manage a secret aviation unit under the auspices of the Intelligence Bureau and CIA, Grewal was the immediate choice.

Following the training stint at Camp Peary, six of the students returned to New Delhi. The two most senior members, Grewal and Wing Commander Chandan Singh, remained for several additional weeks of specialised aviation instruction. Marrero, meanwhile, made arrangements in May 1963 to head for India to conduct the comprehensive air survey broached with Biju Patnaik in their December 1962 meeting. Joining Marrero would be the same CIA air operations officer who had been involved with the earliest drops into Tibet, Gar Thorsrud.

For three months, Thorsrud and Marrero were escorted from the Himalayan frontier to the airborne school at Agra to the Tibetan training site at Chakrata. Much of their time was spent near the weathered airstrip at Charbatia; there they were feted by Patnaik, who offered use of Charbatia — now given the call sign Oak Tree — as the principal site for a clandestine air support operation and immediately secured funds from the Prime Minister for reconstruction of the runway.

Returning to New Delhi, the two CIA men were directed to a hotel room for a meeting with a representative of the Intelligence Bureau, T. M. Subramanian. Known for his Hindu piety and strict

CIA instructor Bruce Walker (centre) with Tibetan students "Sandy" and "Rick" at Camp Hale, 1964. Sandy would later serve as a radioman at Mustang and was imprisoned by the Nepalese authorities in 1974. (Photo courtesy Bruce Walker)

vegetarian diet, Subramanian was one of the two intelligence officers who had been trained at Camp Peary during April.

In the ensuing discussions between the CIA officers and Subramanian, both sides spoke in general terms about the best options for building India's covert aviation capabilities. A subject not discussed was which US aircraft would be the backbone for the envisioned covert unit. Earlier in the spring, this had been the subject of serious debate within the CIA. Wayne Sanford, the senior paramilitary officer in New Delhi, had initially proposed the C-119. Other CIA officials in Washington, however, were keen to present the Indians with the C-46 Commando because other CIA operations in Asia — primarily in Laos — were making use of the C-46 and the Agency had a number of airframes readily available. The latter was ultimately selected.

On 7 September 1963, the Intelligence Bureau officially created the Aviation Research Centre (ARC) as a front to coordinate aviation cooperation with the CIA. Group Captain Grewal was named the first ARC operations manager at the newly completed Charbatia airfield. He was given full latitude to handpick his pilots, all of whom would take leave from the military and belong — both administratively and operationally — to the ARC for the period of their assignment.

In New Delhi, veteran intelligence officer Rameshwar Nath Kao took the helm as the first ARC director. To assist Kao and Grewal, the CIA dispatched Edward Rector to Charbatia in the role of air operations advisor. Qualified as a US Navy dive-bomber pilot in 1940, Rector had joined Claire Chennault's famed Flying Tigers the following year. He would later score that unit's first kill of a Japanese aircraft and go on to become an ace. After switching to the US Army Air Forces (later the USAF), he retired as a colonel in January 1962.

Rector came to Oak Tree with considerable Indian experience. During his Flying Tigers days, he had transited the subcontinent. And in late 1962, following his retirement from military service, he had gone to India on a Pentagon contract to coordinate USAF C-130 flights carrying emergency assistance to the front lines during the war with China.

Now serving with the CIA, Rector was on hand for the initial four aircraft deliveries within a week of ARC's creation. First to arrive at Oak Tree was a pair of C-46D Commandos; inside each was a disassembled U-10 Helio Courier. A five-seat light aircraft, the Helio Courier had already won praise for its short take-off and landing (STOL) ability in the CIA's paramilitary campaign in Laos. Without exaggeration, it could operate from primitive runways no longer than a soccer field. More aircraft deliveries followed, totalling eight C-46 transports and four Helio Couriers by early 1964.

Under Rector's watch, the CIA arranged for the loan of some of the best pilots from its Air America roster to act as instructors for the ARC crews. Heading the C-46 conversion team was Bill Welk, a veteran of the Tibet overflights. For the Helio Courier, Air America Captain James Rhyne was dispatched to Oak Tree for a four-month tour. During this same period, T. J. Thompson, who had been assisting with the Tibetans' jump training at Agra, began work on a major parachute facility at Charbatia. "By the time it was finished," said Thompson, "it was larger than the facilities used by the US Army in Germany."

While the CIA assistance at Chakrata and Charbatia was transpiring under the auspices of the Near East Division, a separate Tibet program had been taking shape since December 1962 under the Far East Division. This program called for the training and infiltration of at least 125 Tibetan agents. Agent training would focus on producing self-sufficient three-man radio teams that could infiltrate Tibet, find support, and build a local underground resistance that could feed and shelter them for extended periods without having to rely on lines of supply from India.

Just as with Establishment 22, Gyalo Thondup was quick to buy into the program and went off to recruit. The CIA, meanwhile, reopened Camp Hale to handle the expected influx. Scrambling to piece together an instructor staff, it found a willing volunteer in Bruce Walker, the great-grandson of Methodist missionaries in China. The CIA had earlier sponsored him for Tibetan language training at the University of Washington's newly organised Tibet program, then in March 1962 sent him for more Tibetan language classes at Sikkim's Namgyal Institute of Tibetology.

By the time Walker returned to the United States in the fall of 1962, he had the basics of spoken Tibetan in hand. Given its investment in his education, the CIA rushed him to Hale to prepare the camp for the first wave of Tibetans. Ken Knaus, chief of the Tibet Task Force in Washington, would again be on hand to offer occasional lectures. There was also a stream of smokejumpers — including brothers Miles and Shep Johnson — available for parachute instruction. The USAF even provided experts to teach survival tips. Overall command of the training would be held by Robert Eschbach, an OSS veteran.

By February 1963, four groups totalling 135 Tibetans (10 more than originally planned) had arrived at Hale. Gyalo had been instructed to restrict these recruits to the younger generation, unlike the crowd of seniors at Mustang and Establishment 22. Although Khampas were still the overwhelming majority, 5 percent were from Amdo, and another 5 percent were from central Tibet.

As scheduled, the Hale training concluded by June 1963. Before the Tibetans could return, however, the CIA shifted the goalposts. The Agency was now looking to hook New Delhi into more meaningful cooperation. Specifically, the CIA wanted to use the covert airlift unit at Charbatia for infiltration. A new operational plan now called for the dispatch of five teams by Indian aircraft and 29 teams overland to the area between Lhasa and the border with Bhutan.

Notified of the revised scheme, New Delhi balked. Though not rejecting the plan outright, the Indians indicated a strong reluctance to participate in any airdrops at the present time. "They wanted us to do the drops," said paramilitary advisor Wayne Sanford, "and not incur Chinese wrath if one was downed." For the CIA instructors at Hale, India's reluctance translated into delays in returning their students to Tibet. Tibetans had been stranded in Colorado once before (when Pakistan had closed its border), but this time the problem was exacerbated by the large size of the contingent. Realising that boredom would soon set in and morale would suffer, the staff quickly expanded the curriculum to include classes on tradecraft such as wiretapping and lectures on Marxist Leninism and the new Tibetan constitution.

By the early autumn of 1963, the Tibetans could absorb no more and were clearly growing impatient. One of the Khampa students, Cheme Namgyal (known by the call sign "Conrad"), was especially frustrated with the delays. "We ended up playing lots and lots of volleyball," he recalled.

After further negotiations, a breakthrough finally came in September 1963. Still looking to draw New Delhi into a substantial role, the CIA now had India's agreement to open a joint operations centre in New Delhi that would direct the dispatch of agents into Tibet and monitor their activities. The revised plan scrapped parachute insertions in favour of overland infiltrations and called for about 20 singleton resident agents in Tibet, plus (to sweeten its appeal to New Delhi) a pair of road-watch teams "to report possible Chinese Communist build-ups" and another six "border watch communications teams" to take up positions along the frontier. Radio reports from the agents and teams would be received at a new communications centre to be built at Charbatia. With the first group of 40 Hale graduates scheduled to return to India in November, the secret struggle for Tibet was starting to reach the simmering point.

15
THE JOELIKOTE BOYS

As the CIA's covert program for Tibet regained momentum toward the end of 1963, strict compartmentalisation among its component projects fell by the wayside. This had become readily apparent to Wayne Sanford, who extended his tour in October 1963 to remain as the US embassy's resident CIA paramilitary advisor responsible for ongoing assistance to Establishment 22. One of his first duties after extending his tour was to escort T. M. Subramanian, the intelligence officer now working under ARC, to Camp Hale. Some of the Hale trainees, it had been decided, would be redirected from agent operations to Uban's guerrillas at Chakrata.

The nuances in this were significant. Establishment 22 was an Indian operation supported by the Near East Division. The Hale agent training, however, had originally been conceived as a unilateral Far East Division project with limited Indian exposure. Now the assets from one division's program were being transferred to another — and the Indians were full partners on both.

Much the same thing had happened to the guerrilla army at Mustang. When first launched by the Far East Division, the Mustang operation had been conducted behind India's back. But when Washington sent the high-powered delegation to India during the war with China, Mullik had been fully briefed, and discussions over the best way of jointly running the guerrillas soon followed.

The CIA and Intelligence Bureau, it was discovered, held widely disparate views on Mustang, which was home to 2,030 Tibetan guerrillas as of early 1963. Less than half of them had been properly equipped during the two previous CIA airdrops. Realising that the unarmed men were a ball and chain on the rest, the Agency devised a plan to parachute weapons to an additional 700 men that would be waiting at 10 drop zones inside Tibet. The purpose of this was twofold. First, it would force them to leave their Mustang sanctuary and take up a string of positions inside their homeland. Second, it would go far toward rectifying the disparity between armed and unarmed volunteers.

When this plan was taken to Mullik, his reaction was poor. Just as the Indians had balked at aerial infiltration for the Hale agents, they preferred no Mustang drops by Indian aircraft (ARC was close to formation at the time), for fear of provoking the Chinese. When the CIA proposed that US aircraft do the job — but insisted on Indian landing rights — New Delhi was again reticent.

Eventually in September 1963, the CIA and Intelligence Bureau came up with a new plan for the unarmed men at Mustang to be reassigned to Establishment 22 at Chakrata. It was also agreed that non-lethal supplies for the armed portion of Mustang — which was estimated at no more than 835 guerrillas — would go overland through India and be coordinated through the New Delhi centre. In addition, some of the Hale graduates would go to Mustang to assist with radio operations. Once again, distinctions between the various Tibet projects were becoming blurred.

During the same month, CIA officers beckoned Mustang leader Baba Yeshi to New Delhi to gain his approval for the reassignment scheme. Unfortunately for the Agency, the chieftain was not happy when he was told that his force would be more than halved. With Lhamo Tsering providing translations, talks remained deadlocked for the next week. Opting to seek the counsel of Khampa leader Gompo Tashi, they shifted the debate to Calcutta. Gompo Tashi had recently returned there after half a year in a London hospital, where he had sought relief from lingering war injuries. Still weak, he refused to take sides.

Defiant, Baba Yeshi went back to Mustang. From the perspective of a Khampa tribal leader, his reluctance to downsize Mustang was both understandable and predictable. In true chieftain fashion, he had spent the previous two years patiently padding his command. The results on several fronts were laudable. The bleak food situation, for example, had been fully rectified. With occasional funds channelled by the CIA, a small team of Khampas purchased meat, butter, and rice at Pokhara and sent the supplies north on pack animals. Baba Yeshi's Khampas also procured local barley for a tsampa mill they established in the Mustang village of Kagbeni. His men were eating; malnourishment was a thing of the past.

The quality of his fighters was also improving. Unlike Mustang's first wave of aged recruits, the steady stream of trainees arriving in Mustang during 1963 were either in their late teens or young adults. Many hailed from central Tibet, providing a more representative mix than the previous Khampa-dominated ranks.

Because most of the young arrivals came with no previous guerrilla experience, the Mustang leadership had spent much of 1963 institutionalising its training procedures. A more formal camp was set up at Tangya to offer between three and six months of drills in rock climbing, river crossing, partisan warfare, and simple tradecraft. Graduates were then posted to one of Mustang's 16 guerrilla companies, each of which had a Hale-trained instructor for refresher courses.

Baba Yeshi had made some personalised gains as well. Because his headquarters at Tangya was uncomfortable during the coldest months, in 1963 he focused considerable energy on establishing a new winter base at the village of Kaisang. Located seven kilometres southeast of Jomsom, Kaisang was tucked at the base of the massive Annapurna. More than just a beautiful vista, the new base included a comfortable two-floor house for Baba Yeshi; it had a vegetable garden, Tibetan mastiffs chained to the front gate, and a Tibetan flag fluttering from a tall staff. Ten guards patrolled the perimeter, screening guerrilla subordinates who wished an audience with their commandant.

Against these gains, precious little had been done to progress the war inside Tibet. In theory, the guerrillas intended to concentrate their cross-border forays during the winter, when the frozen Brahmaputra was easily fordable and the Chinese were less likely to patrol. In reality, hardly any guerrilla activities emanated from Mustang at any time of year. During all of 1963 and most of 1964, not a single truck was ambushed (land mines were occasionally laid, without any known success), and no PLA outposts were attacked. Said one senior guerrilla, "We went on existing for the sake of existence."

With Mustang relegated to a sideshow, the focus of joint Indo–US cooperation shifted to the agent program. To monitor this effort, the New Delhi joint operations centre — dubbed the Special Center — was formally established in November 1963. To house the site, Intelligence Bureau officers arranged to rent a modest villa in the F block of the posh Haus Khaz residential neighbourhood.

Ken Knaus, the first CIA representative to the Special Center, arrived in India during the final week of November. (Once Knaus began handling Tibet programs from India, the Tibet Task Force in Washington was downgraded to a desk function within the China Branch.) On 4 January 1964, Knaus was joined by a sharp Bombay native nicknamed Rabi. A math major in college, Rabi had joined the police force upon graduation but soon switched to the Intelligence Bureau. He had been assigned to its China section and spent many years operating from remote outposts in Assam and NEFA. Now chosen as the Indian representative to the Special Center, he internally transferred to the ARC. More than merely an airlift unit, the ARC was now acting as the section of the Intelligence Bureau that would work alongside the CIA on joint efforts with the Tibet agents and guerrillas at Mustang.

In April 1964, Knaus and Rabi were joined by a Tibetan representative, Kesang Kunga. A soft-spoken former district governor and monk, Kesang — better known as Kay-Kay — came from a landed family in central Tibet. Under Kay-Kay was a small team of Tibetan assistants. Three members were former Hale translators. There was also a pool of eight Hale graduates from the 1963 training class; half provided radio assistance at the Special Center, and the other half performed similar tasks at the radio relay centre being set up at Charbatia.

By the time Kay-Kay got his assignment in the spring of 1964, most of the 135 agent trainees had returned to India from Hale. Two dozen were diverted to Establishment 22 at Chakrata, and another eight manned the radio sets at Charbatia and the Special Center. The remainder — slightly more than 100 — were taken to a holding camp outside the village of Joelikote near the hill station of Nainital.

As the agents assembled at Joelikote — where Rabi promptly dubbed them "The Joelikote Boys" — they were divided into radio teams, each designated by a letter of the alphabet. The size of the teams varied, with some numbering as few as two agents and several with as many as five; contrary to the previous year's plan to dispatch lone operatives, none would be going as singletons. As their main purpose would be to radio back social, political, economic, and military information, the CIA provided radios ranging from the durable RS-1 to the RS-48 (a high-speed-burst model originally developed for use in Southeast Asia) and a sophisticated miniature set with a burst capability and solar cells. The teams would also be charged with gauging the extent of local resistance; when appropriate, they were to spread propaganda and extend a network of sympathisers. Although they were not to engage in sabotage or other attacks, the agents would carry pistols (Canadian-made Brownings to afford the US plausible deniability) for self-defence.

During April 1964, the first wave of 10 radio teams began moving from Joelikote to launch sites along the border. Team A, consisting of two agents, took up a position in the Sikkimese capital of Gangtok. Team B, also two men, filed into the famed colonial summer capital of Shimla. Three teams — D, V, and Z — were sent to Tuting, a NEFA backwater already host to 2,000 Tibetan refugees. Two others — T and Y — crossed into easternmost Nepal and established a camp outside the village of Walung. Another two teams went to Mustang to provide Baba Yeshi's guerrillas with improved radio links to Charbatia.

The 10th set of agents — two men known as Team Q — headed into the kingdom of Bhutan. At the same time they crossed the border, the kingdom's prime minister was coincidentally killed by unknown assailants. As their presence became known — sparking unfounded rumours that the Tibetans were attempting to overthrow the kingdom — the two agents were quietly withdrawn and Bhutan was never again contemplated as a launch site.

Aside from the stillborn Team Q and the two others at Mustang, the other seven teams had been briefed on targets before departing Joelikote. These had been generated by the CIA and Intelligence Bureau; Knaus had access to the latest intelligence for this purpose, including satellite imagery. He and Rabi then consulted with Kay-Kay, who endorsed the missions. All involved testing the waters inside Tibet to determine whether an underground resistance could, or did, exist.

Getting the agents to actually cross the frontier proved a challenge. By the early summer of 1964, three of the teams — in Sikkim, Shimla, and Walung — had barely budged. The second set of agents in Walung, Team Y, had better luck. One of its members, a young Khampa going by the call sign "Clyde," headed alone across the Nangpa Pass for a survey near the Tibetan town of Tingri. Located along the traditional route linking Kathmandu and Lhasa, Tingri was a popular resting place for an assortment of pilgrims and traders; as a result, Clyde attracted little attention. Better still, Tingri was surrounded by cave hermitages that offered good concealment.

Returning to Walung with this information, Clyde briefed his four teammates. Three — Robert, Dennie, and team leader Reg — were fellow Khampas; the last — Grant — was from Amdo. Following the same route used during the survey, the five arrived at the caves and set up camp.

Tingri, they discovered, was ripe for an underground. Venturing into town to procure supplies, the team took volunteers back to its redoubt for ad hoc leadership training. They debriefed the locals for items of intelligence value and used their solar-powered burst radio to send two messages a week back to Charbatia. Settling into a routine, they prepared to wait out the approaching winter from the vantage of their cave.

Good luck was also experienced by the three teams operating from the Indian border village of Tuting. Team D, consisting of four Khampas, arrived at its launch site with one Browning pistol apiece and a single survival rifle. Their target was the town of Pemako, 80 kilometres to the northeast. Renowned among Tibetans for its harsh topography and abundant precipitation, Pemako had barely been penetrated by the PLA.

That same rainfall made the trip for Team D a slog. Covering only part of the distance to their target by late 1964, most of the agents were ready to return to the relatively appealing creature comforts in Tuting. Just one member, Nolan, chose to stay for the winter. Wishing him luck, his colleagues promised to meet again in the spring of 1965.

Much the same experience was recounted by the five men of Team Z. Also targeted toward Pemako, they conducted a series of shallow cross-border forays to contact villagers and collect data on PLA patrols. Finally making a deeper infiltration near year's end, they encountered some sympathisers and the makings of an underground. By that time, most of the agents were eager to return before the approaching winter. Just as with Team D, one of its members, Chris, elected to stay through spring with his embryonic partisan movement.

The final group of agents from Tuting, Team V, was targeted 80 kilometres west toward the town of Menling. Located along the banks of the Brahmaputra, this low-lying region featured high rainfall and lush forests. Many locals in the area, though conversant in Tibetan, were animists, with their own unique language and style of dress.

Despite such ethnic differences, one of Team V's members, Stuart, had a number of relatives living in the vicinity. With their assistance, the team was able to contact a loose underground of resisters. Shielded by these sympathisers — who even helped them steal some PLA supplies when their cache was exhausted — the five men of Team V radioed back their intent to remain through the winter.

Reviewing their progress in November 1964, Knaus, Rabi, and Kay-Kay had some reason for cheer. Of the 10 teams dispatched to date, four had at least some of their members still inside Tibet. All four, too, had identified sympathetic countrymen. Encouraged by these results, the Special Center representatives penned plans to launch a second round of nine teams the following spring, when the mountain passes would be free of snow. Slowly, the secret war for Tibet was shifting from simmer to low boil.

16
BORROWED TIME

On the afternoon of 16 October 1964, the arid desert soil around Lop Nur in central Xinjiang Province rippled as the PRC tested its first nuclear bomb. The detonation had not been unexpected. For the past few months, the UA had been closely tracking China's nuclear program using everything from satellite photographs to a worldwide analysis of media statements made by Chinese diplomats. India had supported this collection effort by allowing the CIA to use Charbatia in April to secretly stage U-2 flights over Xinjiang. By late September, there were enough indications for senior officials in Washington to publicly predict the blast three weeks prior to the event.

Such forewarning did nothing to dampen anxiety in New Delhi. This resulted in a windfall of sorts for the Tibet project, with the CIA using the Indians' more permissive attitude to push for a series of covert initiatives. One sensitive project combined the CIA, the Intelligence Bureau, and the top mountain climbers from both nations (including one Tibetan from Establishment 22). Conceived in late 1964 following the first PRC atomic test, this operation called for placement of a nuclear-powered sensor atop Kanchenjunga, the third tallest mountain bordering Sikkim and Nepal. From its vantage atop the Himalayas, the sensor would theoretically relay telemetry data from intermediate-range ballistic missiles the Chinese were developing at test sites in Xinjiang. Because Kanchenjunga was later deemed too challenging — it is one of the world's hardest peaks to scale, even without the extra weight of sensitive equipment — the placement site was shifted in 1965 to India's Nanda Devi peak. That October, a device was carried near the summit, but before the climbers had a chance to activate its generator, worsening weather forced them to secure the equipment in a crevice until they could return the following spring.

Some of the most tangible Indo–US cooperation was in the expansion of the ARC fleet at Charbatia. By 1964, a total of 10 C-46 transports and four Helio STOL planes had been delivered to the Indians. Late that year, they were augmented by two more STOL airframes that were a unique adaptation of the Helio. Known as the Twin Helio, these planes looked exactly like the single-engine version, but with two propellers placed above and forward of the wings. Developed in 1960 with the CIA's war in Laos in mind, the Twin Helio's engine's placement allowed for unrestricted lateral visibility and reduced the possibility of propeller damage from debris at primitive airstrips.

One of the first two Mi-4 choppers sent from Mumbai to the ARC base at Charbatia in 1965. They initially sported an olive drab colour scheme as seen here. (Photo via M.K. Anand)

Of the planes delivered to the ARC, several received further modifications in India. To provide for an eavesdropping capability, CIA technicians in 1964 transformed one of the C-46 airframes into an electronic intelligence (ELINT) platform. This plane flew regular orbits along the Himalayas, recording Chinese telecommunications signals from inside Tibet. For some of the nine remaining C-46 transports, ARC became a test bed during 1966 for a unique adaptation. Much like the jet packs strapped to Indian Air Force C-119 Flying Boxcars during 1962, four 1,000-pound rocket boosters were placed on the bottom of the C-46 fuselages to allow heavy loads to be safely carried from some of India's highest airfields.

Such cooperation, however, masked tension under the surface. At the highest levels of government, problems were evident by early 1964. Following the assassination of John F. Kennedy the previous November, the new administration of President Lyndon Johnson withheld approval of a five-year military assistance package to India negotiated by his predecessor. Not helping matters was the fact that Johnson was increasingly consumed by the Vietnam War, leaving him little time to thoughtfully contemplate South Asia.

During the following year, bilateral strains were exacerbated by the Indo–Pakistan conflict that autumn. Pakistan initiated hostilities in August when it attempted to seize the contested Kashmir by infiltrating thousands of guerrillas. After that effort faltered, Karachi crossed the frontier with tanks. India responded in kind, leading to some of the bloodiest armour battles since the Second World War.

For the next month, the United States remained in the background as the subcontinent teetered on the edge of all-out war. Relying on the United Nations to broker a ceasefire, Washington did little apart from cut the flow of additional weapons to Pakistan. By effectively walking away from the region, the Johnson administration infuriated both sides: although the special US–Pakistani alliance was now effectively dead, no points had been scored with India.

The Soviet Union, meanwhile, was patiently working overtime to improve ties with New Delhi. In September 1964, it signed a deal not only to sell India the MiG-21 jet but also to allow mass production in Indian factories. The Soviets even impinged on areas of cooperation between the CIA and the Intelligence Bureau. During 1965, Moscow offered — and New Delhi accepted — a pair of Mi-4 helicopters for the ARC.

The deterioration in Indo–US relations had taken place during the watch of Ambassador Chester Bowles, who had replaced Galbraith in the summer of 1963. Bowles, who inherited the CIA's cooperative ventures already in progress, was largely silent about the Agency during his first two years in New Delhi. Wayne Sanford, the CIA paramilitary officer who had provided regular updates for Galbraith, had not even met Bowles for a briefing by the summer of 1965.

But with Indo–US tension gaining momentum, Bowles became more conscious of the damage being done to bilateral intelligence cooperation. In a bid to reverse the estrangement, he lent his support to a September 1965 CIA proposal to provide the ARC with three C-130 transports, an aircraft the Indians had been eyeing for five years. The offer came at a particularly opportune time. At Charbatia, Ed Rector had finished his tour and been replaced as air advisor by Moose Marrero, who had a long history of contact with Biju Patnaik and the original ARC cadre.

As it turned out, Marrero's past ties had only minimal effect. The C-130 deal encountered repeated delays, largely because the irate Indians did not want to remain vulnerable to a fickle US spare-parts pipeline. In a telling request, they even asked Marrero to vacate Oak Tree and relocate to an office at the US embassy compound in New Delhi.

Still attempting damage control, the CIA in 1966 offered a quiet continuation of supplies for its paramilitary projects. As Washington had officially cut all arms shipments to India and Pakistan following the 1965 war, this was a significant, albeit secret, exception. Four flights were scheduled, all to be conducted by a CIA-operated 727 jet transport staging between Okinawa and Charbatia.

The Indians listened to the offer and consented. But in a reprise of conditions imposed on the DC flights of 1962, the government insisted that the flights into Oak Tree be made at low level to avoid radar — and to avoid any resultant publicity from the resurgent anti-American chorus in New Delhi political circles.

As it turned out, the ARC operation at Charbatia was not the only CIA project encountering difficulties. Throughout 1964, Intelligence Bureau director Mullik had been pushing for infiltration of all the Hale-trained agents to establish an underground movement within Tibet. By year's end, the Special Center saw its limited inroads — elements of four teams operating inside their homeland — as a glass half full. Mullik, by contrast, saw it as a glass half empty. Whereas he had once held excessive expectations of a Tibet-wide underground creating untold headaches for China, he now saw the limitations of overland infiltrations — especially by Khampa agents moving into areas where they did not have family or clan support. By the beginning of 1965, Mullik lashed out, claiming that the Tibetans were being coddled by the CIA.

Part of the problem was that Mullik himself was vulnerable and under pressure. In May 1964, ailing Prime Minister Nehru had died in his sleep, denying the 14-year spymaster of his powerful patron. That October, colleagues (and competitors) saw the chance to ease Mullik out of the top intelligence slot. They succeeded, but only to a degree. Although he gave up his hat as bureau director, he retained unofficial control over joint paramilitary operations with the CIA. That position — which was officially titled Director General of Security in February 1965 — answered directly to the prime minister and oversaw the ARC base at Charbatia, the Special Center, Establishment 22, and the sensor mission atop Nanda Devi.

With Mullik growing impatient, the Special Center readied its agents for a second season inside Tibet. Arriving in late 1964 as the new CIA representative at the Center was John Gilhooley, the same Far East Division officer who had briefly worked at the Tibet Task Force's Washington office in 1960. Almost from the start, Gilhooley faced dark news filtering in from Tibet. As soon as the snows cleared in early 1965, members of Team D had departed Tuting and headed back across the border to rendezvous with Nolan, the teammate they had left behind for the winter. Only then did they discover that he had already died of exposure. The remaining three agents returned to India and did not attempt another infiltration.

Much the same was encountered by Team Z. Departing Tuting to fetch Chris, they learned that he had been rounded up during a winter PLA sweep. Radio intercepts monitored at Charbatia later revealed that Chris had refused to answer questions during an interrogation and been executed.

Team Z's bad luck did not stop there. Entering a village later that summer, the men were sheltered in a hut by seemingly sympathetic locals. While they rested, however, the residents alerted nearby Chinese militiamen. As the PLA started firing at the hut, the team broke through the rear planks and fled into the forest. One of the agents, Tex, died from a bullet wound before reaching the Indian border.

Better longevity was experienced by the members of Team V, all five of whom had successfully braved the winter near Menling. By the spring of 1965, four elected to return to India, but Stuart, who had relatives in the area, stayed and was given permission to lead his own group of agents, appropriately titled Team V1. Two new members — Maurice and Terrence — were dispatched from Tuting for a linkup.

By that time, Stuart was living in his sister's house north of the Brahmaputra. During his regular crossings of the river, he used boats in order to avoid Chinese troops guarding the bridges. The new agents, however, chose the bridge option, ran into a PLA checkpoint, and panicked. Drawing their Brownings, they got into a brief firefight before being arrested. The PLA quickly isolated Maurice and forced him to send a radio message back to India claiming that he had arrived safely. On his first message back, however, the Tibetan included a duress code. This was repeated in two subsequent transmissions, after which his handlers ceased contact for fear the Chinese would triangulate the signals coming from Charbatia and expose the base to the press. A warning was then flashed to Stuart, who was able to get back to India.

Team Y, the last of the 1964 teams still inside Tibet, had a similar experience. After successfully living alongside sympathisers near Tingri through the winter, the five agents lobbied the Special Center in early 1965 for permission to rotate back to India. Agreeing to replace them in phases, the Center authorised two of the veterans — Robert and Dennie — to make their way out to Walung.

It came at a bad time. The Chinese had begun a more forceful program of suppression across Tibet, purging collaborators, establishing communes, and increasing military patrols. Robert and Dennie ran headlong into this dragnet. Ditching their supplies, both agents veered deeper into the hills as they evaded toward the Nangpa Pass on the Nepalese border. Unfortunately for the two, the Nangpa is notoriously treacherous through late spring. Dennie ultimately reached Nepal; Robert did not.

Back at Tingri, the rest of Team Y faced the same Chinese patrols. Two replacement agents had already arrived by that time. In need of supplies, team leader Reg left their cave retreat to procure food. Captured upon entering a village, he was forced to lead the PLA back to the team's redoubt. In the ensuing firefight, all were killed except for the lone Amdo agent, Grant. A subsequent sweep rounded up the dozens of sympathisers they had trained over the previous year.

The news was equally bleak for the new teams launched in 1965. At Shimla, the two-man Team C would meet a dark fate upon infiltration. Looking to cross a river swollen by the spring thaw, agent Howard fell in and drowned. His partner, Irving, spent the next three days looking for a better fording point. Cold and hungry, he chanced upon an old woman and her son tending a flock. They led him to an isolated sheep enclosure, then alerted the militia. Irving was soon heading for Lhasa in shackles.

Another trio of agents, Team X, was deployed to easternmost India and targeted against the town of Dzayul. The CIA was eyeing Dzayul because the surrounding forests supposedly hosted displaced Burmese insurgents who could potentially be harnessed against the Chinese. Team X, however, found nobody of interest and came back.

More bizarre was the tale of Team U. The five-man team staged from Towang, the same border town that had factored into the Dalai Lama's 1959 escape and the 1962 war. Three members headed north from Towang toward Cona, where one of the agents had family. Upon reaching their target, they were immediately reported by the agent's own brother. Arrested and bundled off to Lhasa, they were not mistreated but instead were shown films of captured ROC agents, then photos of the captured and killed members of Team Y. After less than a month of propaganda sessions, all three were given some Chinese currency and escorted to the border. After a final warning about "reactionary India," they were allowed to cross unmolested.

Sometimes the agents were their own worst enemy. The two members of Team F, which staged from Walung to Tingri, constantly quarrelled with each other and with local sympathisers. After the more argumentative of the pair was replaced by a fresh agent, the two rushed to cache supplies for the coming winter.

A final pair of Tibetans, Team S, also reached Tingri during the second half of 1965. These two agents, Thad and Troy, had better rapport with the locals than did their peers in Team F. So good was their rapport, in fact, that a local sympathiser offered them shelter in his house until spring. It was with these two Tingri teams in place that the Special Center awaited its third season during the 1966 thaw.

Although the Special Center's agent program had little to boast about, it looked positively dynamic compared with the guerrilla army festering in Mustang. A big part of Mustang's problem was that it was being managed from afar without any direct oversight. The Special Center had assumed handling of the program, but none of its officers had ever actually visited Mustang. The closest they got was when CIA representative Ken Knaus twice visited Pokhara in 1964 to meet Mustang officers. Without an on-site presence, the Agency and Intelligence Bureau had to rely on infrequent reporting by the Tibetan guerrillas themselves. From what little was offered, it was readily apparent that the by-product from Mustang was practically nil.

For the taciturn Mullik, disenchantment with Mustang was starting to run deep. By late 1964, he was alternating between extremes — first insisting that the guerrillas be given a major injection of airdropped supplies, later throwing up his arms and demanding that they all be brought down to India and merged with Establishment 22.

In January 1965, the pendulum swung back — with a twist. Now Mullik was proposing that Mustang be given two airdrops to equip its unarmed volunteers. These weapons would be given on the condition that the guerrillas shift inside Tibet to two operating locations. The first was astride the route between Kathmandu and Lhasa. The second was along the Chinese border road running west from Lhasa toward Xinjiang via the contested Ladakh region.

As before, Mullik was reluctant to use the ARC to perform the supply drops. Knowing that the CIA would be equally reluctant to use its own assets — that would defeat one of the main reasons for creating the ARC in the first place — he offered two sweeteners. First, he promised that the US aircraft could stage from Charbatia. Second, he would allow one ARC member to accompany the flights. This revised proposal went back to Washington, which on 9 April 1965 lent its approval to the airdrop and Mustang redeployment scheme.

Mullik, it turned out, was a moving target. As soon as he was informed of Washington's consent, he reneged on the offer to allow an ARC crew member on the flights. The CIA fired back, insisting that the Indian member was a prerequisite for the missions to go ahead. To this, Mullik had a ready counteroffer: he would provide a cover story if the flight encountered problems.

As Mullik ducked and weaved, Ambassador Bowles urged the CIA to accept the proposal as a way to keep intelligence cooperation on a solid footing. The CIA agreed; the flights would proceed on an all-American basis.

Now that the mission was moving forward, the Agency had to decide on planes and crews. The assignment eventually went all the way to Japan, where the CIA operated a proprietary named Southern Air Transport (SAT). Four cargo handlers were then sent to Okinawa for a week of USAF instruction in high-altitude missions, including time in a pressure chamber, turns on a centrifuge, and classes on cold weather survival. The rest of the crew came from the SAT roster in Japan; none, with the exception of the primary radio operator, had been on the earlier Tibet flights.

Taking a page from the past, SAT decided that the drop aircraft would come from its DC-6 fleet. This was the civilian version of the C-118 that had performed the Tibet missions in 1958; the only difference was a smaller cargo door in the rear. Because the smaller door meant that the supply bundles would also need to be smaller, mechanics fitted the DC-6 with a Y-shaped roller system to double the number of pallets loaded down the length of its cabin; after the first row of cargo was kicked out the door, pallets from the second row would be kicked. It was further decided to carry all the supplies aboard a single plane, rather than fly two missions as originally proposed by Mullik.

Early on 15 May 1965, the DC-6 departed Okinawa and made a refuelling stop at Takhli. Based on requirements generated by the Special Center, most of the bundles were filled with ammunition and pistols, plus a small number of M1 carbines and solar-powered radios. There was also a pair of inflatable rubber boats, to be used for crossing the wide Brahmaputra during summer. Because of the large amount of supplies involved, it was decided to make the drop inside Nepal and within a few kilometres of Tangya rather than at the more distant Tibetan drop zones used during the previous supply missions.

Once at Oak Tree, the plane was taken into an ARC hangar for servicing away from prying eyes. Wayne Sanford had arranged for the provision of fuel and support for the crew. He had also requested the Indians to temporarily suppress their radar coverage along the corridor into Nepal during the final leg of the flight.

For two days, the weather proved uncooperative. Not until the night of 17 May was the full moon unfettered by cloud cover. Not wasting the moment, the heavy DC-6 raced down the runway and lifted slowly into the northern sky.

At Tangya, Baba Yeshi had gathered his officers earlier in the week for a major speech. A massive airdrop was to take place in a valley just east of their position, he said, and each company would be responsible for lifting its share off the drop zone. Although Baba Yeshi had been informed of the quid pro quo conjured in New Delhi — weapons in exchange for a shift to positions astride the roads in Tibet — this was not mentioned in his speech.

Not surprisingly, pulses began to race as word of the impending drop flashed through the guerrilla ranks. With soaring expectations, the officers hurriedly left Tangya to assemble the necessary teams of yaks, men, and mules.

As the DC-6 crossed central Nepal, the pilot took the plane up to 4,848 meters (16,000 feet). The rear door was then opened, allowing frigid air to whip through the cabin. Ahead, a blazing letter signal lit the drop zone in a small bowl-shaped valley. Dropping into a steep bank, the DC-6 came atop the signal and then pulled up sharply. In the rear, the four cargo handlers worked furiously to get the loads out the small door. Only a fraction had been disgorged when they had to halt to allow the pilot to make a sharp turn and realign. It would take yet another pass before the entire cabin was emptied.

On the ground in Mustang, the guerrillas spent the next day collecting bundles scattered across the drop zone, in the next valley, and in the one after that. Several were never found, and rumour had it that the two rubber boats were recovered by local residents and taken to the Crown Prince at Lo Monthang.

Even more harsh than the complaints over the wide disbursement was the disgruntlement over the content of the bundles. Taking Baba Yeshi at his word, those assembled at the drop zone had expected a lavish amount of weapons, enough to fight for 15 years. Dozens of yaks and mules had been organised in what was envisioned to be a major logistical effort. "Just one plane came," lamented one guerrilla officer, "and it delivered mostly bullets and pistols."

Disillusioned, the company commanders took their allotments back to their respective camps and returned to their earlier inactivity. Radio messages were placed to Baba Yeshi over the following months, calling on him to make the shift inside Tibet, but all were answered with delays and excuses. By the end of that calendar year, few cross-border forays of any note had been staged. As far as the US and Indian representatives at the Special Center were concerned, Mustang was living on borrowed time.

17
REVOLUTION

The year 1966 had started on a most inauspicious note. On 10 January, Indian Prime Minister Lal Bahadur Shastri suffered a fatal heart attack. As his body was flown home for cremation, party stalwarts in New Delhi selected Nehru's daughter, Indira Gandhi, as Bahardur's successor. Looking somewhat awkward and shy in public, Mrs Gandhi had been elevated to power precisely because party seniors thought her pliable.

President Johnson, for one, quickly found out otherwise. In March, Gandhi arrived in Washington on her first official foreign trip. Exuding both tact and charm, she earned Johnson's strong support for a major food aid package in exchange for market-oriented economic reforms.

With the Washington summit a success surpassing all expectations, Indo–US relations got back some of their lustre. Sensing an opportunity, the CIA on 22 April sought approval for a major $18 million Tibetan paramilitary package. Part of this was earmarked to maintain the Mustang force for a three-year term. The package also included two C-130 aircraft as ELINT platforms to augment the lone ARC C-46 flying in this role, as well as funding for a 5,000-man increase in Establishment 22.

Most remarkable was the argument the CIA was using to justify its proposal. Moving beyond the lip service paid by Mullik in earlier years, the Agency claimed that the Intelligence Bureau had drawn up plans in 1965 calling for the liberation of Tibet. Reading into this, the CIA suggested that India might be willing to commit Establishment 22 to a second front in the event circumstances in Vietnam sparked all-out hostilities between the United States and China.

In making a linkage between Tibet and Vietnam, the CIA was being politically astute. Rather than justifying the Tibetan operation solely on its own merits, the Agency was now trying to loosely fix it to the coattails of Indochina policy — a topic that resonated at the top of the Johnson administration agenda. All this smacked of geopolitical fantasy. If Mullik, just a few months earlier, had balked at making airdrops to Mustang, it was a good bet that New Delhi would not willingly invite Beijing's wrath by sponsoring a Tibet front if the US and China went to war over Vietnam. Even Ambassador Bowles, an ardent proponent of intelligence cooperation, quickly backpedalled on the Vietnam link.

There was another problem with the CIA's April proposal. With few exceptions, the projects it sought to maintain had been proven ineffectual. Confirming as much was Bruce Walker, the former Camp Hale officer who had arrived in the spring of 1966 to replace John Gilhooley as the CIA representative at the Special Center. In many respects, Walker was presiding over a funeral. Making a token appearance at Hauz Khas once a week, he had few remaining agents to oversee. "The radio teams were experiencing major resistance from the population inside Tibet," he recalls. "We were being pushed back to the border."

A good case in point was Team S. Agents Thad and Troy had started out well, identifying a sympathetic Tingri farmer and bivouacking at his house since the onset of snow the previous winter. Thad had gotten particularly close to his host's daughter; by early spring, her abdomen was starting to show the swell of pregnancy. This sparked rumours among suspicious neighbours, who reported the case to district officials.

Alerted to the possible presence of an outsider, a Tibetan bureaucrat arrived that May to investigate. Quizzed about his daughter's mysterious suitor, the farmer folded. He brought Thad out from hiding, and they took the bureaucrat into their confidence and begged him to keep the matter a secret. Feigning compliance, the official bade them farewell — only to return that same night with a PLA squad. Thad was captured immediately; Troy, concealed in a haystack, surrendered after being prodded with a bayonet.

Giving the PLA the slip, the farmer managed to flee into the hills. Nearby was a cave inhabited by Team S1, which also consisted of two agents who had spent the winter near Tingri. Linking up, the three attempted to run south toward the Sikkimese border. Just short of

ARC C-46 (VT-DRX) at Charbatia, 1966. (Photo from Denis Goodwin/Air Britain Trust via Malcome Fillmore)

the frontier, the trio encountered a PLA patrol and was felled in a hail of bullets.

That left just one pair of agents still inside their homeland. Team F, consisting of Taylor and Jerome, had occupied yet another Tingri cave since the previous year. Even though they kept contact with the locals to a minimum, word of suspicious movement in the hills eventually came to the attention of the Chinese. On 2 November 1966, the PLA moved in for an arrest. The Tibetans held them at bay with their pistols until they ran out of ammunition; both were subsequently captured and placed in a Lhasa prison.

As Team F's radio fell silent, the Special Center was at an impasse. After three seasons, the folly of attempting to infiltrate "black" radio teams (that is, teams without proper documentation or preparation to blend into the community) was evident. Earlier in the year, this growing realisation had prompted the Center to briefly flirt with a new kind of mission. Four agents were brought to the Indian capital from Joelikote and given instruction in the latest eavesdropping devices, with the intention of forming a special wiretap team. For practice, they climbed telephone poles around the Delhi cantonment area by night.

In the end, the wiretap agents never saw service. In late November 1966, the Special Center put team infiltrations into Tibet on hold. Aside from a handful of Hale-trained Tibetans used for translation tasks at Oak Tree, as well as the radio teams already inside Nepal, Joelikote was closed, and the remaining agents reverted back to refugee status. "I was saddened and embarrassed," said Indian representative Rabi, "to have been party to those young men getting killed."

The Special Center had also reached an impasse with its other main concern, the guerrilla force at Mustang. Despite the May 1965 arms drop, Baba Yeshi and his men had resisted all calls to relocate inside Tibet. Though frustrated, the CIA had continued financing the guerrillas for the remainder of that year. This funding flowed along a simple but effective underground railroad. Every month, a satchel of Indian rupees would be handed over by the Agency representative at Hauz Khas. From there, two Tibetans and two Indian escorts would take the money to the Nepal frontier near Bhadwar. Meeting them were a pair of well-paid cyclo drivers also on the Agency's payroll. They hid the cash under false seats and pedalled across the border, where they handed the money over to members of the Mustang force. The money would then go to Pokhara, where foodstuffs and textiles were purchased at the local market and shipped to the guerrillas via mule caravans.

By early 1966, the CIA was still prepared to continue such funding for another three years. In addition, the Agency had not ruled out more arms drops in the future. The catch: Baba Yeshi had one final chance to move his men inside Tibet.

Perhaps sensing that his financiers had run out of patience, the Mustang chieftain was jarred from complacency. Employing vintage theatrics, he gathered his headquarters staff in late spring and announced that he would personally lead a 400-man foray against the PLA.

Traveling north to Tangya, the chieftain and 30 of his loyalists canvassed the nearby guerrilla camps for more participants. Another 30 signed on, including one company commander. Though far short of the promised 400, 60 armed Tibetans on horseback cut an impressive sight as they steered their mounts toward the border. Once the posse reached the frontier, however, the operation began to fall apart. A 15-man reconnaissance party was sent forward to locate a suitable ambush site, and the rest of the guerrillas argued for two days over whether Baba Yeshi should actually lead the raid

Roger McCarthy, the former head of the Tibet Task Force, visits the Taj Mahal with Zeke Zilaitis in 1966. Zilaitis, a former Camp Hale instructor, was assigned at the time as an advisor to Establishment 22 in Chakrata. (Photo courtesy Kevin McCarthy)

across the border. After his men pleaded with him to reconsider, the chieftain finally relented in a flourish. Armed with information from the reconnaissance team, 35 Tibetans eventually remounted and galloped into Tibet.

What ensued was a defining moment for the guerrilla force. Apparently alerted to the upcoming foray through their informant network, Chinese soldiers were waiting in ambush. Pinned in a valley, six Tibetans were shot dead, including the company commander. In addition, eight horses were killed and seven rifles lost. In its six years of existence, this was the greatest number of casualties suffered by the project.

As word of the failed foray filtered back to New Delhi, the Special Center finally acknowledged the limitations of Mustang. On the pretext of not provoking a PLA cross-border strike into Nepal, the guerrillas were "enjoined from offensive action which might invite Chinese retaliation." Any activity in their homeland, they were told, would be limited to passive intelligence collection. The guerrilla leadership, never really enthusiastic about conducting aggressive raids, offered no resistance to their restricted mandate.

By process of elimination, the only remaining Tibetan program with a modicum of promise was Establishment 22. In the first half of 1966, the Agency rotated in a new team of advisors to boost its level of assistance to Chakrata. Replacing Wayne Sanford in the US embassy was Woodson "Woody" Johnson, a Colorado native who had served in a variety of intelligence and paramilitary assignments since joining the CIA in 1951. Working up-country alongside

CIA instructor Henry "Hank" Booth conducting a sniping course at Chakrata, December 1967. (Photo courtesy Jamba Kalden)

CIA case officer Sam Currie at the Nanda Kot base camp, June 1967. The US and India conducted a joint covert operation over several years to place a sensor in the Himalayas to intercept Chinese missile telemetry. An initial attempt to place the device atop Nanda Devi failed in 1965, but an encore effort at Nanda Kot succeeded in May 1967. The SFF provided crucial logistical support to the Nanda Kot effort. (Photo courtesy Sam Currie)

Establishment 22 was Zeke Zilaitis, the former Hale trainer with a taste for rockets, and Ken Seifarth, the airborne specialist on his encore tour with Brigadier Uban's guerrillas.

Boosting its representation a step further, the CIA that summer introduced 49-year-old Tucker Gougelmann as the senior advisor for all paramilitary projects in India. A Marine during the Second World War, he had joined the CIA in 1950 and had run maritime raiding teams in Korea and Vietnam.

By the time Gougelmann got his India assignment in mid-1966, he had a full plate. Part of his time was devoted to managing the mountaineering expeditions aimed at placing a nuclear-powered sensor atop the Nanda Devi summit. Even more of Gougelmann's time was spent arranging assistance for the guerrillas at Chakrata. The Indians were eager to double the number of Tibetans at Establishment 22 and were even calling for the recruitment of Gurkhas into the unit. Reflecting bureaucratic creep, Director General of Security Mullik had come up with a new, more formal name for the outfit — the Special Frontier Force, or SFF — and had given Uban an office in New Delhi.

The SFF had matured considerably since its humble start. One hundred and twenty-two guerrillas made up each of its companies, with five or six companies grouped into battalions (known as a *vikas*) commanded by Tibetan political leaders. With "6" being an auspicious number for Tibetans, the first battalion, known as 6 Vikas, had been officially formed on 26 January 1965.

Though expanding the size of the SFF would be easy in one sense — with thousands of idle refugees eager for meaningful employment — there were problems. Most of the training was being handled by Uban's seasoned cadre; aside from perfunctory oversight provided by Seifarth and Zilaitis, the CIA was relegated to funding and bringing in the occasional instructor from Camp Peary for brief specialist courses. One such instructor, Henry "Hank" Booth, was dispatched in 1967 to offer a class in sniping. The six-week program went well, with the Tibetans proving themselves able shots with the M1903 Springfield rifle. For graduation, Uban held a small ceremony, during which Booth awarded his students a copy of the 1944 US Army field manual for snipers.

What came next was a telling indictment of the relationship between the Tibetans and their Indian hosts. Late that same evening, a fellow CIA officer took Booth to a hill overlooking the SFF cantonment. Below were lights burning bright at five separate camps. The Tibetans were in the process of translating the field manual into Tibetan, with each camp doing a section of the manual. Multiple copies were being made — including hand-drawn reproductions of the diagrams — and exchanged by runners. By sunrise, as Booth departed for New Delhi, each unit had a complete copy of the book, and the Indians moved in to confiscate the manual.

Not helping the relationship between the Indians and the Tibetans was the decision to add Gurkhas to their ranks. The Indians saw this as a means of expanding the mandate and abilities of the force beyond things Tibetan. The Tibetans, however, bristled at the ethnic dilution of their unit. Brigadier Uban recognised the delicacy of juggling two different cultures. "The Tibetans were more ferocious," he reflected, "but the Gurkhas were more disciplined."

Wayne Sanford, who had returned to India for another CIA tour in New Delhi, was less generous in his assessment of the Gurkhas. "We would 'kill' off their leaders during training exercises," he said. "The Tibetans were natural fighters and would move the next best guy into the leader's slot and keep on operating; the Gurkhas were clueless without leadership."

To keep peace within the force, a cap was set at no more than 100 Gurkhas. In addition, the two ethnicities would not be mixed; the Gurkhas would be segregated into their own "G Group" at Chakrata. Though given the same paramilitary training as in the previous SFF cycles, G Group was relegated primarily to base security and administration.

The Tibetan majority, meanwhile, was being rotated along the Ladakh and NEFA border in company-size elements. Several ARC air bases were established specifically to support these SFF operations. In the northeast, the ARC staged from a primitive airstrip at Doomdoomah in Assam. For north-western operations and airborne training, it used a larger air base built at Sarsawa, 132 kilometres south of Chakrata.

Not all the SFF missions were within India's frontier. Back in 1964, an Establishment 22 team had staged a brief but deadly foray from Nepal toward Tingri. In 1966, the force inherited the wiretap mandate originally conjured for the special team selected from Joelikote. Placing the taps posed serious challenges. The lines paralleled the roads built across Tibet, most of which were a fair hike from the border. Once a tap was placed at the top of a pole, a wire needed to run to a concealed cassette recorder. Because the recording time on each cassette was limited, an agent had to remain nearby to change tapes and then bring them back to India for CIA analysis.

The SFF proved up to the task. In a project code-named GEMINI, select members began infiltrating from NEFA with recording gear during mid-1966. To supply them while they waited for the tapes, an ARC C-46 was dispatched to an airfield near Siliguri. Taking off during predawn hours, the plane would overfly the Sikkimese corridor and be at the team's position by daybreak. Flying with the rear door open, the cargo handlers briefly took leave of their oxygen bottles and shawls to push the cargo into the slipstream. On the way home, they would hang a bag of soft drinks out the door in order to have chilled refreshments by the time they returned to base.

The results of GEMINI were mixed. Although the SFF guerrillas were able to exfiltrate without loss of life, the project was put on hold near year's end after a British journalist in Calcutta reported the mysterious flights over Sikkim. "We got miles of tapes," recalled New Delhi officer Angus Thuermer, "but much of it was useless, like Chinese talking about their families back home." Deputy chief of station Bill Grimsley was more upbeat in his assessment: "One never knows where the intelligence will lead in these matters."

Washington apparently agreed. On 25 November, after repeated failed attempts during the first three-quarters of the year, the CIA put a small portion of its $18 million Tibet package up for endorsement. It totalled just $650,000, most of it going to pay for Mustang. This time, the policy makers offered their approval for the paramilitary program to proceed.

Tucker Gougleman, the CIA's senior paramilitary advisor in India. (Photo via Jim Morrison)

Meantime, in the PRC Chairman Mao formally proclaimed a Great Proletarian Cultural Revolution in August 1966. In what was part ideological purge, part power struggle, part policy dispute, Mao steered the nation toward a destructive campaign of sophomoric Marxism and paranoid suspicion, ostensibly to "cleanse its rotten core."

As China descended into this orgy of violence, India watched with understandable concern. With nobody in clear control of Beijing (Mao was prone to prolonged absences from the capital), the Chinese were more dangerous neighbours than ever. Making matters worse, they had successfully tested a nuclear-tipped medium-range ballistic missile in October 1966.

In years past, such conditions might have made India's covert Tibetan assets appear all the more relevant as both a border force and a potential tool to exploit China's turmoil. By the spring of 1967, however, New Delhi had irreversibly soured toward most of its joint paramilitary projects. After all, the black radio teams inside Tibet had already been cancelled, and the Mustang force hardly inspired confidence.

The Indians were also nervous about media revelations concerning the CIA. Never openly embraced, the Agency now had few advocates on the subcontinent. Mullik, who had chaperoned the Tibet projects since the beginning of Indian involvement, had already given up his seat as Director General of Security in mid-1966. His replacement, Balbir Singh, had an independent and forceful personality but only limited clout with the prime minister. For her part, Mrs Gandhi showed little appreciation for the Agency or its assistance. "We became a tolerated annoyance," summed up Woody Johnson.

If any tears were being shed at the CIA, they were of the crocodile variety. Already, the Agency had taken measured steps to disengage itself from Tibet. The Tibet desk, which had been under the Far East Division's China Branch ever since its establishment in 1956, was transferred to the Near East Division. John Rickard, one of four brothers born to missionary parents in Burma (three of whom went to work for the CIA), headed the desk during this period and changed his divisional affiliation to reflect the shift. More than just semantics, the change underscored the fact that the remaining Tibetan paramilitary assets, with rare exception, would probably not be leaving Indian soil. Apart from a single representative at the

Special Center, the Far East Division had been completely excised from the Tibet program.

The CIA also reduced its links to the ARC. Although attrition was starting to take a toll on the planes delivered during 1963 and 1964 — the latest casualty, a Twin Helio, crashed in 1967 — no replacements were budgeted. Tellingly, the Indians opted in 1967 to add the Soviet An-12 transport as the new centrepiece for its ARC fleet.

18
CIVIL WAR

Signs of dissent against Baba Yeshi dated back years. But by 1967, with the Mustang guerrillas sulking and spent, their complaints about him — especially charges that he was pocketing money earmarked for their food allowances — grew louder. Leading the call were six idealistic Hale graduates, including Rara, who had commanded the 1961 jeep ambush. All six later trekked to Darjeeling, where they made their demands known to Gyalo's long-time assistant, Lhamo Tsering.

When word of the complaints got back to Mustang, Baba Yeshi was less than receptive. In years past, his aloof stance would have carried the day. But with the curtailing of offensive action from Mustang, Gyalo and Lhamo Tsering feared that an open scandal in Nepal would provide a ready excuse for the CIA to target funding. Scrambling for a face-saving solution, they determined that Baba Yeshi should get a competent, respected, and untainted assistant.

They eventually settled on Wangdu, the feisty Khampa known as Walt who had trained on Saipan in 1957 and been parachuted back into Kham. After fleeing Tibet for India in January 1959, he had turned his back on the resistance. Bitter, he had refused an earlier offer to join Establishment 22; instead, he had closed himself off at Darjeeling and frittered away the years reading and studying English.

In early 1968, Gyalo called Wangdu down from Darjeeling to his New Delhi house. It took repeated appeals, but the Khampa finally relented. After nearly a decade, he would be re-joining the cause. Baba Yeshi took the arrival of his uninvited deputy relatively well. "Gyalo sent a message emphasizing that Wangdu was there to help and assist," said Kay-Kay, the senior Tibetan representative at the Special Center, "not to replace." Although no warm welcome was offered, neither was there any animosity.

A division of responsibility between the two came easily. With Baba Yeshi spending much of his time at Kaisang, Wangdu headed for Tangya. Low-level intelligence was still being collected by the network of radio agents posted to frontier outposts at Dolpo, Limi, Nashang, and Tsum, so Wangdu had the rest of the guerrillas focus on training for the remainder of the year.

At the beginning of 1969, Lhamo Tsering decided to inspect the guerrillas himself. His findings were heartening. After working together for a year, Baba Yeshi and Wangdu were apparently getting along and in good spirits. Though Wangdu expressed some reservations in private, the threat of a schism within the ranks appeared slim.

Very quickly, however, the atmosphere soured. The precipitating factor: To commemorate the 10th anniversary of the insurrection in Lhasa, a series of events was being planned for Dharamsala in March. Baba Yeshi was invited to attend the Dharamsala memorial services after a stop in New Delhi. Wangdu would be taking his annual home leave at the same time, with Lhamo Tsering left in temporary command.

Baba Yeshi, the first commander of Mustang. (Photo courtesy Roger McCarthy)

Baba Yeshi smelled a putsch in the making but could hardly turn down the invitation from the highest quarters of the Tibetan government-in-exile. When he arrived in the Indian capital, his fears were confirmed. He was greeted with the news that he would be receiving a permanent transfer to Dharamsala to assume the prestigious post of deputy to the security minister in the Dalai Lama's own cabinet. Wangdu, his deputy, would be in charge of the Nepal project.

Baba Yeshi wanted none of it. Resistant to the transfer after almost a month of negotiations in New Delhi, he reappeared in Darjeeling. A few weeks after that, Lhamo Tsering woke to find him at Kaisang. The situation quickly teetered on the edge of confrontation. Baba Yeshi, supported by loyalists among the headquarters staff, demanded his right to properly turn over command to Wangdu

Lhamo Tsering (centre) posing with a Swedish K submachine gun at Mustang, 1968. The other guerrillas wield the M1 Garand. The peak in the background is Annapurna III. (Photo courtesy Lhamo Tsering)

before returning to India. As a compromise, Lhamo Tsering gave him two weeks to sort out his affairs.

After the allotted time, the chieftain departed Kaisang with two dozen bodyguards. But instead of going to his promised seat in Dharamsala, he got as far as Pokhara and stopped. In letters smuggled back to Mustang, he implored his men to rally to his side. A civil war was about to begin.

At the same time trouble was brewing in Mustang, Indo–US intelligence cooperation experienced major changes in structure and personalities. In June 1968, David Blee departed as the New Delhi station chief after more than six years in the post. Replacing him the following month was John Waller, the former deputy station chief in India between 1955 and 1957.

Within two months after his arrival in New Delhi, Waller was confronted with a new counterpart organisation. Intentionally patterned after the CIA, the Research and Analysis Wing (RAW) was officially unveiled on 2 September. RAW took control of the foreign intelligence desk of the Intelligence Bureau, the latter of which was now downgraded to domestic activities. In addition, the head of RAW was given a second hat as Director General of Security overseeing covert paramilitary projects.

Selected as the first RAW chief was R. N. Kao. Previously head of the ARC, the debonair Kao had a long history of close cooperation with US officials. Despite this warm past, Kao was faced with Indo–US relations that were again on a downward spiral. In November 1968, Richard Nixon won the US presidential election, and many Indians recalled his slant toward Pakistan when he was Eisenhower's vice president.

Mrs Gandhi was showing a tilt of her own. Backed into a political corner by 1969, she shrewdly began courting the populist left at home and the Soviet Union abroad. This, combined with the perceived hostility from Nixon, led to outward relations between New Delhi and Washington sinking to their lowest depth in over a decade.

Behind the scenes, intelligence cooperation toward Tibet remained only a shadow of its former self. Arriving in June 1968 as the new CIA representative at the Special Center was John Q. Bellingham. Posted there after a tour in Hong Kong, Bellingham found little to do other than channel monthly payments for Mustang. Indeed, one of his main tasks was managing the denouement of that base. In early 1969, the Indians had made it apparent that their contingency plans no longer involved any participation by Tibetan guerrillas in Nepal. The CIA was of a similar mind-set. When it came time for Washington to review Tibet operations on 30 September, it endorsed a provision to scale back Mustang to a token force.

The Tibetans learned of this pivotal decision indirectly. In early October 1969, Bellingham arrived at the Special Center with the monthly funds for Nepal. As was customary, Kay-Kay came to witness the transfer. Turning to the Indians as he left, the CIA representative offered a comment in passing: "I guess this is one of the last."

Kay-Kay froze. "It was my darkest moment," he later said. No matter how poorly it had fared in the field, the Tibetan leadership had looked on Mustang as the symbolic paramilitary arm of its government-in-exile.

A Royal Nepal Airlines flight took Kay-Kay and two junior Tibetan officers from the Special Center to Pokhara, where they mounted horses and went to bring the news directly to the guerrilla leadership. They arrived at Kaisang in driving rains and found Wangdu in his office. After explaining the decision, Kay-Kay paused for comments, but Wangdu offered only a silent gaze.

Reduced funding was only part of Mustang's troubles. After spending the summer and fall of 1969 stewing at Pokhara, Baba Yeshi had enticed a company of loyalists to move east to Nashang. Tempers were starting to flare between the two factions, leading to the death of two Baba Yeshi followers and five horses. Vowing to expel dissidents, Wangdu placed Baba Yeshi's sympathetic assistant, a hulking Andowa and Hale graduate named Abe, in detention. Abe,

Mustang officers (left to right) Gen Dawa, Gen Gyurme, Rara, and unknown, 1968. (Photo courtesy Lhamo Tsering)

Mustang guerrillas practice with an M18 57mm recoilless rifle, circa 1968. (Photo courtesy Lhamo Tsering)

in turn, got possession of a razor and committed suicide by slicing open the vein in his neck. Incensed, Baba Yeshi retreated to a house in Kathmandu and began plotting his revenge.

In 1970, Lhamo Tsering returned to New Delhi after his prolonged deployment to Nepal. Waiting for him at the Special Center was Bellingham, who was anxious to finalise a formal demobilisation plan for Mustang. Until that point, the CIA was still funding 2,100 guerrillas at a cost of $500,000 a year. Pressed for time, Lhamo Tsering outlined a schedule whereby the force would be cut by a third over each of the next three calendar years. Without delay, Bellingham approved the scheme.

Part of the demobilisation plan involved a rehabilitation program for the guerrillas, to ensure that they would be able to support themselves. Members of the Special Center were immediately deployed to Kathmandu and Pokhara to oversee this program. Their purpose was to ensure that rehabilitation funds would be wisely invested in self-generating enterprises. Although the demobilised guerrillas had few marketable skills, existing Kathmandu-based projects funded by the Dalai Lama and foreign aid groups demonstrated that Tibetan handicraft and carpet factories were profitable ventures.

Drawing on this precedent, the first third of the rehabilitation funds was channelled into two carpet factories in Pokhara. Part of the money was also used to break ground for a 30-room budget hotel in the same town. With a third of the guerrillas dutifully filing out of the mountains to take up employment at these sites, demobilisation appeared to be progressing according to plan.

At Tangya, not everybody was embracing the conversion to civilian life. Wangdu, for one, was game for alternative forms of funding that would allow him to maintain some of his men under arms. In early 1971, he made an unsuccessful bid to garner interest from the Soviet Union.

Ironically, the CIA did not necessarily see Soviet inroads into the subcontinent as a bad thing. "By keeping the Soviets onboard in India," said CIA New Delhi chief David Blee, "they were a counterweight to the Chinese."

Such realpolitik led to previously unthinkable levels of cooperation regarding support to the ARC. With an aging C-46 fleet and no C-130 ELINT platforms forthcoming, the ARC inventory by 1967 was dominated by the Soviet-made Mi-4 chopper and An-12 transport. Whereas this transformation might have had the CIA howling in earlier years, the Agency was now perfectly willing to assist the Indians with their new Soviet hardware. In 1968, for example, Agency technicians installed oxygen consoles in the unpressurised An-12 cabins for use during SFF parachute training. Because this aircraft had an extremely fast cruising speed — more than double that of the C-46 — CIA airborne advisor Alex MacPherson was dispatched to India that spring to train an ARC cadre in high-speed

Mustang guerrillas in training, circa 1968. (Photo courtesy Roger McCarthy)

exit techniques. Two years later, CIA technicians were back in India to modify an ARC An-12 with ELINT gear.

CIA support for the SFF, meanwhile, was declining fast. One of the last CIA-sanctioned operations took place in 1969, when four SFF commandos were trained in the use of sophisticated "impulse probe" wiretaps. Buried underneath a telephone line, the tap transmitted conversations to a solar-powered relay station established on a border mountaintop in NEFA, which in turn relayed data to a rear base farther south. Although several taps were installed successfully, two SFF members disappeared on a 1970 foray, and further infiltrations were halted. By the following year, the PLA detected the extent of the tampering and started rerouting its lines away from the border.

CIA instructor Henry "Hank" Booth (standing left), SFF Dapon Jamba Kalden (centre) and Brigadier Mishra with the top marksmen from an M1903 Springfield sniping course at Chakrata, December 1967. (Photo courtesy Jamba Kalden)

By early 1971, direct CIA contact with the SFF was almost non-existent. This came as tension between India and Pakistan was once again on the rise. The reason was the humanitarian disaster unfolding inside East Pakistan, where a heavy-handed campaign to suppress secessionists (who wanted independence from the western half of the bifurcated nation) had led to a deluge of refugees into India.

The situation had New Delhi's full attention not only because of the humanitarian ramifications but also because it presented a chance to cripple its arch-rival. During previous wars with Pakistan, fighting had focused on the western front. Now the Pakistani government not only had to keep that flank protected but also had to rush reinforcements to the eastern side of the subcontinent. Logistically challenged, the Pakistanis were getting whipsawed in the process.

Compounding Pakistan's woes, the Indian government was quietly supporting scores of resistance fighters from East Pakistan. Playing a major role in this was Major General Uban (he had finally gotten his promised second star), who was now considered one of India's most seasoned unconventional warfare specialists on account of the nine years he had spent with the SFF. Taking temporary leave of his Tibetans, the general was placed in charge of a guerrilla training program for 10,000 East Pakistani — soon to be called Bangladeshi — insurgents.

Uban made room at Chakrata for a training site for the Bangladeshis. By that time, the SFF had grown to 64 Tibetan companies. Despite this increase, the force had not seen any serious combat since its inception. Worse, Uban learned that seven companies were being misused for traffic control in Ladakh.

Protesting this abuse of his elite unit, Uban lobbied to incorporate his men into contingencies against East Pakistan. By fall, the Indians were already well on their way to completing plans for a major combined arms campaign to liberate that territory. Though Uban made a strong case for the SFF's inclusion — his men could act as guerrillas with plausible deniability, he argued — such a decision would

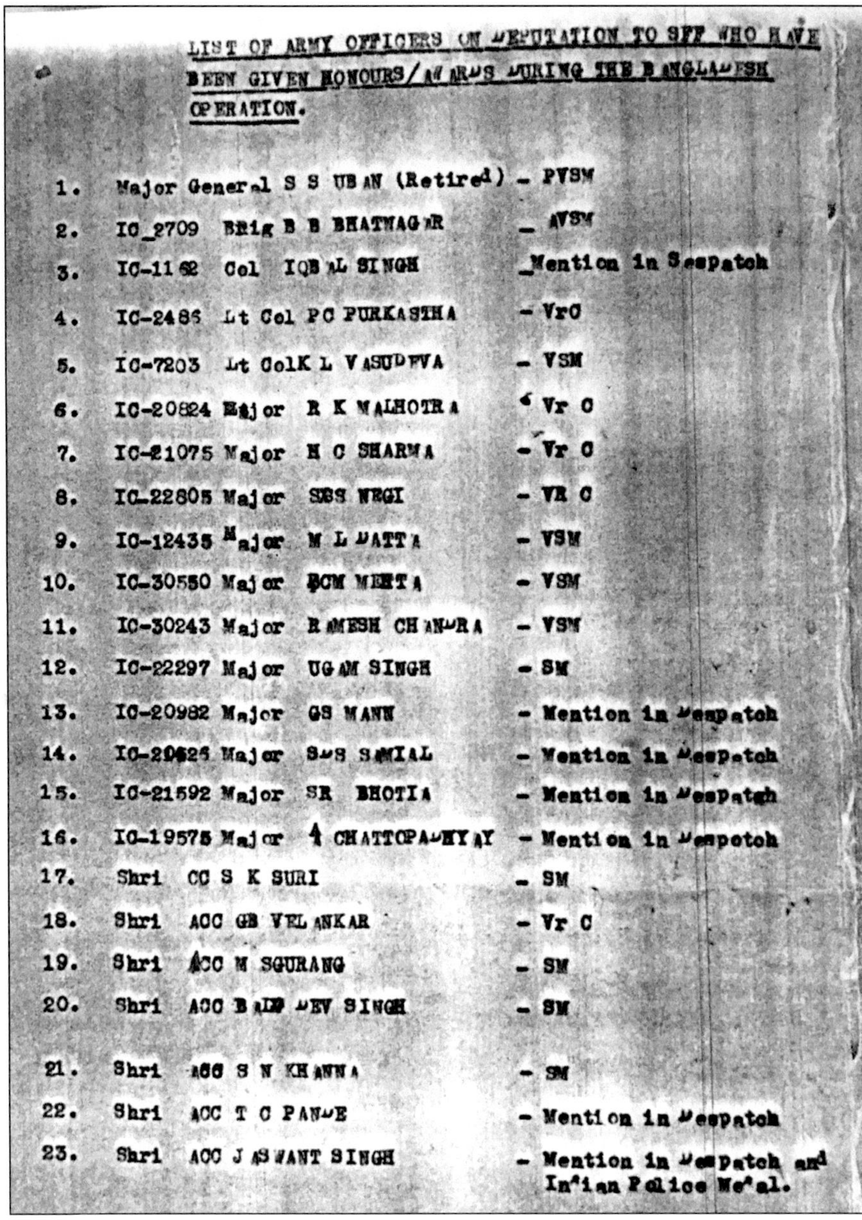

LIST OF ARMY OFFICERS ON DEPUTATION TO SFF WHO HAVE BEEN GIVEN HONOURS/AWARDS DURING THE BANGLADESH OPERATION.

1. Major General S S UBAN (Retired) - PVSM
2. IC_2709 Brig B B BHATNAGAR - AVSM
3. IC-1162 Col IQBAL SINGH - Mention in Despatch
4. IC-2486 Lt Col PC PURKASTHA - VrC
5. IC-7203 Lt Col K L VASUDEVA - VSM
6. IC-20824 Major R K MALHOTRA - Vr C
7. IC-21075 Major H C SHARMA - Vr C
8. IC-22805 Major SBS NEGI - VR C
9. IC-12435 Major M L DATTA - VSM
10. IC-30550 Major BCM MEHTA - VSM
11. IC-30243 Major RAMESH CHANDRA - VSM
12. IC-22297 Major UGAM SINGH - SM
13. IC-20982 Major GS MANN - Mention in Despatch
14. IC-20625 Major SDS SAMIAL - Mention in Despatch
15. IC-21592 Major SR BHOTIA - Mention in Despatch
16. IC-19575 Major A CHATTOPADHYAY - Mention in Despatch
17. Shri CC S K SURI - SM
18. Shri ACC GB VELANKAR - Vr C
19. Shri ACC M SGURANG - SM
20. Shri ACC BALDEV DEV SINGH - SM
21. Shri ACC S N KHANNA - SM
22. Shri ACC T C PANDE - Mention in Despatch
23. Shri ACC JASWANT SINGH - Mention in Despatch and Indian Police Medal.

Indian Army document listing officers on deputation to the SFF during Operation EAGLE, 1971. (Author's collection)

SFF commandos in a makeshift armada advancing on Ramgamati during Operation EAGLE, 24 December 1971. (Photo courtesy Jamba Kalden)

SFF commandos using Bulgarian-made AK-47s during Operation EAGLE, 1971. (Photo courtesy S.S. Uban)

be controversial. Until that point, there had been an unwritten rule that the SFF would not be used for anything other than its intended purpose against China. There were also Tibetan attitudes to consider. Tibet, noted several members of the force, had no quarrel with Pakistan. Rather, Tibet had benefited from assistance offered by the East Pakistani authorities, recalled senior political leader Jamba Kalden.

As word flashed to Dharamsala, senior Tibetan officials were in a quandary. If they did not agree with Uban's proposal, they feared that the Indians would see them as ungrateful; with CIA support largely dissipated, they could ill afford to alienate their primary benefactor. Although some in the Dalai Lama's inner circle felt that they should demand a quid pro quo — participation against East Pakistan in exchange for Indian recognition of their exiled government — the idea was not pushed. Quietly, Dharamsala offered its approval.

By late October 1971, an ARC An-12 airlift began shuttling nearly 3,000 Tibetans to the Indian border adjacent to East Pakistan's Chittagong Hill tracts. To reinforce their deniable status, the guerrillas were hurriedly given a shipment of Bulgarian-made AK-47 assault rifles. Joining them was a small cadre of Indian Army officers; not by coincidence given Uban's own background, many came from the artillery corps.

At the border, they assembled at Demagiri. Normally a quiet frontier backwater, Demagiri by that time was overflowing with refugees. As the Tibetans turned it into a proper military encampment, they made plans to divide into three columns and initiate operations. Their exact mission had been the subject of prior debate. India's military staff had wanted them to perform surgical strikes, such as destroying the key Kaptai Dam. Uban, in contrast, saw them doing something "more worthy," such as joining forces with his Chakrata-trained Bangladeshi insurgents and seizing Chittagong port. This was vetoed by the top brass because neither the SFF nor the Bangladeshis had integral heavy weapons support. After further discussion, it was decided that the SFF would be charged with staging guerrilla raids across the Chittagong Hill tracts, known for their thick jungles, humid weather, and leech-infested marshes. This promised to be a difficult mission for the mountain-faring Tibetans.

The hills held another, more deadly, challenge. Based along the tracts was a Pakistani composite brigade, including part of a battalion of elite commandos, the Special Service Group. Not only did this brigade threaten the flank of one of the Indian corps massing to move against Dacca, but it could conceivably open an escape route to nearby Burma.

At the beginning of the second week of November, the SFF began Operation EAGLE. Taking leave of Demagiri, the guerrillas used 19 canoes to shuttle across the Karnaphuli River and steal into East Pakistan. Coming upon an outpost that night, the Tibetans overran the position while the Pakistanis were eating. Boosted by their swift victory, they made plans to hit the next post the following morning.

Listening over the radio, General Uban was anxious. As he moved into Demagiri to coordinate both the SFF and his Bangladeshi force, he had few qualms about the Bangladeshis — they were native boys and could live off the land — but he knew that the Tibetans were untested under battle conditions and careless in open march. In addition, their newly introduced Indian Army cadre was not accustomed to guerrilla tactics.

Very quickly, his fears were confirmed. On 14 November, the lead element of Tibetans came running back toward the Indian border. Dhondup Gyatotsang, Uban learned, had been shot dead by a Pakistani sniper. The cousin of Mustang commander Wangdu and a Hale graduate, Dhondup had been one of the most senior political leaders in the force. After his body was brought back to Demagiri and placed upon a funeral pyre, Uban got on the radio and barked at the Tibetans to resume their advance. "I told them not to come back until the position was taken, " he said.

The strong words had an effect. Reversing course, the SFF split into small teams and curled behind the Pakistanis in classic guerrilla fashion. Using both their Bulgarian assault rifles and native knives, they smashed their way into the town of Barkal. "After that," remembers Uban, "they were unstoppable."

By the time all-out war was officially declared early the following month, the SFF had been inside East Pakistan for three weeks. Multiple Indian corps blitzed from all directions on 3 December, forcing Pakistani capitulation within two weeks; Bangladesh's independence would soon follow. At the time of the ceasefire, the Tibetans were within 40 kilometres of Chittagong port and had successfully pinned down the Pakistani brigade in the border hills. Taking leave of their normal anonymity, the SFF paraded through Chittagong to ecstatic Bangladeshi masses. A total of 23 Indian officers and 45 Tibetans would be awarded for their gallantry; 580 Tibetans received cash bonuses. Their victory had had a cost, however. Forty-nine Tibetans had paid with their lives for the birth of a nation not their own.

19
A PASS TOO FAR

Fallout from the Bangladeshi operation was swift. The CIA lodged a protest against the RAW over the use of Tibetans in Operation EAGLE. R.N. Kao hardly lost any sleep over the matter; with US financial and advisory support to the SFF all but evaporated, the Agency's leverage was nil.

More serious were the protests against Operation EAGLE from within the Tibetan refugee community. In this instance, it was Dharamsala that was under fire, not the RAW. Facing mounting criticism for having approved the deployment, the Dalai Lama made a secret journey to Chakrata on 3 June 1972. After three days of blessings, most ill feelings had wafted away.

As this was taking place, John Bellingham was approaching the end of his tour at the Special Center. He had just delivered the second instalment of rehabilitation funds, which arrived in Nepal without complication. With this money, two Pokhara carpet factories had been established, and construction of a hotel in the same town was progressing according to plan. Another carpet factory was operating in Kathmandu, as was a taxi and trucking company.

By the summer of 1973, with one-third of the funds still to be distributed, the CIA opted not to deploy a new representative to the Special Center. Because Bellingham had moved next door as the CIA's chief of station in Kathmandu, and because he was already intimately familiar with the demobilisation program, it was decided to send him the Indian rupees in a diplomatic pouch for direct handover to designated Tibetans in Nepal. Although this violated the Agency's previous taboo against involving the Kathmandu station, an exception was deemed suitable in this case, given the humanitarian nature of the project.

The money was well spent. That November, ex-guerrillas formally opened their Pokhara hotel, the Annapurna Guest House. Bellingham and his wife were among its first patrons.

Although all the promised funds had been distributed, the CIA was not celebrating. Wangdu had dipped into extra money saved over previous years, defied orders to completely close the project, and retained six companies — 600 men — spread across Mustang. Worst of all, not a single weapon had been handed back.

All this was happening as a new set of geopolitical realities was conspiring against the Tibetans. President Nixon, besides having frosty relations with India, was dedicated to normalising ties with the PRC. In February 1972, he travelled to Beijing and discussed this possibility with Chinese leaders, who were slowly distancing themselves from the self-inflicted wounds of their Cultural Revolution. Although the phaseout of Mustang was not directly linked to this visit — as many Tibetans have incorrectly speculated — it is equally true that Washington had little patience for a continued Mustang sideshow, given the massive stakes involved with Sino-US rapprochement.

The SFF contingent that participated in Operation EAGLE boards a commercial transport ship in Chittagong bound for Calcutta, 18 January 1972. (Photo courtesy Jamba Kalden)

The Nepalese government, too, was getting a dose of realpolitik. In January 1972, King Mahendra suddenly died and was succeeded by his son, Birendra Bir Bikram Shah Dev. Looking around the subcontinent, Birendra had reason for concern. Pakistan had been dismembered only a month earlier, and the Indians had signed a cooperation treaty with the Soviet Union the previous August. This led the new monarch to believe that it was in his kingdom's interest to offset a stronger India by fostering goodwill with Beijing. In November 1972, he dispatched his prime minister to the Chinese capital; in December 1973, Birendra himself made the trip.

Following these diplomatic developments, Wangdu's residual force at Mustang counted no allies of note by the beginning of 1974. Sensing an opportunity, the Nepalese government geared up to move forcefully against the long-standing affront to its sovereignty in Mustang. Playing a supporting role in this was deposed chieftain Baba Yeshi. Ever since retreating to Kathmandu in early 1970, he had been in intermittent contact with a small band of loyalists in Nashang. He had also been in touch with the Nepalese authorities and offered them assistance in confronting his rival, Wangdu. Though eager to do so, the Nepalese military, as yet untested in combat, was biding its time until conditions were right.

In the spring of 1974, there arose just such conditions. As he had done in previous years, Lhamo Tsering travelled overland to Pokhara to inspect ongoing rehabilitation projects in that town. Although his trips had not been controversial in the past, this time Kathmandu saw him as a useful pawn. On 19 April, he was arrested at the Annapurna Guest House and taken to the town's police station.

With Lhamo Tsering in detention, the Royal Nepalese Army dispatched a lieutenant colonel to Jomsom to initiate a dialogue with Wangdu. At the time, the Tibetans held the strategic high ground at Kaisang. But with Lhamo Tsering behind bars, Wangdu was in a conciliatory mood. Venturing down from Kaisang with a coterie of bodyguards, he offered to turn in 100 weapons in exchange for Lhamo Tsering's release. The Nepalese, suddenly emboldened, rejected the offer. With bad feelings all around, Wangdu retreated to his headquarters.

Realising that they needed more muscle, the Nepalese began mobilising military reinforcements from around the kingdom. During June, an infantry brigade massed at Pokhara, then began walking north in driving rains to join one company already at Jomsom. Making the same hike was an artillery group consisting of a howitzer, a field gun, and a mortar.

As they started to reach critical mass, the government troops delivered an ultimatum to Wangdu. His guerrillas had until 26 July (later extended by five days) to hand in their weapons; after that, the army vowed to forcibly disarm them. To add emphasis, a team of Baba Yeshi loyalists, working alongside the Nepalese, sent surrender leaflets to Kaisang. "You cannot push the sky with your finger," read one.

Almost until the 11th hour, the sabre rattling had little effect. But upon hearing of the impending confrontation, the Tibetan authorities in Dharamsala intervened. The Dalai Lama recorded a personal plea, and a senior Tibetan minister rushed the tape to Mustang and played it in front of the guerrilla audience. Hearing their leader implore them to disarm, the warriors broke down. Four of the six companies came out of the mountains and did as instructed. At Kaisang, one Khampa officer shot himself in the head rather than turn over his rifle. Two other guerrillas leaped to their deaths in the swift waters of the Kali Gandaki.

Still at large was Wangdu, backed by a pair of companies commanded by deputies Rara and Gen Gyurme. The surrender deadline had expired, and the Nepalese were contemplating their next move. Still looking to employ carrot over stick, they couriered appeals to Kaisang during early August, promising a festive celebration at Jomsom if Wangdu bowed out gracefully. When that failed, they began moving against the guerrilla headquarters.

Undaunted, the Tibetans at Kaisang unpacked a recoilless rifle. They had never used this weapon inside Tibet during all the preceding years, but they now sent a round impacting into a nearby hillside. Intimidated, the Nepalese scurried back to Jomsom.

Wangdu, meanwhile, had beckoned Rara and Gen Gyurme for what was to be their final meeting. He would make a dash west toward India with 40 followers, he told them. His two deputies were to delay the Nepalese for eight days to allow him sufficient time to escape.

By that time, the Nepalese were gearing up for a second foray against Kaisang. Advancing at night, they surrounded the headquarters at 0300 hours. When they made a final push after sunup, however, they found only a handful of Tibetans present; Wangdu was not among them.

Determined to get serious, the army made plans for a major sweep north across Mustang. Marching along the east bank of the Kali Gandaki, a single Nepalese battalion eventually reached Tangya by the end of August. In an anti-climax, the remaining guerrillas surrendered without a fight. Searching the camp, the government troops found few weapons; the rest had been cached, they presumed. At the same time, the smaller pro-Baba Yeshi faction at Nashang turned in its arms. There were no firefights at that location either. Apart from two Nepalese who succumbed to altitude sickness, nobody died during the operation.

Wangdu, however, was still at large. Correctly assuming that the last two company commanders were co-conspirators in his escape, the Nepalese invited Rara and Gen Gyurme to Pokhara to review the status of the rehabilitation projects. After three nights at the Annapurna Guest House, they were taken away in chains to join Lhamo Tsering.

Though they had yet to capture the Mustang leader, the Nepalese authorities had a pretty good idea where he was heading. During the march north, the government battalion had spotted a band of horsemen riding west. Assuming that Wangdu might be destined for India, Kathmandu alerted its 4th Brigade posted along the north-western border of the kingdom. Because there were only a limited number of passes along the frontier with India, the troops were especially vigilant at those locales.

Their calculations proved correct. During the second week of September, a line of horsemen was seen approaching the 5,394-meter Tinkar Pass separating Nepal and India. Only meters from the Indian border, a Nepalese sergeant took the column under fire. Two were killed and one severely wounded; the rest escaped across the frontier. Uncertain as to the identity of the corpses, the Nepalese flew in Baba Yeshi. He positively identified Wangdu, and the traitorous chieftain had the bodies buried on the spot.

At Pokhara, the last Mustang guerrillas were directed to temporary resettlement centres while the Nepalese authorities debated their future. Half ultimately left for India; of these, nearly 100 joined the SFF. For the remainder, favouritism was shown toward Baba Yeshi's followers formerly at Nashang; a camp was built for them near Kathmandu, with funds from the United Nations. Those loyal to Wangdu, by contrast, were given barren plots near Pokhara and, due to government intransigence, had no access to United Nations funding.

That was still far better than the prison cells holding Lhamo Tsering, Rara, and Gen Gyurme. Four other unrepentant guerrillas soon joined them, including the wounded member from Wangdu's escape party and a Hale-trained radioman named Sandy. They were taken to Kathmandu for trial, where the authorities were deaf to pleas for leniency. All received life sentences.

At the Special Center in New Delhi, the Tibetan and Indian representatives had been monitoring Mustang's death throes as best they could. Until the final days of July, four of their radio teams in Nepal had been sending back regular updates. Once those fell silent, gloom set in among the operatives at Hauz Khas.

With a whimper, their secret war in Tibet had come to an end.

20
SECOND WIND

For the SFF, changes ensued in the wake of Operation EAGLE. Major General S.S. Uban retired as inspector general in January 1973. Elevated in his stead was a seasoned paratrooper, Major General Tirath Singh Oberoi. Joining the force as its commandant, or second-in-command, was Brigadier Rai Singh Yadav.

Among its indigenous members, one change involved the recruitment of females. In 1973, 500 Tibetan women joined the force as its 34th Company, where they trained to be radio operators, nursing assistants, and clerical staff. To boost their morale, in July 1977, 51 of them were given airborne training at Sarsawa. Included in this batch was Denchen Wangmo, the wife of senior political leader Ratuk Ngawang, who kept secret from the parachute instructors the fact that she was three months pregnant.

Another change involved the resumption of assistance from the US. Looking to patch over its earlier protests regarding Operation EAGLE, the CIA deployed two airborne instructors to India in the spring of 1975. The first was Alex MacPherson, the same advisor who had completed an earlier tour in Charbatia. Though born in Chicago, MacPherson had lived most of his life in Scotland and spoke with a thick Scottish brogue. After initially serving in the British Army, he had joined the USAF Air Commandos in 1963 and became an expert free faller before shifting to the CIA in 1968.

The second was former smokejumper Bruce Lehfeldt. From 1968 to July 1974, he had worked with airborne commando teams in Laos as part of the major CIA paramilitary program in that kingdom.

In late 1974, both Lehfeldt and MacPherson had been informed of the need to develop modified parachutes for use by the SFF where they to jump in the thin air on the high Tibetan plateau. As a training substitute, drop zones were to be used in Ladakh, some as high as 4,848 meters (nearly 16,000 feet) above sea level.

Ultimately, three parachutes prototypes were developed, including a 28-foot chute made of non-porous cloth, an enlarged version of the T-10 parabolic chute, and a 34-foot conical chute. Testing took place at the Naval Air Facility at El Centro, California, through the first quarter of 1975, after which the two advisors took the sample equipment to India for further trials. This culminated in a jump in Ladakh from 32,000 feet with bottled oxygen, whereupon an elated Lehfeldt instantly regretted his decision to take off his mask after landing at a 16,000-foot drop zone. "I was like a fish out of water," he recalled, "gasping in the thin air."

Once in-country testing was concluded and the chutes handed over, the ARC in 1976 ran freefall training for an initial contingent of SFF commandos. Aside from adding this skill set, however, the SFF in fact was seeing less action in the field. In 1974, the unit had been guarding the border near Nepal to stem an influx of Chinese-trained insurgents. Following Kathmandu's suppression of Mustang, however, it was feared that the SFF might stage reprisal forays against the Nepalese. To prevent this, India pulled its Tibetan commandos away from that border.

The following year, a second ruling prohibited the SFF from being posted within 10 kilometres of the Tibet frontier. This came after a series of unauthorised incursions and cross-border shootings, including a four-hour fire fight in Ladakh during 1971 that resulted in two SFF fatalities.

By the late 1970s, the future of the SFF was no longer certain. With Indo-Chinese tensions easing somewhat, there was criticism that maintenance of a Tibetan commando force was

The Dalai Lama inspects Chakrata, 3 June 1972. To his left (in the dark suit) is SFF Commandant T.S. Oberoi; on his right (in the light suit) is SFF Inspector General S.S. Uban. (Photo courtesy S.S. Uban)

The Dalai Lama and SFF Inspector General S.S. Uban at Chakrata, 3 June 1972. (Photo courtesy S.S. Uban)

CIA airborne advisors Bruce Lehfeldt (left) and Alex MacPherson in Leh, 1975. (Photo courtesy M.K. Anand)

an unnecessary expense. However, the SFF was soon given a new mission: counterterrorism. Because the Tibetans were foreigners, and therefore did not have a direct stake in Indian communal politics, they were seen as an ideal, apolitical counterterrorist force. In 1977, RAW chief Kao deployed 500 SFF commandos to Sarsawa for possible action against rioters during national elections. After the elections, which went off without major incident, 60 Tibetans were retained at Sarsawa for counterterrorist duties.

Three years later, when Indira Gandhi (and Kao) returned to power, the SFF's war against terrorism received a major boost. In 1981, over 500 trainees were sent to Sarsawa for counterterrorist instruction. Upon graduation, they formed what was dubbed the Special Group. While this group was theoretically under the SFF, significantly no Tibetans were counted among its members; rather it consisted of Gurkhas and Indians. Select members of the group would be sent to Israel for three weeks of additional instruction in 1983.

The Special Group would soon see action across India. In June 1984, one of its companies was used during an abortive attack against Sikh extremists holed up in the Golden Temple in the

ARC officer M.K. Anand (left) and ARC Director T.S. Subramaniam pin Indian Air Force freefall wings on SFF graduates from the first freefall course at Charbatia, 1976. While serving in the ARC, Anand in 1968 became the first military skydiver in India. (Photo courtesy M.K. Anand)

General T.T. Raina (centre), the Chief of the Army Staff of the Indian Army, gets a briefing at Chakrata during the handover ceremony from SFF Inspector General T.S. Oberoi (left) to Major General H.K. Bhardwaj (right), June 1975. Bhardwaj would serve as SFF Inspector General through August 1981. (Photo via Jamyang Norbu)

The first class of SFF female paratroopers at Charbatia with ARC instructors, April 1977. (Photo courtesy Tenzin Yeshi)

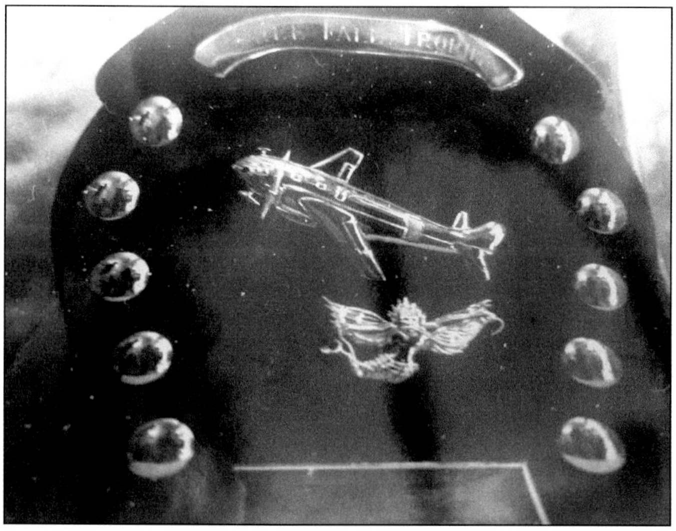

Freefall trophy presented to the best SFF student during the first freefall course at Charbatia, 1976. A Tibetan Garuda deity is featured on the trophy. (Photo courtesy M.K. Anand)

Punjab. The temple was subsequently retaken in a bloody army operation, leading Indira Gandhi's Sikh bodyguards from the Delhi police to assassinate the Prime Minister later that year.

The Tibetan mainstream of the SFF, meanwhile, continued to see action across the northern frontier. In 1977–78, three additional Tibetan battalions were raised at Chakrata; these were rotated among posts in Ladakh, Sikkim, and Doomdoomah air base in Assam. In 1984, SFF members were used in Operation Meghdoot while battling Pakistan for control of the Siachen Glacier; just like after the Bangladesh operation, there were protests in Dharamsala for taking losses outside of the struggle to liberate the Tibetan homeland.

The SFF would also go on to play a significant role in the 1999 Kargil War. Recognised as expert mountaineers, 80 SFF commandos were used on Khalubar and Point 5500 to scale near-vertical ridges and secure ropes for Indian Army soldiers to capture the peaks.

Dapon Ngesang, who served as the senior political leader in the SFF from 1981–87. By that time, the SFF had reverted to using standard Indian Army jump wings and jump status indicator badges. (Photo courtesy Jamba Kalden)

SFF female parachutists at Charbatia, 1977. The male SFF instructor (third from left) wears a freefall badge on his right chest pocket. (Photo courtesy Tenzin Yeshi)

The first SFF female paratroopers and the SFF leadership cadre pose with Indian Prime Minister Indira Gandhi, April 1977. (Photo courtesy Tenzin Yeshi)

Company leader Jamyang Tsering (front left) with an SFF static-line parachute class, 1977. (Photo courtesy Jamba Kalden)

This reportedly came at the cost of at least 18 Tibetan lives. Recalled Brigadier Gurdip Singh Uban, the son of the original SFF Inspector General who was serving as their commandant during the war: "So many [Tibetans] were sent; so few got through."

By that time, the SFF counted eight battalions. Of this number, six of them — 1, 2, 3, 5, 6, and 7 Vikas — were wholly comprised of Tibetan troops. The Special Group, consisting almost exclusively of Indians and tasked by RAW with covert operations both inside and outside the border, was given the cover designation of 4 Vikas. Meantime, the Gurkha members of the SFF in January 1999 were gathered into a segregated battalion known as 1 Archers.

Not until 2020 would the SFF fully emerge from the shadows. This came about following heightened border tensions with China around Ladakh, leading to an SFF deployment on Gurung Hill as part of Operation SNOW LEOPARD. While patrolling in this sector on 31 August, company leader Nyima Tenzin from 7 Vikas stepped on a landmine and lost his life. A second Tibetan, Tenzin Londhen, was seriously injured in the blast. Their sacrifices soon came to be widely lauded by Indian politicians and in the media. But while the SFF's existence had now been openly acknowledged and their cause boosted, their homeland has yet to be set free.

SOURCES AND BIBLIOGRAPHY

This book is based heavily on interviews conducted during the 1995–2000 timeframe as part of the research for *The CIA's Secret War in Tibet* (University Press of Kansas, 2002) co-authored with the late James Morrison. Relevant documents were obtained from the US State Department Foreign Relations of the United States series, the Foreign Broadcast Information Service, the Joint Publication Research Service, and the Declassified Documents Reference System.

Published works that were helpful include *Tears of the Lotus* by Roger McCarthy (McFarland & Company, 1997), *Orphans of the Cold War* by John Kenneth Knaus (PublicAffairs, 1999), *Phantoms of Chittagong* by S.S. Uban (Allied Publishers, 1985), and *Echoes from Forgotten Mountains* by Jamyang Norbu (publisher pending).

The author would specifically like to acknowledge the unwavering guidance provided by Mohinder Kumar Anand, the late Tashi Choedak, the late Jamba Kalden, the late Roger McCarthy, the late S.S. Uban, Bruce Walker, and Jamyang Norbu from the High Asia Research Center.

The following persons generously provided information, either through interviews or correspondences, for the chapters in this volume (in alphabetical order):

Harry Aderholdt, Roland Andersen, William Andesevic, Athar, Kaydor Aukatsang, Surindar Kumar Bajaj, Subodh Bhardwaj, Truman Barnes, Ed Beasley, David Blee, Henry Booth, William Broe, Lyle Brown, Kenneth Cathey, Don Cesare, John Condon, John Cool, Walter Cox, James Critchfield, Pat Dailey, Lawrence Dalley, William Demmons, Pema Doka, Tsering Dolkar, John Fogarty, Thomas Fosmire, John Greaney, William Grimsley, Kalsang Gyatotsang, Gen Gyurme, Mary Hawthorne, Neese Hicks, Frank Holober, John Hoskins, Donyo Jagotsang, Lobsang Jamba, Franke Janke, Miles Johnson, Shep Johnson, R.N. Kao, James Keck, Karen Keen, Robert Kleyla, John Kenneth Knaus, M.S. Kohli, Princess Kukula, Kesang Kunga, Bruce Lehfeldt, Robert Linn, Bill Lively, Barbara McCarthy, Kevin McCarthy, James McElroy, Jerome McEntee, Kenneth Millian, Billie Mills, Harry Mustakos, Cheme Namgyal, Prithvi Pant Negi, George Patterson, Richard Peterson, Eli Popovich, Anthony Poshepny, Willard Poss, Doug Price, Harry Pugh, Tashi Punzo, John Reagan, Ralph Redford, James Rhyne, John Rickard, Tom Sailor, Wayne Sanford, Charles Ken Seifarth, Connie Siegrist, Jack Shirley, Ray Stark, Don Stephens, Jack Stiles, Howard Stone, Ron Sutphin, Bista Temba, Tendar, Angus Theurmer, Thomas T.J. Thompson, Gyalo Thondup, Jentzen Thondup, Gar Thorsrud, Sonam Topden, Lhamo Tsering, Wangchuk Tsering, Lobsang Tsultrim, John Turner, Gurdip Uban, Henri Verbrugghen, Jack Wall, John Waller, Pema Wangdu, Temba Wangyal, Gen Wongya, Tenzin Yeshi, Sioux Zilaitis, and David Zogbaum.

ABOUT THE AUTHOR

Ken Conboy is currently country manager for a private security and risk consultancy in Jakarta. Prior to that, he served as deputy director at the Asian Studies Center, an influential Washington-based think tank, where his duties included writing policy papers on economic and strategic relations with the nations of South and Southeast Asia. The author of nearly 20 books about Asian military history and intelligence operations, Conboy's most recent titles include a three-volume series for Helion on the war in Laos. Conboy, a graduate of Georgetown University's School of Foreign Service and of Johns Hopkins' School of Advanced International Studies, was also a visiting fellow at Chulalongkorn University in Bangkok.